Enterprise Service Bus

Enterprise Service Bus

David A. Chappell

O'REILLY®

BEIJING · CAMBRIDGE · FARNHAM · KÖLN · PARIS · SEBASTOPOL · TAIPEI · TOKYO

Enterprise Service Bus
by David A. Chappell

Published by O'Reilly Media, Inc., 1005 Gravenstein Highway North, Sebastopol, CA 95472.

O'Reilly Media books may be purchased for educational, business, or sales promotional use. Online editions are also available for most titles (*safari.oreilly.com*). For more information, contact our corporate/institutional sales department: (800) 998-9938 or *corporate@oreilly.com*.

Editor:	Mike Hendrickson
Production Editor:	Emily Quill
Cover Designer:	Edie Freedman
Interior Designer:	David Futato

Printing History:

June 2004:	First Edition.

 This book uses RepKover™, a durable and flexible lay-flat binding.

ISBN: 0-596-00675-6 (standard printing)
0-596-00814-7 (Sonic Software printing)

Contents

Foreword

Integration is making a comeback—perhaps it never even left. In this book you'll be introduced to the next generation of integration, called Enterprise Service Bus (ESB). ESB is really exciting in that it introduces battle-ready integration principles in a new way using open standards, messaging, and loosely coupled Service Oriented Architecture (SOA) principles.

The costs of using proprietary integration solutions will soon become something of the past. Integration solutions will always be required, but companies can look forward with enthusiasm knowing that upcoming solutions will be based on open standards and common integration principles, especially in the area of web services and SOA. Soon, the new game in town will be integration products competing on who best supports systemic requirements (scalability, availability, performance, etc.), and not on specific product features. Not only that, the new desire to push toward SOA forces organizations to rethink their existing environment and create architectures that are based on coarse-grained, loosely coupled, shared services. However, we all know that performing the magic of "gluing" these services together is no small task. It requires new thinking in both business and technology solutions. And, in the past, because there were virtually no integration standards and few agreed-upon repeatable integration patterns, proprietary integration products were really the only option.

Now that's all about to change, and that is what this book is about. What I like about this book is that Dave shows us how ESB brings integration solutions to those of us who want to focus on integration architectures and solutions. The ESB concept, as the backplane of a highly distributed integration network, allows us to think about the architecture and the best way to design and architect our solutions using an event-driven SOA, without having to deal with specialized integration approaches and becoming middleware surgeons. It allows us to focus on how we want to architect our solutions without conforming our requirements to what a product offers.

There are two areas in this book that particularly excite me. First, as an architect of enterprise Java™ solutions I am excited about the synergy between the ESB and Java Business Integration (JBI/JSR-208). JBI combined with an ESB is a godsend to those who have felt locked into proprietary integration products and solutions. JBI increases the proliferation of integration technology by providing a standards-based container environment in which integration processing elements run as services. These processing elements may include BPEL engines, XSLT transformers, routing engines, dispatchers, and any other integration feature engine you can think of. An ESB can provide its own JBI container environment or can integrate with one provided by another vendor. What's very cool about this is that it enables an ecosystem where ESB vendors such as Sonic can now focus on coordination, transport, and routing of a highly distributed and consistently managed SOA backplane, while at the same time providing an environment in which JBI processing engines can flourish.

Second, as a design-patterns person I am also excited by this book's use of ESB components in pattern-based approaches to integration, which are used to explain the capabilities of an ESB. Even more interesting is that Dave chose to leverage and extend the "Gregor-grams" from the *Enterprise Integration Patterns* book by Gregor Hohpe and Bobby Woolf. In the EIP book, there is a wonderful use of visuals to depict various patterns for enterprise messaging. The ESB patterns used throughout this book show the visual construction of loosely coupled, service-based integration patterns to create larger-grained solutions, or micro-architectures, which leverage the ESB architecture to uniquely solve complex integration problems in simple ways. This concept alone is reason enough to buy this book. The visual metaphor lends itself wonderfully to composing integration solutions and really helps the integration architect represent the architecture visually and form a complete ESB solution. The nice thing about any loosely coupled, messaging-based solution is that you tend to add new feature elements as requirements dictate. Using patterns to compose the ESB features allows you to not only add the integration features as needed, but also to see the visual architecture as it evolves.

I really think SOA built upon ESB is the next wave in integration. Read this book and decide for yourself. It is sure to open up new ways of thinking about solving any and all of your integration challenges.

—John Crupi
Sun Distinguished Engineer
Coauthor, *Core J2EE Patterns*
Bethesda, MD
April 2004

Preface

Welcome to *Enterprise Service Bus*. I hope you enjoy reading this book as much as I enjoyed writing it. Being part of a new technology evolution is very exciting, and now that you are beginning to explore the concept of the Enterprise Service Bus (ESB), you can become a part of it, too. The ESB provides a highly distributed, event-driven Service Oriented Architecture (SOA) that combines Message Oriented Middleware (MOM), web services, intelligent routing based on content, and XML data transformation. ESBs are being used to solve integration challenges in many unique ways, as we will explore throughout this book.

About This Book

Over the past few years, I (along with many of my coworkers) have had the invaluable opportunity of working closely with IT professionals who were trying to build or buy something like an ESB. As part of the research for this book, I met, spoke with, and interviewed many IT leaders across a variety of industries to gain an understanding of their integration challenges, and of how they are applying ESB integration concepts to uniquely solve them. The concepts in this book draw from that experience.

This book represents a new direction for O'Reilly books. It is the first of a new "Enterprise Series" of books from O'Reilly. This book is targeted to integration architects, project managers, CIOs, CTOs, and basically anyone who has a need to integrate applications and who understands the bigger picture of the integration issues within their IT organization.

At the same time, this book will also be valuable to everyday IT developers who need to understand ESB technology for their individual integration projects. As we will see in the first few chapters, the new "integration architects" are actually everyday IT developers, and the ESB concept brings the power and capability to solve their integration needs into their reach.

This book provides an architectural overview of the ESB concept, and includes discussions of many practical uses and integration patterns that explain how an ESB can be applied toward today's application integration challenges. Ideally, readers of this book should possess some knowledge of technical concepts, but this is not a hard requirement. The introductory chapters provide a conceptual overview, including the requirements, drivers, and catalysts that have fostered the emergence of this new technology category.

My intent in this book is to explain the ESB concept with just the right amount of detail that is suitable for individuals across many disciplines within an IT organization and with varying levels of technical and business acumen. This book takes a different tack from my previous O'Reilly books, and from most O'Reilly books in general, in that there are no code samples to speak of. You will, however, find a considerable number of diagrams that explain architectural concepts of the ESB.

Although this book represents a slightly new direction for O'Reilly, it also possesses a trait that O'Reilly books have become known for: the "Missing Manual" approach to a particular technology. The ESB is being rapidly adopted across a variety of industries. Many middleware, integration, and infrastructure vendors have also gotten "on the Bus" and are either shipping an ESB already, or have plans to build one. A big part of the ESB is its commitment to standards-based integration. An ESB is designed and built from the ground up with standard components and standard interfaces. However, there is no specification for the ESB itself. This book will serve as a guide to define what an ESB is, as viewed through the eyes of those of us who pioneered the ESB concept and have been working with IT professionals on real-world ESB-based integration solutions. Even other vendors who want to join in with the growing ESB market trend, and are trying to figure out exactly what an ESB is, are welcome to use this book as a guide.

Overview of the Chapters

Chapter 1, *Introduction to the Enterprise Service Bus*, gives an overview of the ESB, including the many characteristics that define it. It also explains the evidence of industry adoption and market attraction of this new concept in service-oriented integration.

Chapter 2, *The State of Integration*, provides a summary of the drivers, both business and technical, that have contributed to the need for a new approach to integration. It also examines some surprising statistics showing that, in general, the enterprise is far from connected, and it explores the shortfalls of Enterprise Application Integration (EAI) approaches to date. It explains the characteristics of an "accidental architecture" which helps you to identify your own architecture issues. Lastly, it explains how the ESB concept draws from best practices of previous integration approaches, and shows that you can refactor toward an ESB and away from an accidental architecture in incremental steps.

Chapter 3, *Necessity Is the Mother of Invention*, examines some key concepts of the ESB, including the many requirements, technology drivers, and forces in the IT climate that led to the creation of the ESB concept. This is explained in the context of the recent history of the evolution of the ESB, illustrating the point that an ESB is not merely an academic exercise; it is born out of necessity, based on real requirements and difficult integration problems that couldn't be solved by any preexisting integration technology. The discussion concludes with a high-level study of an ESB deployment, in which a manufacturer exposes inventory management and supply chain optimization functionality to its remote distributors as shared services through an ESB. This study, along with many others, will be revisited in more technical detail in later chapters.

Chapter 4, *XML: The Foundation for Business Data Integration*, explores the use of XML as a means for providing the mediation between diverse data structures and formats as data is passed between applications. It also examines how ESB-enabled data transformation and content-based routing services can support an XML data exchange architecture that insulates individual applications from changes in data structures, as integrated business processes improve over time.

Chapter 5, *Message Oriented Middleware (MOM)*, explains Message Oriented Middleware and its role in an enterprise integration strategy. A MOM is a key part of the ESB architecture, as it provides the underpinnings to the network of virtual channels that an ESB uses to route messages throughout an extended enterprise and beyond. This chapter explains how the definition of a MOM has evolved to support the highly diverse and distributed topologies and open standards that an ESB integration requires. (In other words, it's not your Mom's MOM.) The chapter goes on to explain the key differences between the low-level coding of using a MOM versus the higher-level configuration aspects of using an ESB.

Chapter 6, *Service Containers and Abstract Endpoints*, explains the details of what makes an ESB an ESB. The ESB provides an architecture that brings together all the concepts described in previous chapters into an infrastructure that can span an extended enterprise and beyond. This chapter describes the ESB *service container*—a key enabler of the highly distributed, event-driven SOA—and its concept of endpoint abstraction.

Chapter 7, *ESB Service Invocations, Routing, and SOA*, covers the service invocation model—i.e., the underlying framework that provides the SOA in an ESB. We will discuss multiple forms of process routing, including the concept of itinerary-based routing and the role it plays in enabling a highly distributed SOA across independently deployed services.

We will also discuss some fundamental ESB services such as content-based routing and XSLT transformation, and explore how service types can be defined and then reused for different purposes through elements of configuration. Finally, we will see how additional capabilities can be layered on top of an ESB through an advanced service, such as an XML persistence service and an orchestration service.

Chapter 8, *Protocols, Messaging, Custom Adapters, and Services*, examines how the ESB can extend its MOM core to create the flexibility in protocols necessary to connect to applications in an adaptable and non-intrusive way. This includes an explanation of how XML and SOAP messaging can be integral parts of an ESB strategy, yet also be flexible enough to carry other data formats such as EDI X12 messages. This chapter also shows the details of a partner integration using an ESB, and examines the use of third-party adapters and custom integration services for integrating with SAP.

Chapter 9, *Batch Transfer Latency*, explores the most common form of integration being done today: bulk data transfer and batch updating using Extract, Transform, and Load (ETL) techniques. We will discuss the business impact of the latency and reliability issues associated with this integration method, and examine the prescriptive steps for migrating toward real-time integration using an ESB in the context of a case study using pattern sketches.

Chapter 10, *Java Components in an ESB*, examines the various Java components in an ESB. The ESB is a platform-neutral concept, and could be implemented without any Java involved. However, a good ESB should take advantage of Java components due to the large adoption of Java-based technology across IT departments. A fairly extensive list of specifications that are utilized within an ESB comes out of the Java Community Process (JCP) on a regular basis; this could be the subject of a whole other book. Some Java specifications are particularly worth calling attention to because they have a special impact on the operation of an ESB. Chapter 10 will discuss the following specifications and their impact on making an ESB a more effective integration environment:

- Java Business Integration (JBI): A specification describing the way integration components, such as ESB services, can be plugged together in a vendor-neutral and portable fashion.

- J2EE Connector Architecture (JCA): A specification that defines how to use a standard set of interface contracts for creating adapters to connect into, and interact with, enterprise applications.

- Java Management eXtensions (JMX): A specification for remote management defining the means by which an application can interface with a management infrastructure and management consoles.

Chapter 11, *ESB Integration Patterns and Recurring Design Solutions*, examines some common uses of an ESB in integration scenarios. The ESB concept already has a number of common uses that solve some very common and challenging integration problems. These include the Validate, Enrich, Transform, Operate (VETO) pattern and its derivatives, a "two-step XRef" pattern, and several variations of backend integration patterns that are driven by enterprise portal requirements, such as a federated query/response pattern and forward caching using an ESB caching service.

Chapter 12, *ESB and the Evolution of Web Services*, provides an overview of the evolving web services specifications (including the WS-* family of specifications), and explains how web services and ESBs will move forward together.

The Appendix contains the list of vendors who are currently offering or are promising to offer an ESB product in the future. I will try my best to keep this up to date with subsequent printings of the book.

The Bibliography contains references to other books, specifications, and web links that were used in supporting research for this book.

Notational Conventions for ESB Integration Patterns

Throughout this book, integration patterns are often utilized to describe how concepts are put to use in an ESB. Some up-front explanations of the term "pattern" and this book's use of pattern notation are warranted.

A *pattern* is a popular concept in software construction. The concept of using a pattern to build things actually originates from other engineering disciplines that predate computers and software, and was originally made popular by Christopher Alexander, author of *A Pattern Language*.

When building a skyscraper, for example, there are certain repeatable methods to connect the steel girders. These methods can then be used in a larger architecture to form a building. Patterns for creating software architectures are similar, and have been explored in books such as *Design Patterns* by Erich Gamma, et al., and *Patterns in Enterprise Application Architecture* by Martin Fowler. More recently, the idea of messaging patterns has been popularized by Gregor Hohpe, et al., in *Enterprise Integration Patterns*, a great book that describes a series of integration patterns that are built upon low-level, message-oriented middleware.

When building a service-oriented integration network using an ESB, there are certain ways to combine individual integration components—for example, by using a data transformation service or content-based routing service to form repeatable and reusable patterns that can be built upon throughout the integration substrate. Chapter 11 conveys some examples of common integration patterns being used in ESB deployments today, and other chapters also explore ESB integration patterns in the context of the concepts being discussed. Although this book by no means covers all the patterns in use today, it should give you an idea of how an ESB can combine integration components to solve a variety of everyday integration problems. Refer to the links on this book's O'Reilly web page, *http://www.oreilly.com/catalog/esb*, for an ongoing list of ESB patterns, and for errata on the existing ones.

A pattern description must follow certain conventions so that it is easily identifiable, easily understood, and easily communicated among engineers when discussing the larger issues that patterns can help to solve. This book uses the following form when describing patterns. (Some of this is borrowed from Alexander's, Hohpe's, and Fowler's books.)

Pattern Name
> The name of the pattern. This makes it easily identifiable and referenceable in other patterns, and helps to provide a vocabulary for engineers to use when discussing architectures that make use of patterns.

Problem Statement
> A summary of the problem that the pattern solves.

Forces
> Circumstances surrounding the problem that contribute to the need for the solution the pattern offers.

Sketch
> A drawing or diagram that illustrates the pattern in a simple, understandable form.

Solution
> A description of how the pattern solves the proposed problem.

Alternative Approaches
> Other approaches, which are often less than adequate, that could have been used to solve the problem.

Variations
> Alternate ways to apply or augment the pattern. Variations can also manifest themselves as choices that can be made in the makeup of the pattern, such as publish-and-subscribe versus point-to-point messaging models. Variations can often result in a whole new pattern with a unique name.

You won't necessarily find these as headings when reading through the patterns, but each pattern has these elements whenever possible.

Diagramming Notations

To describe the integration patterns used in this book, a simple set of glyphs were created to visually represent the different components of an ESB. These glyphs borrow from the work done by Gregor Hohpe, et al., in *Enterprise Integration Patterns*. These "Gregorgrams," as they have come to be known, are gaining rapid adoption in the industry as a means for describing messaging components and common integration patterns.

This book uses some of the glyphs from *Enterprise Integration Patterns*, and also supplies a whole new set of glyphs that represent many of the higher-level concepts and constructs used by the ESB. There is a parallel between the icons in *Enterprise Integration Patterns* and the concepts they represent, and the icons in this book and the ESB concepts that they represent. Many of the integration patterns described in *Enterprise*

Integration Patterns—such as content-based routers, load-balanced queue receivers, or routing slips—are implemented as custom messaging client code built on top of a messaging infrastructure. An ESB provides these same capabilities as built-in functionality, either as part of the bus directly or as an out-of-the-box service to be plugged into the bus. Therefore, the glyphs used in this book represent those pluggable services and are designed to be plugged together to form ESB diagrams. The diagrams can represent abstract pattern sketches or physical deployment characteristics, or can be a combination of both.

A legend showing all the glyphs that were created for use by this book is shown in the included reference card. The glyphs in this book were designed with these goals in mind:

- To create a visual diagramming notation for explaining the core concepts of an ESB
- To allow you, the integration architect, to have a common means of designing your own integration patterns using an ESB
- To have a visual pattern language for documenting integration designs for legacy purposes

With these primary goals in mind, the icons also have these secondary uses:

- To show physical deployment characteristics of an ESB architecture
- To show message flow and business process routing for messages as they travel across an ESB
- To abstractly illustrate a pattern sketch for an integration environment, which describes the steps that a business message goes through as it travels across the various components of an automated business process

I plan to keep an updated set of these glyphs at *http://www.oreilly.com/catalog/esb*. They will be packaged as templates that can be plugged into Visio and PowerPoint so you can use them to diagram your own ESB architectures and integration patterns.

Figure P-1 shows examples of using the glyphs to show the details of individual ESB components. This figure will be explained in more detail in Chapter 6.

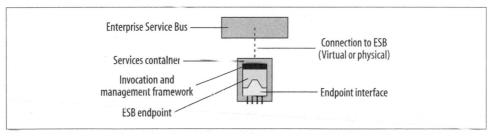

Figure P-1. Generic ESB endpoint

These glyphs can be combined to show composite components, as illustrated in Figure P-2.

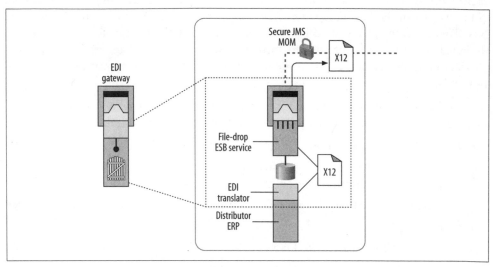

Figure P-2. Diagramming notation used to show the subcomponents of a composite ESB service

The diagramming notation can also be used to abstractly describe the components that make up an integration pattern, in the form of a pattern sketch. The particular pattern sketch convention was made popular by *Enterprise Integration Patterns*, and is akin to the way a rebus puzzle is formed. See Figure P-3.

Figure P-3. Rebus puzzle

When the rebus puzzle concept is applied to an integration pattern sketch, it can show the components that make up the pattern, and the steps that a message goes through as it follows the pattern (i.e., passes through the steps of a business process). This is illustrated in Figure P-4.

These glyphs can also be used together to show illustrations of physical deployment characteristics. For example, Figure P-5 shows different types of applications being plugged into different *ESB segments*, which may be different departments or business units, or separated by geographic location.

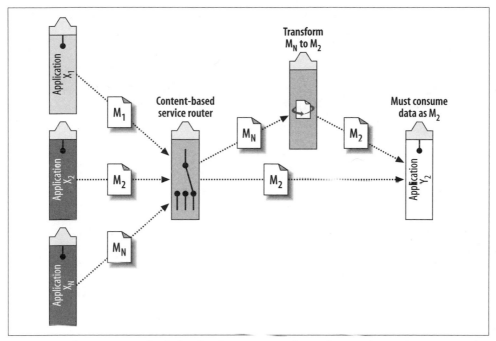

Figure P-4. Abstract pattern sketch showing the components that make up an integration pattern and the stages of processing for a message

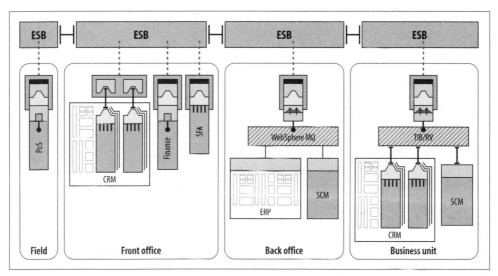

Figure P-5. An ESB diagram showing physical deployment characteristics of geographic separation, and different application endpoint types

The notation can also be used to represent flow of data across an ESB, either as messaging distribution or as multiple steps in an ESB process flow, as illustrated in Figure P-6 and Figure P-7, respectively.

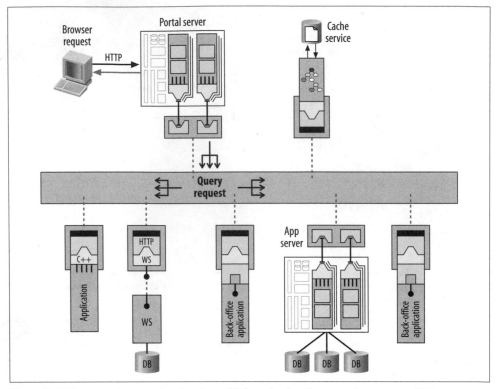

Figure P-6. Diagramming notation showing publish-and-subscribe messaging across an ESB

Finally, the visual representations of the abstract patterns, the process flow descriptions, and the physical characteristics of the bus and its components may be combined, as illustrated in Figure P-8.

Some of these diagrams may look complex at first; their meanings should become clearer when they are used to explain the concepts of the ESB throughout the book. Seeing the concepts illustrated in these diagrams will help you to understand what an ESB is, and how it is being used in real integration projects today.

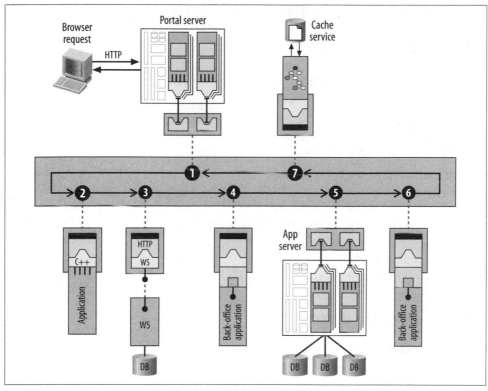

Figure P-7. Diagramming notation showing multiple steps in a process flow

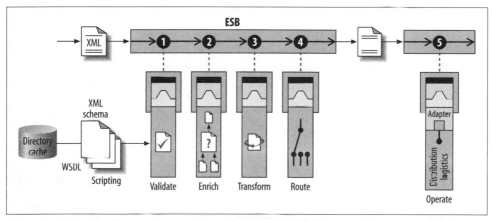

Figure P-8. Using the diagramming notation to describe the abstract pattern definition combined with the process flow definition

Conventions Used in This Book

The following typographical conventions are used in this book:

Plain text
> Indicates menu titles, menu options, menu buttons, and keyboard accelerators (such as Alt and Ctrl).

Italic
> Indicates new terms, URLs, email addresses, filenames, file extensions, pathnames, directories, and Unix utilities.

`Constant width`
> Indicates commands, options, switches, variables, attributes, keys, functions, types, classes, namespaces, methods, modules, properties, parameters, values, objects, events, event handlers, XML tags, HTML tags, macros, the contents of files, or the output from commands.

`Constant width bold`
> Is used to show emphasis in code examples.

We'd Like to Hear from You

Please address comments and questions concerning this book to the publisher:

> O'Reilly Media, Inc.
> 1005 Gravenstein Highway North
> Sebastopol, CA 95472
> (800) 998-9938 (in the United States or Canada)
> (707) 829-0515 (international or local)
> (707) 829-0104 (fax)

We have a web page for this book, where we list errata, examples, and any additional information. You can access this page at:

> *http://www.oreilly.com/catalog/esb*

To comment or ask technical questions about this book, send email to:

> *bookquestions@oreilly.com*

For more information about our books, conferences, Resource Centers, and the O'Reilly Network, see our web site at:

> *http://www.oreilly.com*

Acknowledgments

Over the course of writing this book, I interacted with countless people, all of whom helped me in some way toward getting this book written. First, I would like to thank those who provided creative input into the content of the book and provided answers to my questions along the way: Jeanne Abmayr, Dennis Attinger, Jonathan Bachman, Jon Chappell, Ray Christopher, Rob Conti, Glen Daniels, Tim Dempsey, Gary Hemdal, Mitchell Horowitz, Sonali Kanoujia, Rajiv Kotyan, Trip Kucera, Luis Maldonato, Jaime Meritt, Paul Moxon, Stephen Neal, Matt Rothera, George St. Maurice, Mike Theroux, Jamison Tomasek, and Hub Vandervoort.

Of special note I would like to recognize Jonathan Bachman, Gary Hemdal, and Hub Vandervoort for their creative input and participation in helping to formulate the visual diagramming notation that is used in this book.

Also, I would like to thank those who provided substantial feedback during the review period: Jean-Michel Coeur, Paul Connaughton, John Crupi, Bill Cullen, Tim De Borger, Chris Ferris, David Grigglestone, David Hentchel, Gregor Hohpe, Rick Kuzyk, Ted Neward, Ken Schwarz, Gordon Van Huizen, Leonard Walstad, and Bill Wood.

Of particular note are these reviewers, who provided by far the most thorough and constructive feedback: David Hentchel, Gregor Hohpe, Leonard Walstad, and Bill Wood.

Lastly, I would like to acknowledge the many members of the Sonic Software engineering team, including Bill Cullen, Jaime Meritt, and Bill Wood, for their innovation and contributions to the creation and ongoing development of the ESB as a technology concept.

Introduction to the Enterprise Service Bus

Across all industries, executives are demanding more value from their strategic business processes. What process is strategic to a given company may vary dramatically by industry, but a common theme is that CEOs want their IT organizations to measurably improve the flow of data and information driving key business decisions. Whether it's a financial services firm seeking a competitive advantage by guaranteeing a higher volume of faster foreign exchange trades, a retail chain looking to accelerate the flow of store data back to brand managers at corporate headquarters, or a building materials supplier striving to optimize order flow through a complex distribution chain, there are common and significant technical challenges to be overcome. Information is locked up in applications within different departments and organizations, and it is both time-consuming and costly to pry that data loose. In short, the enterprise is far from integrated.

The past several years have seen some significant technology trends, such as Service Oriented Architecture (SOA), Enterprise Application Integration (EAI), Business-to-Business (B2B), and web services. These technologies have attempted to address the challenges of improving the results and increasing the value of integrated business processes, and have garnered the widespread attention of IT leaders, vendors, and industry analysts. The Enterprise Service Bus (ESB) draws the best traits from these and other technology trends.

The ESB concept is a new approach to integration that can provide the underpinnings for a loosely coupled, highly distributed integration network that can scale beyond the limits of a hub-and-spoke EAI broker. An ESB is a standards-based integration platform that combines messaging, web services, data transformation, and intelligent routing to reliably connect and coordinate the interaction of significant numbers of diverse applications across *extended enterprises* with transactional integrity.

An *extended enterprise* represents an organization and its business partners, which are separated by both business boundaries and physical boundaries. In an extended enterprise, even the applications that are under the control of a single corporation may be separated by geographic dispersion, corporate firewalls, and interdepartmental security policies.

SOA in an Event-Driven Enterprise

In an *event-driven enterprise*, business events that affect the normal course of a business process can occur in any order and at any time. Applications that exchange data in automated business processes need to communicate with each other using an event-driven SOA to have the agility to react to changing business requirements. An SOA provides a business analyst or integration architect with a broad abstract view of applications and integration components to be dealt with as high-level services. In an ESB, applications and event-driven services are tied together in an SOA in a loosely coupled fashion, which allows them to operate independently from one another while still providing value to a broader business function.

> In the realm of SOA, events are represented in an open XML format and flow through a transparent pipeline that's open to inspection and subject to intermediation...
>
> — John Udell, *InfoWorld*

Service components in an SOA expose coarse-grained interfaces with the purpose of sharing data asynchronously between applications. Using an ESB, an integration architect pulls together applications and discrete integration components to create assemblies of services to form composite business processes, which in turn automate business functions in a real-time enterprise.

An ESB provides the implementation backbone for an SOA. That is, it provides a loosely coupled, event-driven SOA with a highly distributed universe of named routing destinations across a multiprotocol message bus. Applications (and integration components) in the ESB are abstractly decoupled from each other, and connect together through the bus as logical endpoints that are exposed as event-driven services.

With its distributed deployment infrastructure, an ESB can efficiently provide central configuration, deployment, and management of services that are distributed across the extended enterprise.

A New Approach to Pervasive Integration

The common goal of applying technologies such as SOA, EAI, B2B, and web services is to create an architecture for integration that can be pervasive across an extended enterprise and beyond. For an integration infrastructure to achieve this pervasiveness, it must have the following characteristics:

- It must adapt to suit the needs of general-purpose integration projects across a variety of integration situations, large and small. Adaptability includes providing a durable architecture that is capable of withstanding evolutions in protocols, interface technology, and even process modeling trends.

- It must link together applications that span the extended enterprise using a single unified approach and a common infrastructure.

- It must extend beyond the boundaries of a single corporate IT data center and into automating partner relationships such as B2B and supply-chain scenarios.

- It must have simplicity of design and low barriers to entry, enabling the everyday IT professional to become a self-empowered integration architect.

- It must provide an SOA across the pervasive integration that enables integration architects to have a broad, abstract view of corporate application assets and automated business processes.

- It needs the flexibility and ability to react to and meet the needs of changing business requirements and competitive pressures.

 In an ESB, applications and event-driven services are tied together in an SOA in a loosely coupled fashion. This allows them to operate independently from one another while still providing value to a broader business function.

The ESB architecture addresses these needs, and is capable of being adopted for any general-purpose integration project. It is also capable of scaling pervasively across enterprise applications, regardless of physical location and technology platform. Any application can plug into an ESB network using a number of connectivity options, and immediately participate in data sharing with other applications that are exposed across the bus as shared services. This is why the ESB is often referred to as an *integration network* or *integration fabric*.

An ESB provides a highly distributed approach to integration, with unique capabilities that allow individual departments or business units to build out their integration projects in incremental, digestible chunks. Using an ESB, departments and business units can continue to maintain their own local control and autonomy in individual integration projects, while still being able to connect each integration project into a larger, more global integration network or grid.

SOA for Web Services, Available Today

Web services have bestowed newfound importance on service-oriented architectures by providing a standards-based approach to interoperability between applications. The main objective of web services has been to provide a service abstraction that allows interoperability between applications built using disparate platforms and environments. The achievement of this goal will provide an easier path to pervasive integration between applications.

With the advent of the ESB there is now a way to incorporate web services and SOA into a meaningful architecture for integrating applications and services into a backbone that spans the extended enterprise in a large-scale fashion. An ESB makes web services, XML, and other integration technologies immediately useful with the mature technology that exists today.

The core tenets of SOA are vital to the success of a pervasive integration project, and are already implemented quite thoroughly in the ESB. The web services standards are trending in the right direction, but remain incomplete with respect to the enterprise-grade capabilities such as security, reliability, transaction management, and business process orchestration. The ESB is based on today's established standards in these areas, and has real implementations that are already being deployed across a number of industries. The ESB is quite capable of keeping in step with the ongoing evolution of the web-services equivalents of these capabilities as they mature. Chapter 12 provides a more detailed discussion on this subject.

Conventional Integration Approaches

An ESB applies web services and other complementary standards by combining them with technology concepts and best practices learned from EAI brokers. However, an ESB is more than simply a web-services veneer on top of the same old EAI hub.

Traditional formalized approaches to integration have their pros and cons. Figure 1-1 shows some of the high-level traits of integration approaches, which range from the least desirable on the lower left point of origin, to the most desirable on the upper right quadrant.

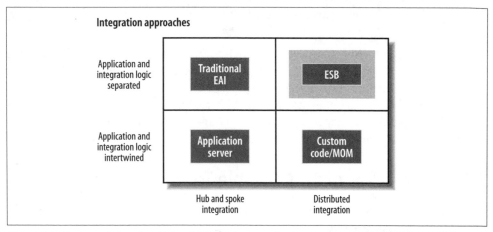

Figure 1-1. Characteristics of traditional EAI brokers, application servers, vanilla MOM, and ESB

Traditional EAI brokers, which include those that are built upon application servers, use a hub-and-spoke architecture. A hub-and-spoke architecture has the benefit of centralized functions, such as management of routing logic and business rules, but does not scale well across departmental or business unit boundaries. Chapter 2 will examine the huge price of early attempts at integration using EAI hubs, as well as their moderate success.

Application servers can interoperate through standard protocols, yet they link things together in a tightly coupled fashion, and intertwine the integration logic and application logic together.

EAI brokers provide increased value by separating the application logic from the integration and process routing logic, yet still suffer from the hub-and-spoke architecture.

Message Oriented Middleware (MOM) provides the ability to connect applications in a loosely coupled, asynchronous fashion. However, MOM by itself requires low-level coding in an application. Using a traditional MOM, along with custom coding techniques, can get you a long way toward a distributed integration solution. However, without a higher level of abstraction of the routing logic, this approach also suffers from having integration logic hard-wired and intertwined with the application logic. Depending on the MOM being used, even the distributed characteristic might be limited because some traditional MOM infrastructure is not capable of spanning physical network boundaries very well.

Finally, in an ESB, services can be *configured* rather than coded. Process flow and service invocations can transparently span the entire distributed bus. An ESB provides a highly distributed integration environment that spans well beyond the reach of hub-and-spoke architectures, and a clear separation of business logic and integration logic such as routing and data transformation. An ESB architecture forms an interconnected grid of messaging hubs and integration services, with the intelligence and functionality of the integration network distributed throughout.

Chapter 6 further describes the contrast between integration using an application server architecture and integration using an ESB. MOM concepts are discussed in Chapter 5. "The Accidental Architecture" in Chapter 2 continues to discuss the separation of business process routing and business logic.

Requirements Driven by IT Needs

A key characteristic of an ESB is to provide the underpinnings to support the needs of distributed, loosely coupled business units and business partners automating supply chains. These capabilities in an ESB were born out of necessity, as a result of middleware vendors working with industry professionals who were trying to create an architecture for large-scale integration. These industry professionals included IT architects in large corporations, and innovators in the e-Marketplace trading hub community who needed to build a B2B trading exchange backbone based on shared services, messaging, XML, and numerous connectivity options, while adhering to industry standards for each component. Chapter 3 will discuss the many catalysts that contributed to the creation of the ESB concept.

At the same time, the biggest needs that had yet to be addressed included how to effectively provide integration capabilities such as application adapters, data transformation, and intelligent routing in a way that could be used for general-purpose integration projects across a variety of integration situations. Also required was a more universal technology and an architectural approach that could be used to connect applications beyond the needs of individual tactical integration projects.

IT professionals had been disappointed by some previous technology trends such as CORBA and EAI. CORBA had the right idea with SOA, but turned out to be too complex to implement and maintain due to its reliance on tightly coupled interfaces between applications and services. EAI also suffered from steep learning curves and expensive barriers to entry on individual projects (more on this in the next chapter). What was really needed was a simple approach to SOA, with an architecture that could be adapted to suit the general needs of any integration effort, large or small. In addition, there needed to be a durable architecture that was capable of withstanding evolutions in protocols, interface technology, and even process modeling trends. The ESB concept was created to address all these needs.

Industry Traction

Since ESB was first introduced in 2002, the ESB approach to integration has been adopted by numerous significant vendors in the middleware, integration, and web-services markets. Its acceptance continues to grow steadily.

Analyst firms such as Gartner Inc., IDC, and ZapThink have been tracking and writing about the ESB technology trend since early 2002. In a report issued in 2002 (DF-18-7304), Gartner Inc. analyst Roy Schulte wrote the following:

> A new form of *enterprise service bus (ESB)* infrastructure—combining *message-oriented middleware*, *web services*, *transformation* and *routing intelligence*—will be running in the majority of enterprises by 2005.

> These high-function, low-cost ESBs are well suited to be the backbone for service-oriented architectures and the *enterprise nervous system*.

Those four pillars—MOM, web services, transformation, and routing intelligence—represent the foundation of any good ESB. This book will focus on the role of each piece and many other required components as we explore the ESB. We will examine what the ESB can do for an enterprise, and the role that each basic component plays. We will also explore some advanced topics, including architectural overviews of practical uses across a number of industries.

Vendors Adopting the ESB

A number of middleware and integration vendors have either built, or are in the process of building, something that matches the description of the ESB. And the list is growing all the time. The Appendix lists all the known vendors. Some vendors say they are providing an ESB already; some have announced plans to create one; some are just using the terminology in marketing materials but don't really have anything substantial behind it.

This technology category is destined to become as hot as application servers were in the late '90s, when more than 25 vendors were competing for the same technology space.

A few vendors in this list deserve special mention. Sonic Software pioneered the concept, and shortly thereafter a number of other smaller vendors got on board, saying they also were providing an ESB or were in the process of building one. Once the incumbent integration companies such as webMethods, SeeBeyond, and IBM finally got "on the Bus" and announced their intent to build an ESB, the ESB term really began to get widespread notice as a growing technology category with staying power.

At the time of this writing, Microsoft has not publicly made any statements regarding its Indigo project and the term ESB. However, some journalists and analysts made that connection when Indigo was first announced. A November 30, 2003 *ComputerWorld* article, "Developer interest piqued by Microsoft technologies," quoted Roy Schulte of Gartner Inc. regarding Indigo:

> Roy Schulte, an analyst at Gartner Inc. in Stamford, Conn., noted that Indigo is a superset of Microsoft's Messaging Queuing (MS MQ) technology, as well as the company's Component Object Model (COM), COM+, .Net remoting and Web services support. "Think of this as a simplification, a unification of communication middleware on behalf of Microsoft's plan," he said, adding that he sees Indigo as a very good enterprise service bus (ESB).

Indigo is based on messaging and has the notion of combining MSMQ and web services. That could provide the basis for a messaging bus. However, the rest of its integration capabilities are locked into BizTalk, which is a hub-and-spoke integration server. To qualify as an ESB, both a distributed message bus and distributed integration capabilities need to exist.

If nothing else, the completion of Indigo will make applications and services built on the Microsoft platform even more attractive as endpoints to connect into an ESB. The inclusion of Indigo into the Microsoft platform and development environment will facilitate making applications capable of being loosely coupled and messaging-aware.

Characteristics of an ESB

Due to the fast flurry of vendors trying to gain attention in the growing ESB product category, combined with the number of industry analysts and journalists reporting with their opinions on it, understandably there is much confusion as to what an ESB actually is. This section serves to outline the main characteristics of an ESB.

Pervasiveness

As illustrated in Figure 1-2, the ESB can form the core of a pervasive grid. It is capable of spanning an extended enterprise and beyond, having a global reach across departmental organizations, business units, and trading partners. An ESB is also well suited for localized integration projects, and provides flexible underpinnings enabling it to adapt to any type of integration environment.

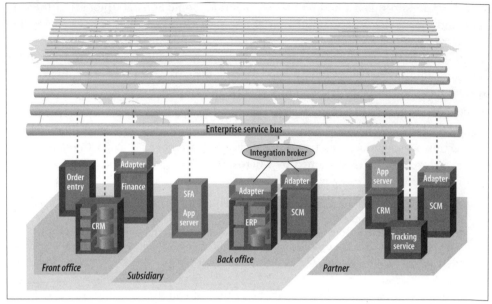

Figure 1-2. ESB forms a pervasive grid that can span a global enterprise network

Applications plug into the bus as needed, and are capable of having visibility and of sharing data with any other applications or services that are plugged into the bus. While web-services interfaces are an integral part of an ESB architecture, all applications do not have to be modified to become true web services to participate in the ESB. Connectivity is achieved through multiple protocols, client API technologies, legacy messaging environments, and third-party application adapters.

Standards-Based Integration

Standards-based integration is a fundamental concept of an ESB. For connectivity, an ESB can utilize J2EE components such as the Java Message Service (JMS) for MOM connectivity, and J2EE Connector Architecture (JCA or J2CA) for connecting to application adapters. An ESB also integrates nicely with applications built with .NET, COM, C#, and C/C++. In addition, an ESB can easily integrate with anything that supports SOAP and web-services APIs, which includes de facto standard web-services toolkit implementations such as Apache Axis. For dealing with data manipulation, an ESB can use XML standards such as XSLT, XPath, and XQuery to provide data transformation, intelligent routing, and querying of "inflight" data as it flows through the bus. For dealing with SOA and business process routing, an ESB can use the Web Services Description Language (WSDL) to describe abstract service interfaces, and Business Process

Execution Language for Web Services (BPEL4WS), WS-Choreography, or some other XML-based vocabulary such as ebXML BPSS, to describe abstract business processes.

Don't worry if you don't know what all these buzzwords mean. Though this book is not intended to be an exhaustive reference or tutorial on all these individual technologies, they will be explained in sufficient detail in the context of how they relate to an ESB.

These standards-based interfaces and components are put together in a meaningful way that comprises an open-ended pluggable architecture. An ESB provides an infrastructure that supports both industry-standard integration components as well as proprietary elements through the use of standardized interfaces. Figure 1-3 shows a simplified view of an ESB that is integrating a J2EE application using JMS and JCA, a third-party packaged application using a JCA-compliant application adapter, a .NET application using a C# client, and two external applications using web services.

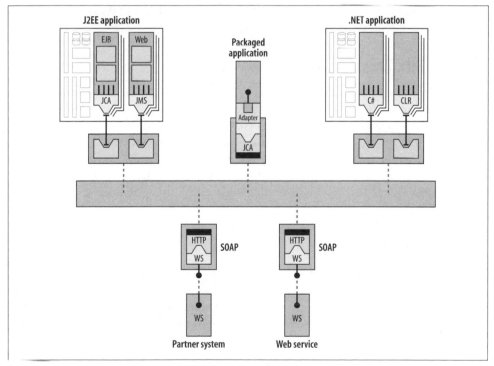

Figure 1-3. An ESB integrating a variety of disparate technologies

Highly Distributed Integration and Selective Deployment

The ESB draws from traditional EAI broker functionality in that it provides integration services such as business process orchestration and routing of data, data transformation, and adapters to applications. However, integration brokers are usually highly centralized and monolithic in nature. The ESB provides these integration capabilities as individual services that can work together in a highly distributed fashion, and can be scaled independently from one another. In Chapter 6 you will learn more about the ESB "service container," a core concept of the ESB, which allows the selective deployment of integration services.

Distributed Data Transformation

A key part of any integration strategy is the ability to readily convert data formats between applications. Many applications do not share the same format for describing similar data.

Data transformation is inherently part of the bus in an ESB deployment. Transformation services that are specialized for the needs of individual applications plugged into the bus can be located anywhere and accessible from anywhere on the bus. Because the data transformation is such an integral part of the ESB itself, an ESB can be thought of as solving the *impedance mismatch* between applications.

Extensibility Through Layered Services

An ESB gives you all the required core capabilities for virtually any integration project, and can be augmented with layered technology to handle more specific uses. For example, specialized capabilities such as Business Process Management (BPM) software can process workflow-related business processes, and collaboration servers can provide specialized services for managing business partners. Specialized third-party translators can provide data conversion from external data formats such as EDI into a target Enterprise Resource Planning (ERP) system or onto the general bus as an internal canonical XML representation.

Event-Driven SOA

In an ESB-enabled, event-driven SOA, applications and services are treated as abstract service endpoints, which can readily respond to asynchronous events. The SOA provides an abstraction away from the details of the underlying connectivity and plumbing. The implementations of the services do not need to understand protocols. Services do not need to understand how messages are routed to other services. They simply receive a message from the ESB as an event, and process that message. The ESB gets the message to anywhere else it needs to go.

In an ESB SOA, custom integration services may be created, extended, and reused as ESB functionality. Application endpoints, which are exposed as services, can be constructed together with specialized integration enablers to form composite services and process flows that can be recombined and reused for various purposes, with the goal of automating business functions in a real-time enterprise.

Chapter 7 will discuss SOA in the ESB in more detail.

Process Flow

An ESB's process flow capabilities range from simple sequences of finite steps to sophisticated business process orchestration with parallel process execution paths using conditional splits and joins. These can be controlled by simple message metadata or through the use of an orchestration language such as BPEL4WS.

The process flow capabilities of the ESB make it possible to define business processes that are local to an individual department or business unit, and that can also coexist within a larger integration network. This is something a hub-and-spoke integration broker or a BPM tool can't do very well on its own. Chapter 7 will examine the details of a distributed processing capability that provides highly distributed business process orchestration without the need for a centralized processing or rules engine.

Process flow in an ESB can also involve specialized integration services that perform intelligent routing of messages based on content.

Because the process flow is built on top of the distributed SOA, it is also capable of spanning highly distributed deployment topologies (even spanning oceans at times) without the need to be painfully aware of the physical network boundaries or multiple protocol hops between applications and services on the bus (Figure 1-4).

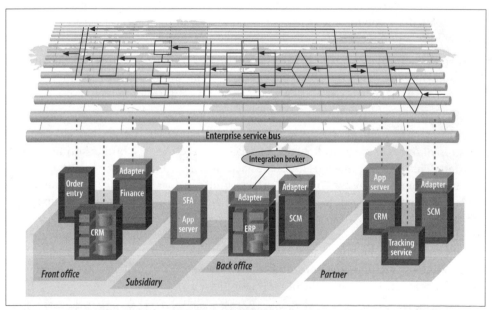

Figure 1-4. Orchestration and process flow spanning highly distributed deployment topologies across physical and logical boundaries

Security and Reliability

The connections between nodes on the ESB are firewall-capable. The security between applications and the ESB, and even between the ESB nodes themselves, is capable of establishing and maintaining the most stringent authentication, credential-management, and access control.

Reliability is achieved by having an enterprise-capable MOM at the core of the ESB. The MOM core provides asynchronous communications, reliable delivery of business data, and transactional integrity. As you will learn in Chapter 5, this is not your traditional MOM technology from a decade ago. Requirements have evolved and matured since then, and a MOM core of an ESB must be capable of meeting today's requirements.

Autonomous but Federated Environment

Traditional hub-and-spoke EAI broker approaches tend to have organizational boundary problems, which are sometimes caused by the physical limitations of the EAI broker's incapability of easily spanning firewalls and network domains. More importantly, even if a hub-and-spoke architecture is capable of being stretched out across organizational boundaries, it still does not allow the local autonomy that individual business units need to operate semi-independently of one another. One of the biggest problems associated with extending the reach of integration beyond the departmental level is the issue of local autonomy versus centralized control.

As part of the business culture in most large corporate environments, each department or business unit needs to operate independently of one another. However, they still rely on shared resources, and reporting and accounting information that funnels into a common business function.

In such an environment, it is not reasonable to impose an integration strategy that requires all message traffic to flow through a centralized message broker sitting in headquarters. This is not simply a technical obstacle; it is a corporate culture issue as well. In an environment of loosely coupled business units, it does not make sense for things such as business process flow between localized applications, or security domains, to be managed by a single centralized corporate IT function. Loosely coupled business units within an organization need to operate independently of one other. Each should have its own IT function and not have to think in terms of routing all its message traffic, or delegating control of its business rules and security domains, through a centralized integration broker at one location or the other (Figure 1-5).

Local business units and departments need to have control over their own local IT resources, such as the applications running at their site. The integration infrastructure should support deployment topologies to support that business model with practicality. The ESB provides this deployment model, allowing for local message traffic, integration components, and adapters to be locally installed, configured, secured, and managed,

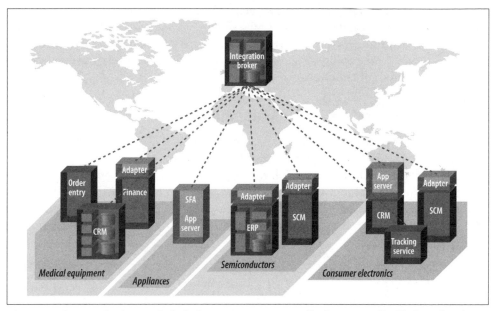

Figure 1-5. Separate business units lack the necessary autonomy if using a centralized hub-and-spoke integration broker

while still being able to plug together the local integration domains into a larger federated integration network with an integrated security model (Figure 1-6).

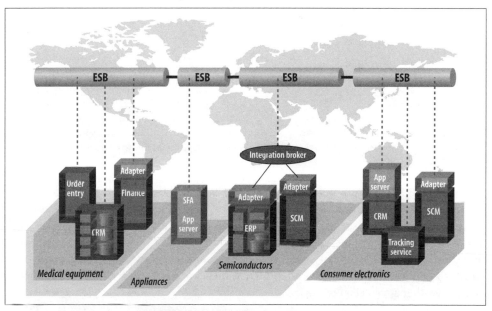

Figure 1-6. Autonomous and federated, an ESB allows organizations to cooperatively federate operations across organizational boundaries

The distributed characteristics of the ESB are achieved by abstraction of endpoint definitions from the physical deployment details and underlying wire protocols, along with orchestration and routing of data between those endpoints. The federated characteristics are achieved by the ability of the ESB to segregate and selectively traverse application domains and security boundaries.

Remote Configuration and Management

In some business models it doesn't make sense to have local IT staff at each remote location, although there is still a need for a loosely coupled, autonomous yet federated integration network. To illustrate this point, let's examine a simple case study for an ESB deployment in the retail industry. A video rental chain can have hundreds or thousands of remote locations that all contain the same set of applications, and all operate in the same fashion with regard to inventory management, accounting, and reporting (Figure 1-7).

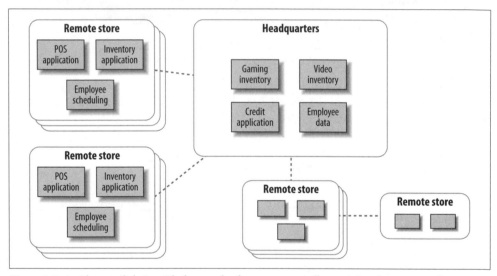

Figure 1-7. A video retail chain with thousands of remote stores, all containing the same set of applications

Using an ESB, an integration blueprint can be established to handle the local communication between the applications at a remote store. This includes the interface definitions to in-store applications, the routing of message traffic and message channel management, and security permissions. It may also include integration components such as an application adapter, protocol adapter, or data transformation. This integration blueprint, or template, can be deployed and customized at each site and act independently of all the other stores (Figure 1-8).

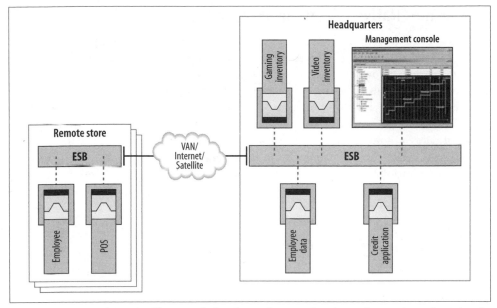

Figure 1-8. ESB configuration blueprint deployed at each remote location and remotely configured and managed

This remote deployment blueprint capability is not unique to retail—it has applications across other industries as well. The unified remote management of federated integration realms is a key contributor to the success of any ESB deployment in a highly distributed environment.

SECURE, RELIABLE MESSAGING LINKS

In addition to sharing data between applications locally at each store, these remote stores need to share information with headquarters to do accounting and reporting, credit management, and tracking of employee data. The remote stores may also need to share information with each other. For example, a large video chain may want to offer a service whereby a consumer can rent a video from a store close to home, and return it to another store near the office. Therefore, stores in the same geographic area need to be able to share information about the rental in a near real-time fashion. Because of the latency and resiliency issues of satellite networks between the remote stores and headquarters, it's not feasible to just maintain a constant centralized access point for all rental information. That transient information about what you just rented two hours ago needs to be shared, or be accessible with an integrated data-sharing link between the remote stores.

Because the link between the headquarters and the remote stores is achieved using reliable messaging, the interrupts in network service due to unreliable satellite links are compensated for by the messaging layer. Also note that it is possible for the stores to link among themselves using a secure and reliable messaging channel across an Internet connection.

XML as the "Native" Datatype of the ESB

XML is an ideal foundation for representing data as it flows between applications across the ESB. The data that is produced and consumed by a vast array of applications can exist in a variety of formats and packaging schemes. While it is certainly possible for the ESB to carry data using any form of packaging or enveloping scheme that you like, there are tremendous benefits to representing in-flight data as XML, including the ability to use specialized ESB services that combine data from different sources to create new views of data, and to enrich and retarget messages for advanced data sharing between applications. Chapter 4 will explore a fundamental benefit of XML—the ability to insulate an organization from the need to synchronize upgrades between applications—and will discuss the philosophy behind distributed XML transformation services in more detail.

Real-Time Throughput of Business Data

An ESB eliminates latency problems by providing real-time throughput into in-flight data as it travels between applications across the ESB. Currently, one of the most popular integration methods is nightly batch processing. However, bulk batch-processing integration strategies, nightly or otherwise, are prone to high margins for error and can cause delays in information retrieval. The resulting high latency in getting up-to-date information can be costly. Chapter 9 discusses the details of this, and explores how an ESB can be used to refactor your organization from nightly batch processing toward real-time throughput of business data.

Operational Awareness

Operational awareness refers to the ability of a business analyst to gain insight into the state and health of business operations. An infrastructure that allows the timely tracking and reporting of data as it flows across an organization in the form of business messages in a business process is an invaluable tool in helping to achieve operational awareness. A separate category of products known as Business Activity Monitoring (BAM) has emerged to address the many issues of operational awareness.

One of the benefits of using XML as the native data format for the ESB is that messages are not treated as opaque chunks of data. If all data between applications and services is formatted as XML documents, underpinnings are provided by the ESB that allow you to layer advanced capabilities on top of the ESB to gain real-time insight into the business data that flows through your enterprise. These capabilities, whether they are inherently part of the ESB or are enabled as an extension of it, represent a natural part of the common infrastructure that includes the routing, process flow, and underlying plumbing, and that don't require a separate third-party BAM product be bolted onto the side.

Auditing and tracking capabilities that are a base part of an ESB allow you to monitor and track the health of your business processes and the flow of messages throughout your SOA. Value-added services such as data caching, data collection and aggregation, and visual rendition of XML data can create a substrate for generating operational alerts, notifications, and reporting that can provide real-time insight into the state of your business as the data traverses your enterprise (Figure 1-9).

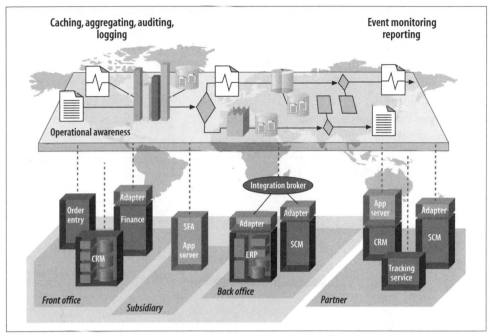

Figure 1-9. Value-added services enabling operational awareness provide real-time insight into live business data

Tracking and reporting of data in the ESB is made possible by defining auditing and tracking points within a process flow, which in turn provide insertion points for collecting important content from business messages as they travel through a business process. Examples of trackable data are the business messages themselves, and the process events indicating whether a message has passed through a particular set of business process steps.

Advanced value-added services can provide the data collection services, the query mechanisms, and the reporting capabilities that enable all this data to be gathered and presented in a meaningful way. XML persistence services can provide caching and aggregation points that can collect data to be transformed for the purpose of providing data to feed into other applications, or to feed into human-readable reporting mechanisms that can be used by business analysts. This means that data flowing through the ESB can be analyzed in real time to produce live information about the nature of your business—for example, to provide a realistic snapshot of where your inventory is at all times within a supply chain.

Incremental Adoption

One of the primary differentiating qualities of an ESB is its ability to allow incremental adoption, as opposed to being an all-or-nothing proposition. In the post-Y2K spending slowdown, budgets for multimillion-dollar IT projects are just not what they used to be. There is some indication that IT funding is getting freed up to solve the short-term tactical integration needs, but budgets are still being highly scrutinized at an executive level. At the same time, however, there is still a desire to implement larger corporate-wide strategic initiatives—all of which rely heavily on integration and reuse of existing IT assets.

Figure 1-10 illustrates how an ESB can be used for small projects that each build into a much larger integration network. We'll see how this is accomplished as we delve into the details throughout this book.

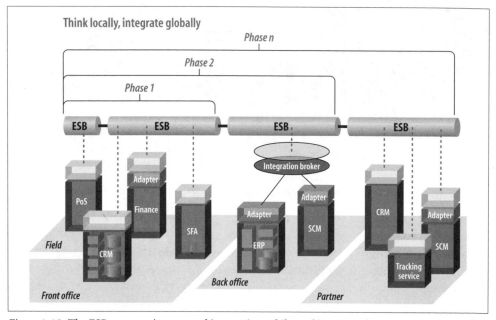

Figure 1-10. The ESB supports incremental integration, while working toward a more strategic goal

The federated/autonomous capabilities of the ESB also contribute to the ability to adopt an ESB one project at a time. Incrementally staged deployments of ESB integration projects can provide immediate value while working toward the broader corporate initiatives.

This notion of incremental adoption is also further supported by the ability to bridge into an existing integration broker hub and legacy message brokers. Integration broker hubs and their traits are explored in more detail in Chapter 2.

Adoption of ESB by Industry

Many nascent technologies suffer from the issue of gaining adoption by trying to find a problem to solve. ESB concepts, on the other hand, have evolved out of necessity via industry-leading architects working with vendors in the technology community to define and build it, so ESB has been adopted as it has been built. ESBs are already being put to use in a variety of industries, including financial services, insurance, manufacturing, retail, telecom, energy, food distribution, and government. Here are some examples.

Financial Services

- A leading subprime lender implemented an ESB to reduce application processing costs by 60%. This was accomplished by creating a unified view of customer and lending data across an eCredit system, third-party credit bureaus, and their back-end systems.

- Leading banks have implemented Straight Through Processing of financial transactions using an ESB, at a considerable saving over manual processing.

- A Derivatives Trading system relies on an ESB to process more than 100,000 transactions a day for 1,200 users, accounting for several billion dollars in revenue.

Insurance

- The world's largest life and health reinsurer, with $20 billion in annual revenue, generated significant savings using an ESB as a business process management solution to streamline the exchange of back-office transactional information between the main headquarters and the insurance brokers who market and manage their policies.

Manufacturing

- A manufacturer of countertops and flooring is using an ESB to improve supply chain predictability and reduce out-of-stock conditions by implementing a co-managed inventory system and "availability to promise" (ATP) query system. In phase 1 of the deployment, the ESB is being used to link the manufacturer and 60 of its distributors in a supply-chain network.

  The deployment model of the ESB allows the manufacturer to deploy ESB service containers at the distributor sites. This is an alternative to deploying an integration broker at each remote distributor.

- A major manufacturer of lighting, televisions, and medical imaging equipment is using an ESB to create a unified integration backbone to connect all its data centers across its global business units, and to create a unified view of product data and billing information to customers worldwide.

Retail

- Using a standards-based, centralized management framework, a national retail video chain is in the process of adopting an ESB infrastructure to dynamically configure and manage 1,800 remote stores from a central management and configuration console.

- The world's largest mail-order company ($12 billion in revenue) relies on an ESB to order products from its many suppliers.

Telecom

- A web portal at a major phone carrier relies on an ESB to provide real-time analytics on click-through tracking (two-hour response versus 30-day response), processing 16 million messages per day.

- The second-largest U.S. telecom carrier provider, a $43 billion company, uses an ESB to provide information from internal systems to competitive carriers.

Energy/Utility

- A $10 billion electric utility firm implemented an ESB, connecting systems both internally and with government-imposed applications. Information is provided in real time for billing, system management, executive reporting, and regulatory-mandated information sharing with its competitors.

Food Distribution Network

- A major European food distribution network (a £1.2 billion division) implemented an ESB in eight weeks and saved $3 million using a centralized hub-and-spoke integration broker approach. The ESB automates the distribution network by managing the buying, selling, and logistical coordination of the supply chain that ranges from the distribution of meats and produce to the grain that feeds the livestock.

  In this food distribution network, the ESB is integrating applications spanning three different operating companies and many third-party trading partners, resulting in increased operational efficiency, significant cost savings, and an easier methodology to integrate new systems.

Government

- A U.S. government agency is working with an ESB to integrate multiple government systems to comply with the USA PATRIOT Act. The PATRIOT Act allows the government to track transactions for the purpose of preventing money from getting to terrorists. The project involves using the ESB as the integration between portal servers and various backend systems across multiple government agencies to provide a unified view of data.

Summary

In summary, an ESB has the following characteristics:

Pervasiveness.   An ESB can be adapted to suit the needs of general-purpose integration projects across a variety of integration situations. It is capable of building out integration projects that can span an entire organization and its business partners.

Highly distributed, event-driven SOA.   Loosely coupled integration components can be deployed on the bus across widely distributed geographic deployment topologies, yet are accessible as shared services from anywhere on the bus.

Selective deployment of integration components.   Adapters, distributed data transformation services, and content-based routing services can be selectively deployed when and where they are needed, and can be independently scaled.

Security and reliability.   All components that communicate through the bus can take advantage of reliable messaging, transactional integrity, and secure authenticated communications.

Orchestration and process flow.   An ESB allows data to flow across any applications and services that are plugged into the bus, whether local or remote.

Autonomous yet federated managed environment.   An ESB supports local autonomy at a departmental and business unit level, and is still able to integrate in a larger managed integration environment.

Incremental adoption. An ESB can be used for small projects.   Each individual project can build into a much larger integration network, which can be remotely managed from anywhere on the bus.

XML support.   An ESB can take advantage of XML as its "native" datatype.

Real-time insight.   An ESB provides the underpinnings to enable real-time insight into live business data. BAM enablement is built right into the ESB fabric.

You should now have enough information about ESBs to whet your appetite. In the later, more detailed chapters, you will learn more about the underlying technical aspects. The next few chapters will discuss the evolution of the ESB, its current state of integration, the benefits of adopting XML in a generic data exchange architecture to mediate between diverse data representations, and asynchronous messaging and MOM.

2

The State of Integration

A number of factors, both business and technical, have led to the need for a new approach to integration. There are business drivers such as changes in economic conditions, regulatory compliance, and the introduction of new disruptive hardware technology such as Radio Frequency Identification (RFID) tags, all of which foreshadow significant changes in the way businesses view application integration and data sharing. These drivers seem at odds with the current state of integration within enterprises, which is not as advanced as you might think. As we will explore in this chapter, the majority of applications that ought to be integrated simply aren't, and those that are integrated suffer from overly complex integration approaches that have grown unmanageable over time, due to a lack of a cohesive integration strategy that can be applied broadly.

Here are some current business drivers that are affecting the need for a broad-scale integration solution:

Economic drivers. These have changed the shape of IT spending. Economic trends have caused IT departments to focus on the applications that are available and getting them to work together somehow.

Top priority: Integration. Survey results show that integration continues to be at the top of the list of priorities for CIOs.

Regulatory compliance. Sarbanes-Oxley, the PATRIOT Act, and FCC regulations are forcing corporations to build the internal infrastructure required to track, route, monitor, and retrieve business data in more detailed ways than ever before.

Straight-Through Processing (STP). The goal of STP is the elimination of inefficiencies in business processes, such as manual rekeying of data, faxing, paper mail, or unnecessary data batching. In industries such as financial services, this helps to achieve near-zero-latency processing of financial transactions.

Radio Frequency Identification (RFID). Seen as the next evolution of bar codes, RFID has the potential to generate new kinds of data in large volumes, which then needs to be routed, transformed, aggregated, and processed.

Unfortunately, the current state of corporate integration environments does very little to facilitate forward progress in these areas. This has left IT leaders to search for broader integration solutions. Problems with the current state of integration include:

The general lack of a well-connected enterprise. This prevents the business from moving forward with automating business processes, which in turn hinders its ability to react quickly to changing business requirements.

The Accidental Architecture. The accidental architecture is a de facto integration approach that develops over time, as a result of not having a coherent corporate-wide strategy for integration. This represents an ongoing legacy of point-to-point integration solutions, each with its own flavor of connectivity and integration. The accidental architecture represents a brittle, rigid infrastructure that is not cohesive and cannot readily withstand new additions or changes to the integration environment.

ETL, batch transfer, and FTP. Extract, Transform, and Load (ETL) techniques using FTP file transfers and nightly batch jobs are still the most popular means of "integration" today. These processes involve nightly dump-and-load operations on the data that sits in various applications. Due to the latency and the margins of error associated with this practice, organizations never really have a good snapshot of their critical data.

The perils of the past with integration brokers. Expensive integration broker projects of the late 1990s have had nominal success and left organizations with silos of proprietary integration domains.

This chapter will examine these factors. In addition, it will explain the benefits of refactoring to an ESB through incremental adoption, while leveraging best practices learned from integration broker technologies.

Business Drivers Motivating Integration

IT Spending Trends

Economic trends have caused IT departments to focus on making things work with applications they have available to them today. In the year leading up to Y2K, the majority of IT spending was focused on Y2K preparation, which included buying packaged applications that were Y2K-ready.

The subsequent economic downturn, whether attributed to post-Y2K, post-Internet-bubble, 9/11, or wartime uncertainty, has led to dramatic changes in IT spending. This has had a particular impact on integration, both positively and negatively. IT budgets are not what they were in pre-Y2K years. No longer do IT managers have the luxury of multimillion-dollar budgets to spend on integration broker software and services, with projects that could take 18–24 months to show results. IT spending has now become highly visible at the executive level, and individual projects are being highly scrutinized.

Only the projects that are critical to business viability are getting funded. Corporations are demanding tangible results and ROI within the 3–6 month timeframe on a per-project basis, though they still maintain the strategic goal of improving overall operational efficiency.

Integration as a High-Ranking Priority

A new era of frugality does not decrease the need for improvement in business processes or the need for integration. The business drivers are still there: the need for improved process cycle times, the need to reduce inventory levels, and the need to eliminate duplicate IT services, to name a few.

An IDC report[*] surveyed 557 CIOs about their high-level priorities for 2004. The report said this about integration:

> Of what might be called "market driver" trends, integration has replaced security as the highest priority in IT planning for 2004 in North America among IT and executives interviewed in June 2003.

The report also notes that integration and security rank third and fourth, respectively, among the highest priorities of CIOs, just behind "Infrastructure replacement/upgrade" and "IT cost-cutting."

That total percentage was influenced by the fact that 21% of "midmarket" companies ranked integration important, even above infrastructure replacement/upgrade and IT cost-cutting. Table 2-1 shows the answers to the question: "Which of the following issues do you expect to have single-highest priority in 2004? Select one."

Table 2-1. Importance of integration by industry (% of respondents)

	Total	Financial Services	Manufacturing	Government/ Education/ Healthcare Delivery	Services	Telecom/ Broadcast	Transportation/ Utilities	Retail/ Wholesale Distribution	Other
Infrastructure replacement/ upgrade	21.0	17.0	24.0	26.0	17.0	15.0	26.0	29.0	8.0
IT cost cutting	20.0	23.0	24.0	18.0	16.0	31.0	22.0	14.0	8.0
Integration	16.0	16.0	17.0	9.0	20.0	15.0	30.0	4.0	15.0
Security	12.0	18.0	9.0	16.0	12.0	8.0	-	14.0	12.0
Internet-related projects	9.0	11.0	6.0	10.0	9.0	4.0	11.0	7.0	8.0

[*] IDC, *Integration Standards Trends in Program Development: It All Depends on What the Meaning of "Open" Is*, November 2003 (document #30365), *http://www.idc.com*.

Table 2-1. Importance of integration by industry (% of respondents) (continued)

	Total	Financial Services	Manufacturing	Government/ Education/ Healthcare Delivery	Services	Telecom/ Broadcast	Transportation/ Utilities	Retail/ Wholesale Distribution	Other
Linux	4.0	1.0	4.0	3.0	8.0	8.0	-	-	-
Optimization Software (e.g., storage management)	4.0	4.0	6.0	4.0	1.0	8.0	-	11.0	4.0
Mobile devices	2.0	-	1.0	3.0	4.0	-	-	-	8.0
Wireless networking	2.0	1.0	2.0	3.0	2.0	4.0	-	-	4.0
Other/don't know	10.0	9.0	8.0	8.0	11.0	8.0	11.0	22.0	35.0
N=	557	82	109	116	143	26	27	28	26

Regulatory Compliance

Sometimes the need for integration is forced upon you, whether you like it or not. Even in hard times, when IT budgets are tight, infrastructure revamping for the purposes of integration still must be done to comply with government regulations. As most IT folks would attest, there's plenty going on just trying to maintain the status quo without having to worry about new integration strategies. However, there's nothing like the prospect of jail time and stiff fines to get the attention of senior management.

Due to regulatory compliance issues, companies in some industries must make information available to competitors and must audit information access. For example, in the telecom industry, the Incumbent Local Exchange Carriers (ILECs) need to provide information to competitive LECs. Energy utilities need to provide billing information to competitors. Healthcare agencies and privacy laws require tracking customer record access for audit purposes. This requires making your disparate data readily available in a standard format using a standard protocol.

Here are some areas in which regulatory compliance is a driver.

Telecom

An FCC regulation requires that all telecom providers expose certain aspects of their customer data with the local phone carriers. One major telecom provider was having stiff fines imposed upon it for not complying with this requirement. Obviously, even a major company cannot afford to pay that amount of money on an ongoing basis. Many issues and high costs are associated with sharing information that is required by law, and filtering out what is *not* required by law. Therefore, a simplistic approach cannot meet the needs of compliance while still protecting sensitive corporate data. You need fine-grained filtering and selective data transformation to provide only the necessary data (and perhaps only at the last possible minute) to minimize the potential leverage your competitors can get as a result of this access. All of this requires fine-grained access and control over process flow.

The telecom provider mentioned previously needed a standards-based integration solution capable of scaling out to the small providers, using a variety of protocols that would allow the smaller providers to adopt the integration strategy. To fill this need, the company ended up adopting an ESB.

Sarbanes-Oxley

The Sarbanes-Oxley Act of 2002, designed to protect investors by improving the accuracy and reliability of corporate disclosures, imposes new reporting requirements and introduces higher accountability on the part of corporate decision-makers and their enterprises. Sarbanes-Oxley compliance requirements pose some real challenges. They include cost considerations, logistical complexities, data collection and management issues, and the timely reporting of accurate data, regardless of where the data exists across an enterprise.

Government

The U.S. federal government had set a goal to become paperless by 2003. At a U.S. government CIO council summit in January of 2003, Brand Niemann, chair of the CIO Council XML Web Services Working Group, said this about the driving force behind XML adoption for integration in the U.S. government:

> The Government Paperwork Elimination Act of 1998 requires federal agencies, by October 2003, to allow individuals or entities that deal with the agencies the option to submit information or transact with the agency electronically, when practicable, and to maintain records electronically, when practicable.

Regulatory compliance has driven a tremendous amount of energy and focus on integrating backend systems and data sources across government agencies. As we will see when we examine the ESB in a portal environment in Chapter 11, an ESB integration network can provide significant value when acting as the intermediate integration technology between the portal and the multitude of backend sources.

Straight-Through Processing (STP)

Straight-Through Processing (STP) refers to the ability to enter transactional data only once for a business process that spans systems and organizations. In other industries, STP may be known as "flow-through provisioning," "paperless acquisition," or "lights-out" or "hands-free" processing.

The goal of achieving STP is to eliminate inefficiencies in business processes, such as manual rekeying of data, faxing, paper mail, or unnecessary batching of data. Examples of things that hinder STP today include rekeying a purchase order into a credit verification system, or the batching of transactions for periodic processing.

STP is an important driver within financial services, telecommunications, and utilities. In financial services, the goal of "T+1" refers to settlement of trades within one day of execution. Automating routine operations helps companies to reduce costs throughout the order or trade lifecycle, to service customers more quickly, and to effectively manage business risks.

Radio Frequency Identification (RFID)

Radio Frequency Identification (RFID) tags are changing the way businesses track goods and supplies throughout their supply chains. RFID tags also promise to help automate supply chains by eliminating the need to have a person unpack crates and pallets to scan bar codes to check the contents. The amount of message traffic that will get generated as a result of RFID-tagged goods passing through readers situated in warehouses and loading docks is going to generate large volumes of data that will need to be captured, routed, transformed, and turned into something meaningful for a business.

"Smart shelves" in retail stores that contain RFID readers will be able to track stock in real time and automatically generate replenishment orders when shelves get low. These shelf readers will also know, for example, when a customer picks up a particular item, then puts it back on the shelf in favor of a different item. This type of data can be valuable to the manufacturer of the item that was reshelved.

Leading retailers such as Wal-Mart and Tesco, as well as the U.S. Department of Defense, have already mandated RFID tagging at the carton level from their large suppliers. The ultimate goal is to drive down the price of the tags themselves such that it is feasible to tag individual items such as a toothbrush or a can of soda. This will significantly increase the number of messages that get generated as a pallet of goods passes by a reader. This volume of data could not be generated with a person manually scanning a bar code one carton at a time. An ESB can act as a buffer to capture the bursts of messages that occur as a pallet passes by a reader at a loading dock. Applications that were not designed to handle that amount of data can be protected by the messaging layer of an ESB, which can distribute the workload across multiple backend applications or queue up the messages until they can be processed.

The increased granularity in messages due to item-level RFID tags can also be a problem for applications that were not designed to handle data at a granularity beyond the carton level. An ESB can provide special caching, aggregation, and transformation services that can collect the fine-grained data and aggregate it into the carton-level summaries that an application may be looking for.

The EPCglobal organization is driving the standardization of the RFID tags, the readers, and the software that integrates the readers to applications. To share RFID data widely, integration rules will need to be defined for the network of readers and interested applications across the supply chain. To avoid flooding the entire network with RFID data, filtering and aggregation rules must be distributed as close to the RFID event generating points as possible. The ESB is an ideal integration platform to remotely configure and manage the rules that control the flow of data.

The Current State of Enterprise Integration

This section will explore the details of how enterprise applications are integrated, or not integrated, today. This includes a discussion of a prevailing problem across many organizations: the accidental architecture.

The Enterprise Is Not Well Connected

Over the past two decades, numerous distributed computing models have arrived on the scene, including DCE, CORBA, DCOM, MOM, EAI brokers, J2EE, web services, and .NET. However, indications are that only a small percentage of enterprise applications are connected, regardless of the technology being used. According to a research report from Gartner Inc.,[*] that number is less than 10%.

Another statistic is even more surprising—of the applications that are connected, only 15% are using formal integration middleware. The rest are using the ETL and batch file-transfer techniques, which are largely based on hand-coded scripting and other custom solutions. More information on ETL and batch file transfer, including their associated problems, can be found in Chapter 9.

The Accidental Architecture

The Gartner 15% statistic provides a sobering data point that illustrates the true state of integration today. How are the other 85% of applications connected? A very common situation that exists in enterprises today is what I refer to as "the accidental architecture." The accidental architecture is something that nobody sets out to create; instead, it's the result of years of accumulating one-of-a-kind pointed integration solutions. In an accidental architecture, corporate applications are perpetually locked into an inflexible integration infrastructure. They continue to be treated as "silos" of information because the integration infrastructure can't adapt to new business requirements (Figure 2-1).

Most integration attempts start out with a deliberate design, but over time, other pieces are bolted on and "integrated," and the handcrafted integration code drifts away from the original intent. Through incremental patches and bolt-ons, integrated systems can lose their design integrity, especially if the system is maintained by a large number of people to whom the original design intent may not have been well communicated. It's a

[*] Statistics from Gartner Inc., "Integration Brokers, Application Servers and APSs," 10/2002.

fact of life that individual point-to-point integrations will drift away from consistency, as engineers make "just this one little change" that's expedient at the time. Eventually it becomes difficult to even identify the points for making changes, and to understand what the side effects would be as a result. In a deployed system this can lead to disastrous results that will negatively affect your business.

Adhering to standards for integration creates a baseline of intended functionality for you to comply with. If the infrastructure is proprietary, rather than based on standards, it can become problematic to retain the intended design and guiding principles over time. While it's easier to take a proprietary platform and bend the rules, this usually results in more "diversity" that later gets bolted on. However, you should keep in mind that simply adhering to standards will not necessarily prevent you from building an accidental architecture.

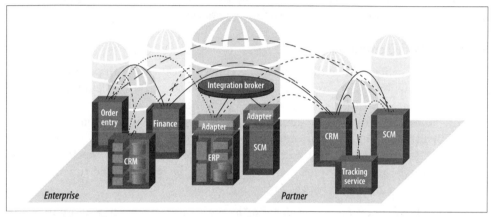

Figure 2-1. The accidental architecture perpetuates the treatment of corporate applications as "silos" of information

The technology behind an accidental architecture can vary. The solid, dashed, and dotted lines in Figure 2-1 represent different techniques used to connect the applications. These techniques can include FTP file transfer, direct socket connections, proprietary MOM, and sometimes CORBA or another type of Remote Procedure Call (RPC) mechanism. Some of the targeted point-to-point solutions may even have XML envelopes defined already, either SOAP-based or otherwise, for carrying the data between the applications being integrated.

The integration broker at the center of the diagram represents an island of integration that connects some applications at a departmental level. However, this does not imply that it is being used to connect *everything* together. The integration broker is usually relegated to being just another piece of infrastructure in the mix, the result of a well-funded project that achieved moderate success, but then didn't continue to integrate everything as promised.

The accidental architecture represents an investment in infrastructure that is rigid and does not provide a durable, cohesive approach to integration. It is not capable of addressing your organizational needs as well as it should. Making changes to the accidental architecture can become increasingly challenging over time, as the number of point-to-point solutions increases. This usually also means that interdependencies between applications are extremely tightly coupled. Making a change to an application's representation of its data means that you also need to change all the other applications that need to share that data. This restricts your ability to quickly adapt your business processes to changes and new business opportunities. These tightly coupled, hard-wired interfaces are not the only problem with an accidental architecture. Further complications arise due to control flow, or orchestration of communication between the business applications, being hardcoded into the applications themselves. This increases the tight coupling and fragility between systems, makes changing business processes even more difficult, and can contribute to vendor lock-in for applications.

Departmental and organizational issues

Technological deficiencies in the accidental architecture can have a ripple effect of manpower coordination issues across the organization. Whether the problem is tightly coupled interfaces or hardcoded orchestration, going back and retrofitting changes into existing applications can be a daunting task. It often requires scheduling lots of meetings with the different development groups that own the applications—just to agree upon what to do and when to do it. If the applications, and their respective development groups, are physically spread out across geographic locations and time zones, the coordination of application changes becomes even more difficult.

Sometimes the application is considered a "legacy" system, in which you are unwilling or unable to make changes simply because it has been put into maintenance mode. There is a common saying that the definition of a "legacy application" is something that you installed yesterday. Even if you have full access to and control over the source code of an in-house application, it can become increasingly difficult over time to make changes as developers move on to other projects or leave the company. As we will see in Chapter 4, an ESB significantly lessens the impact of changing data schemas and formats over time.

Moving forward with an accidental architecture

Even if you have established a good corporate practice for making and tracking changes to application data and interfaces, there are other drawbacks to continuing with the accidental architecture. Using different connectivity technologies means that the security model is probably ad hoc, so there is no sure way to establish and enforce corporate-wide security policies. There are no consistent APIs to rely upon for plugging in new applications, and there's no common ground upon which to establish and build best practices in integration. Recent conversations with an IT leader identified the following problems with accidental architectures:

Unreliability. The communications between the applications are probably not capable of taking advantage of asynchronous reliable messaging. If one of the communication links between two applications within a larger business process fails, the entire process may have to be transactionally backed out and restarted. We will learn more about the advantages of loosely coupled, asynchronous reliable communications in Chapter 5.

Performance and scalability analysis. Whether you are doing preemptive capacity planning or trying to analyze an existing performance problem, the accidental architecture makes it much more difficult due to the many subsystems and their different operational characteristics. The typical reaction is usually an ad hoc, "throw resources at it until it works right" solution, resulting in excessive spending on disks, CPUs, RAM, etc.

Troubleshooting in general. There is no single way to provide adequate diagnostics and reporting. The accidental architecture requires having lots of highly skilled troubleshooters around to debug all the production problems, which tends to increase the overall Total Cost of Ownership (TCO) dramatically. The greater the variation in implementation of the subparts, the broader the expertise needed to figure it all out when it fails. Also, establishing a consistent baseline to describe the proper intended behavior is a challenge.

Redundancy and resiliency. There is no way to ensure that all components of this morass meet with your definition of acceptable redundancy, resiliency, and fault tolerance. This means that it is difficult to define achievable Service-Level Agreements (SLAs) for new functions that depend on connected backend systems

Billing holes. If your system carries data that can represent billable services (as in the telecom business), there's a good possibility that events of billable interest are being lost in the accidental architecture. So, you may be losing revenue and not even know it.

Monitoring and management. There is no consistent way to monitor and manage an accidental architecture. Suppose that your system of integrated applications has to run 24/7, and that your staff is paying attention to the operational monitoring tools and making course corrections. These tools won't all work in the same way, and training (and retraining) the staff on the myriad disparate microsolutions can become very expensive. Simply installing an enterprise-wide operational management tool doesn't automatically provide introspection into the integration infrastructure, and the accidental architecture does not usually provide all the control points that may be needed.

In summary, the accidental architecture represents a rigid, high-cost infrastructure that does not address your organization's changing needs, and suffers from the following disadvantages:

- Tightly coupled, brittle, and inflexible to changes
- Expensive to maintain due to multiple point-to-point solutions

- Changing one application can affect many others
- Routing logic is hardcoded into the applications
- No common security model; security is ad hoc
- No common API (usually)
- No common communications protocol
- No common ground on which to establish and build best practices
- Difficult to support asynchronous processing
- Unreliable
- No health monitoring and deployment management of applications and integration components

As you know, an accidental architecture is created over years, and will not be replaced or fixed by any one action. As the demand increases for integration projects, solutions need to become more flexible, less complex, and cheaper to operate—not the other way around. The accidental architecture gives your more agile competitors an advantage, and renders you unable to realize new business opportunities in a reasonable timeframe.

You need a cohesive architecture, changes to practices, and standards to address a problem of this magnitude. The ESB provides the architecture and the infrastructure, and lets you adopt it on a project-by-project basis. Adopting an ESB is not an all-or-nothing, rip-and-replace solution. Rather, you can adopt it incrementally while still continuing to leverage your existing assets—including the accidental architecture and integration brokers—in a "leave and layer" approach (see the later section "Leave and Layer: Connecting into the Existing EAI Broker").

ETL, Batch Transfers, and FTP

Extract, Transform, and Load (ETL) techniques such as FTP file transfers and nightly batch jobs are still the most popular means of integration today.

This often involves nightly dump-and-load operations on data that sits in various applications. The problem is that there is great potential for data to get out of sync between systems. The recovery process from failure of a dump-and-load can sometimes take more than a day to reconcile. And in a global economy with businesses that run 24/7, there is no "night" anymore anyway—so when can you run your batch job?

Other issues are associated with nightly batch processing as well. Due to the latency of nightly batch jobs, the best-case scenario is a 24-hour turnaround time when analyzing critical business data. This delay can severely hinder your ability to react to business events in a timely manner.

Sometimes, the end-to-end processing across multiple batch-oriented systems can take up to a whole week to complete. The overall latency involved in the processing of data from the source to the target can prevent you from collecting meaningful data that can provide insight into your current business situation. In the case of a supply chain, for example, this can translate to never knowing the true state of your inventory.

Chapter 9 will present a detailed case study covering both the technology and the business implications of batch transfers via FTP, and will explore how an ESB can help you escape the predicaments imposed by this architecture.

Integration Brokers

Hub-and-spoke integration brokers, or EAI hubs, offer alternatives to the accidental architecture. Integration brokers have been in existence since the middle to late '90s, and are built upon MOM backbones or application server platforms.

Some of the companies in the integration-broker market include:

SeeBeyond	IBM
webMethods	TIBCO
Ascential (Mercator)	BEA (more recently)
Vitria	

Integration brokers can help with the accidental architecture by providing centralized routing between applications, using a hub-and-spoke architecture. Furthermore, they allow the separation of business processes from the underlying integration code through the use of Business Process Management (BPM) software. This is all good news so far.

However, there are drawbacks to integration broker approaches. A hub-and-spoke topology doesn't allow regional control over local integration domains. BPM tools that are built on top of a hub-and-spoke topology can't build choreography or business processes that can span departments or business units. The integration broker may be limited by the underlying MOM in its ability to cross physical network LAN segment boundaries and firewalls.

Many companies have adopted hub-and-spoke integration broker solutions for their integration strategies. These technologies have a high cost and questionable success. Expensive integration broker projects of the late 1990s have had nominal success and left organizations with silos of proprietary integration domains. A study produced by Forrester Research in December 2001* shows the following statistics:

- Integration projects average 20+ months to complete
- Fewer than 35% of projects finish on time and on budget
- 35% of software maintenance budget is spent maintaining point-to-point application links
- In 2003, Global 3500 was expected to spend an average of $6.4 million on integration projects

---

* Statistics from Forrester Research, "Reducing Integration Costs," 12/2001.

This study was undertaken during a time when EAI was at the peak of its inflated expectations, and there is little indication that the statistics have improved significantly since then. Note that the $6.4 million per year was a prediction of the average that companies would spend on integration for the following year. I get regular validation of this figure when speaking to IT leaders about these kinds of problems.

By today's budgetary standards, EAI broker projects are expensive. The integration software costs are prohibitive—usually ranging from $250,000 to $1 million per project for the software licensing alone. This typically carries with it a heavy consulting services component, which is often five to twelve times the cost of the software licenses.

The initial high start-up cost of an integration broker is aggravated by the fact that the skills learned in one project are not easily transferable to the next. Due to the proprietary nature of traditional EAI broker technology, there is often a steep learning curve, sometimes of six months or so, associated with each project. The usual approach to try and offset this is to hire specialized consultants who are already trained on the proprietary technology. Of course, highly specialized = highly paid. This is a large contributor to the heavy consulting costs (the other large contributor being the complexity of the technology installation, configuration, deployment, and management). And once the project is done, the consultants are gone.

The implementation time for integration projects is commonly in the 6–18 month timeframe. This means that, by the criteria set previously for short-term, project-based funding, the implementation time eclipses the strategic window that the project was intended to take advantage of.

The proprietary nature of integration brokers combined with the high cost of consulting usually results in either vendor lock-in or an expensive restart for each subsequent project. This means that even with successful projects, growth and scale are daunting. And in the event that you become unhappy with a vendor or an implementation, you're faced with the dilemma of either sticking with what you have, or facing a complete restart that includes either hiring more consultants or investing in a new learning curve. Because of all this, an IT organization is usually left with an island of integration that can't easily expand into new projects. In summary, the integration broker has proven to be just another piece of technology within the accidental architecture, rather than the solution for it.

As we learn more about the details of integration brokers, we will see that technical barriers contribute to the problems listed here. Also, a number of non-technology-based factors contribute to the growing need to adopt an ESB.

Leveraging Best Practices from EAI and SOA

Before we go and sacrifice our previous efforts, throw away every preceding technology, and throw up our hands in defeat, there *is* a way to leverage some good lessons learned from integration brokers and still move away from the accidental architecture—and that is with the adoption of the ESB. Best practices in integration, which have been refined through experience with integration brokers, can now be combined with standards-based infrastructure based on XML, web services, reliable asynchronous messaging, and distributed ESB integration components. These collectively form an architecture for a highly distributed, loosely coupled integration fabric to deliver all the key features of an integration broker, but without all the barriers.

Migrating away from the accidental architecture and refactoring toward a uniform and consistent integration backbone using an ESB involves the prescriptive steps described in the following sections.

Adopt XML

While an ESB is certainly capable of transporting many types of data formats, adopting XML as the means for exchanging data between applications (Figure 2-2), as has been done in some traditional EAI approaches, can have numerous benefits. As we will see in Chapter 4, leveraging XML can provide insulation from making global changes to data structures and interfaces across the accidental architecture all at once. The ESB can further facilitate that process by examining the content of XML messages and allowing control over where they are delivered, sometimes altering the path of delivery to include additional services that modify or augment the message.

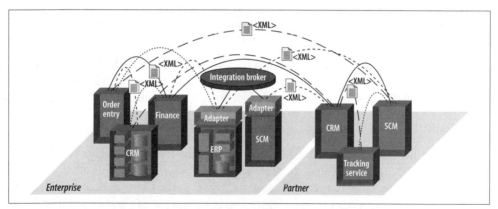

Figure 2-2. The ESB approach uses XML as the means for sharing data between applications

Adopt Web Services and Implement SOA

Thinking and planning in terms of an SOA is a fundamental step in refactoring toward an ESB. As illustrated in Figure 2-3, the introduction of service-level interfaces provides a common layer of abstraction that creates a separation between the interfaces and the implementation. This eases the construction of composite business process definitions composed of coarse-grained service interfaces, using a common interface definition mechanism such as Web Services Description Language (WSDL).

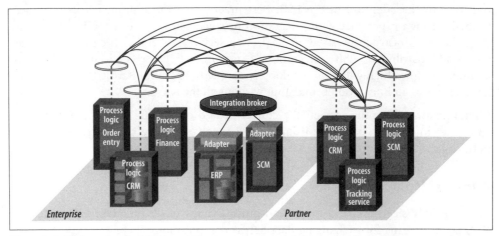

Figure 2-3. Web services and SOA provide a common layer of abstraction that creates a separation between the interfaces and the implementation

While abstraction of service-level interfaces is a step in the right direction, the result is still a bit hard-wired in that the routing logic is tied into the applications (note that in Figure 2-3, the "Process Logic" is still glued in with the applications). Conventional wisdom in web services approaches has been to mimic the client/server model. Even in a distributed network of web services, one application is always a "client" of another. The paradigm requires the abstraction layer to also include glue code that says "invoke method a( ) on service X, then invoke method b( ) on service Y…" and so on.

What has been missing in web services implementations to date is the notion of separation of the process routing logic from the interface definition and application logic. As illustrated in Figure 2-4, the ESB provides that separation, while still fully leveraging an SOA.

By separating the interface definition and the process routing logic, we begin to see the bus layer of the ESB form (Figure 2-5). By bringing the business process routing logic and the interface definition into the bus layer, applications can continue to focus on their own implementation logic. As we saw in Chapter 1, the ESB is actually divided into multiple layers of functionality. It provides a solid backplane of reliable, asynchronous, message-based communications between applications. This backplane is also where process routing can become intelligent, via the addition of conditional decision points based on the inspection of XML content within a message. This intelligent routing is administratively defined, can be altered, and may be supplemented with value-added integration services such as data transformation. The ESB provides an extensible network of integration services that can be extended ad infinitum, yet still can be built incrementally.

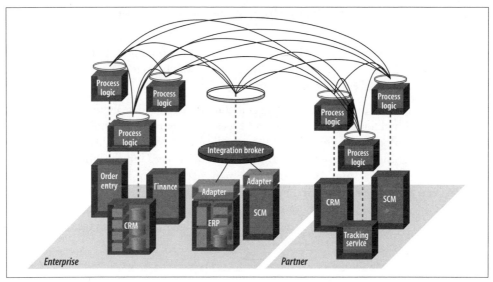

Figure 2-4. The ESB separates business process routing logic from the interface definitions and service implementations

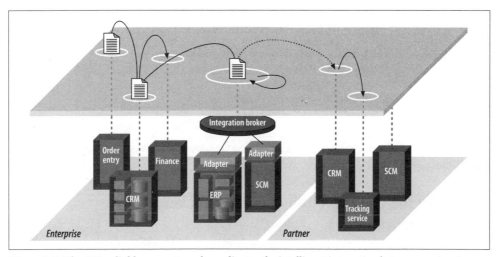

Figure 2-5. The ESB reliably connects and coordinates the intelligent interaction between services in an SOA

Refactoring to an ESB

Getting from the accidental architecture to a uniform integration infrastructure on a global scale may seem like a daunting task. It's not realistic to get everything ready and then flip a switch to get all your applications onto the new infrastructure. This has been a major reason why organizations continue to add on to the accidental architecture as the status quo, even with the knowledge that they are only perpetuating its associated problems.

An ESB provides capabilities that help ease the pain of introduction. Chapter 9 will drill down into a particular case study of how to migrate away from a preexisting integration solution that was based entirely on FTP and nightly batch jobs.

Let's now revisit our discussion of the accidental architecture. In Figure 2-6, the solid, dotted, and dashed lines represent different types of connection technologies and communications protocols used to integrate the applications. Note that there is an existing "island of integration" represented by the integration broker, and that the link between the Point-of-Sale (PoS) application and the Finance application is using FTP file transfer. The link between PoS and the Enterprise Resource Planning (ERP) system had previously been upgraded to use SOAP over HTTP as a protocol, as had the link between the Sales Force Automation (SFA) and the Customer Relationship Management (CRM) applications.

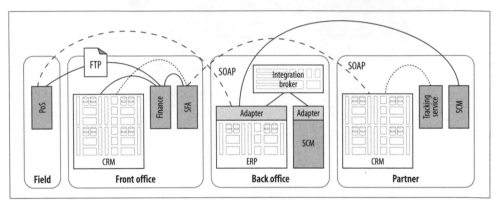

Figure 2-6. Representative accidental architecture using SOAP communications, FTP, and hand-rolled sockets, and including an integration broker

Introduce the ESB at an Individual Project Level

The ESB can be introduced at a departmental level or on a per-project basis. Adopting the ESB at the project level allows you to get accustomed to doing standards-based integration using ESB service containers, with full confidence that the project will fit into a larger integration network and align with the corporate strategic goals of enterprise-wide integration.

The first step in our example ESB adoption is to integrate the front office. In Figure 2-7, the front office CRM, Finance, and SFA are connected into the ESB via "service containers." These containers are key components of the ESB architecture, and are explained in detail in Chapter 6. The nature of the integration through ESB service containers may vary. The interface between the container and the application may be accomplished using a third-party application adapter; the container may expose XML data, which is described using WSDL; or it may be implemented as completely custom-written code.

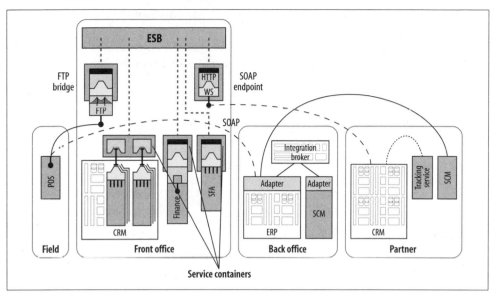

Figure 2-7. The ESB can be adopted on a per-project basis without disrupting the path of point-to-point solutions

But perhaps what's more interesting is not what's already been integrated into the ESB, but what hasn't been. Figure 2-7 shows that the lines of communication for the existing FTP and SOAP protocols, which were once connected to the front office applications, now run directly into bus components that are configured especially for communicating using those protocols. Applications that are still "outside" of the bus—in this case, the PoS and the partner CRM—can communicate with the front office applications that are integrated "inside" the bus without requiring any changes, and without any knowledge that they are participating in an ESB infrastructure. Note that the PoS is now connected to an FTP bridge on the ESB, and the CRM application at the partner site now talks to a web service endpoint that is configured as part of the bus.

An ESB has been introduced without affecting every combination of point-to-point communication that the ESB-enabled applications had previously connected with. The applications plugged into the bus have been migrated over to use a single interface to the ESB integration container, and have dispensed with the other types of communication links they previously had to manage and maintain.

As we will see in Chapter 9, even the newly integrated applications within the domain of the bus can be migrated over to full ESB awareness at their own pace and in accordance with their individual development project timelines.

Propagate the ESB Across a Widely Distributed Enterprise

In the next phase of our ESB adoption, the PoS applications are ESB-enabled at each of the remote locations, removing the dependency on the unreliable FTP link. This can be as simple as installing an ESB container at the remote location and plugging into the ESB at headquarters, or it can involve a "mini" integration environment among several applications at each remote site. The two ESB nodes can now be connected using a secure link that is based on reliable messaging (Figure 2-8).

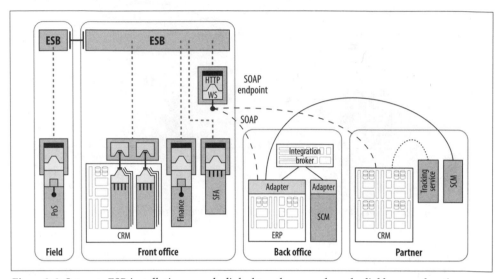

Figure 2-8. Separate ESB installations may be linked together securely and reliably across locations

Furthermore, the remote locations can continue to operate within their own segregated integration environments, but still selectively share data as needed. For example, the remote locations may be independently owned and operated retail stores belonging to a collective franchise. They have no need to share information about their daily operations, but they do need to share data such as price updates and inventory information. The remote ESB nodes can be connected together with the ESB network at headquarters, and can selectively expose message channels to each other to share price updates and so on.

Leave and Layer: Connecting into the Existing EAI Broker

The third phase of our ESB adoption project involves bridging into a department that has already been partially integrated with a hub-and-spoke EAI broker. As noted previously, adopting an ESB is not an all-or-nothing proposition. As illustrated in Figure 2-9, the ESB allows an IT department to protect its investment in an existing EAI broker project by bridging it into the ESB installation.

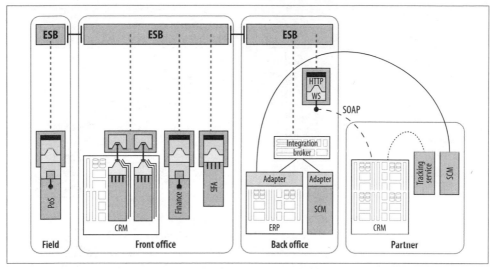

Figure 2-9. The "leave-and-layer" approach allows an ESB to bridge into existing EAI broker installations

Bridging to the EAI broker can occur in several ways. It can be accomplished by using a web services interface, or by binding together the underlying messaging channels. Depending on the implementation of the ESB and the EAI broker, the ESB may even be able to sit on top of the EAI broker's underlying message queue infrastructure, thus partially replacing the EAI broker functionality while retaining the lower-level message channels.

Partner Integration

The final step in our ESB adoption is dealing with the issue of integrating with business partners. As illustrated in Figure 2-10, this could involve leaving the SOAP link as is, or it could involve installing an ESB node at the partner site as well. The decision of which approach to use could depend entirely on how close a relationship your organization has with the partner, whether the partner would allow you to install software at their site, or whether they already have an ESB that can link with yours.

Layered services that are plugged in as an extension of an ESB can manage the logistics of the partner link. For example, a specialized partner manager service could manage the details of ongoing collaborations with partners on a per-partner basis. These details could include which higher-level business protocol is being used (e.g., ebXML, Rosetta-Net, etc.) as well as conversational state, such as the current state of a message exchange, whether an acknowledgment message is expected, and how much time delay is acceptable to receive a business-level response from a partner.

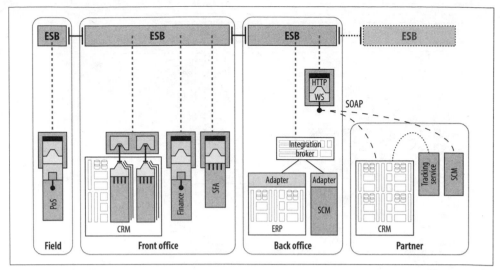

Figure 2-10. The ESB may individually manage SOAP links with business partners, or may link to another ESB node at that site

Summary

This chapter covered the following issues:

- A number of drivers contribute to the need for a broad-scale, general-purpose integration infrastructure.
- The accidental architecture is the dominant design in use today. In this kind of system, the enterprise is currently not very connected at all.
  - Only 10% of applications are linked.
  - Of these, only 15% use any kind of middleware.
  - To date, distributed computing technologies have perpetuated, not solved, the accidental architecture problem.
- Hub-and-spoke EAI brokers have had moderate success. However, they:
  - Are largely proprietary
  - Failed to provide organizations with a standardized integration platform that could be applied to general-purpose use across an enterprise
- The ESB draws value from lessons learned in EAI broker technology.
- Integration is a departmental and corporate culture issue as much as it is a technical issue.
- The ESB allows incremental adoption to occur in accordance with the individual needs of departmental development schedules.

Necessity Is the Mother of Invention

3

The ESB is a new architecture for integration that is flourishing in corporations around the world. To many casual observers, the ESB as a technology category seems to have come out of nowhere. In reality, though, the ESB has not just "happened." Over time, many catalysts helped it develop and evolve, and lessons were learned from past technology approaches that extend back more than a decade.

This chapter will examine some key concepts of the ESB, including the many requirements, technology drivers, and forces in the IT climate that led to the creation of the ESB concept. All of this will be discussed in the context of the recent history and evolution of the ESB. This discussion will illustrate the point that an ESB is not merely an academic exercise; it was born out of necessity, based on real requirements arising from difficult integration problems that couldn't be solved by any preexisting integration technology. The discussion will conclude with a study of an ESB deployment, with a manufacturer exposing inventory management and supply chain optimization functionality to its remote distributors as shared services through an ESB.

Sometimes solving a problem requires looking at previous attempts at solutions and learning from their drawbacks. Entire trends had to come about as predecessors to ESB for the IT and vendor communities to have something to point at and say, "I like that," "I don't like that," or "That's what I've been trying to build on my own." The Greek philosopher Plato is credited for the phrase "Necessity is the mother of invention." The ESB is a shining example of invention fostered by necessity. In this chapter we will explore those necessities, and how an ESB addresses them.

The ESB concept is the next generation of integration middleware, capable of being applied to a much broader range of integration projects than what could be handled by specialized integration brokers. However, it should be stated that ESB is not just EAI plus web services, nor is it MOM plus web services. A number of recognized trends, both technology-driven and business-driven, have had an equal share of influence on the evolution of the ESB.

Enterprise Application Integration (EAI). A number of lessons, both good and not so good, have been learned from EAI. As we have seen, there are various downsides and painful lessons.

Much of the goodness inherited from EAI is in the "best practices" in data transformation and manipulation that can be carried forward into XML technologies and brought forward into an ESB architecture.

e-Marketplaces and vertical trading hubs. During the Internet bubble, this technology category was destined to change the model of how companies do business. The expectation was that e-Marketplaces would be universally adopted, inevitably replacing EDI with something more efficient and more accessible, and allowing companies of all sizes to participate in a supply chain. And while the e-Marketplace trend didn't garner the world's lasting attention as much as its early proponents had hoped, its existence on the hype curve caused businesses and IT culture to evaluate new ways of doing business electronically with other business partners.

This trend also helped foster the recognition of a need for open standards for protocols and service discovery mechanisms. e-Marketplaces were the first to introduce the model of a loosely coupled, distributed federation of individual companies operating autonomously, but still working together in a supply chain in a collaborative fashion. The e-Marketplace showed the IT sector that supply chains can be improved.

Java Message Service. JMS is a standard for APIs and behavioral semantics of MOM. The popularity of JMS as a part of the J2EE platform has brought messaging into the mainstream, and has created a marketplace for competing vendors building new messaging systems from the ground up based on today's requirement of communicating reliably and securely across the Internet.

Application servers. Application servers are important to an enterprise as a means for hosting business logic. They are not a key foundation component of the ESB per se, but they can be integrated using an ESB network. They are being listed here as a catalyst of the ESB concept in that they have nurtured the evolution of some important standards, such as the servlet environment for dynamic processing of requests, JDBC for database connectivity, and the J2EE Connector Architecture (JCA) for a standardized interface to application adapters.

Y2K, and post-Internet-bubble economics. Y2K readiness caused an increase in IT spending, with a significant shift toward the purchase of packaged Y2K-ready applications in favor of applications developed in-house. All the hype and excitement around emerging technologies during the Internet bubble led to continued IT spending. Nowadays, the post-Internet-bubble period has caused a major corporate reevaluation of big IT spending, and a shift toward trying to make things work with the existing applications and with a much smaller budget—even smaller and more highly scrutinized than in pre-Y2K times. The ESB is well suited for the new economics of integration, both in a monetary sense and in practical application.

One common question I get is "Why isn't an ESB built on an application server platform?" In the ESB approach to integration, the integration broker functionality itself is not layered on top of the application server. Integration capabilities are deployed as independent services alongside of, or independently of, the application server. There are a number of reasons for this. One is to avoid the over-bloating of functionality. Application servers are not necessarily the best place for every new technology trend that comes along. An ESB requires a lighter-weight container for deploying integration services without having to install an entire application server stack everywhere. And there are other reasons too: the core architecture of an application server isn't designed for hosting loosely coupled services. The deployment model isn't optimized for dynamic reconfiguration and deployment. The code-centric model embeds things into application code that should be dynamically configured, either explicitly or implicitly. The deployment and management model isn't appropriate for distributed deployment of heterogeneous services. A more detailed discussion of this issue is found in Chapter 6.

Web services and SOA. Web services are an industry effort to provide platform-independent SOA using interoperable interface descriptions, protocols, and data communication. Web services are a key core concept of the ESB, and the ESB can be thought of as a middleware manifestation of SOA design principles as applied to integration.

Evolution and maturation of standards in support of integration and interoperability.

In addition to web services, there are important standards for XML, security, and reliable messaging. The development and adoption of standards, along with communities of supporting vendor implementations, have matured enough to make the benefits of standards-based integration become a reality.

The accidental architecture. As we now know, the accidental architecture is something that nobody sets out to create, yet everybody has. We examined the accidental architecture in Chapter 2, and explored how the ESB can help a system migrate away from the accidental architecture in incremental chunks.

The Evolution of the ESB

The creation of the ESB has been an evolutionary process. As we just discussed, a number of events in the industry had their part in catalyzing the creation of the ESB (Figure 3-1). This does not mean to imply that the predecessors of ESB were bad or failed technologies. Each contributing technology in the ESB ancestry was the best available for its time and continues to have its "meritt"[sic]. The ESB draws positive influences from its predecessor approaches, and avoids the downsides.

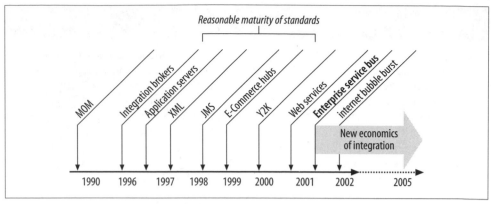

Figure 3-1. ESB catalysts: a timeline of technology and other events affecting the creation of the ESB

The invention of the ESB was not an accident. The ESB is a result of vendors working with forward-thinking customers who were trying to build a standards-based integration network using a foundation of SOA, messaging, and XML. These customers came from the end-user IT community in the manufacturing business, and from e-Marketplace infrastructure and trading exchange companies such as CommerceOne and GE Global Exchange Services (GE GXS).

The ESB in Global Manufacturing

A global company in the manufacturing sector is an example of an end-user IT organization that helped to catalyze the ESB. This manufacturing company is made up of at least five different major business units located around the world. Their goal was to have a common integration backbone based on message-oriented middleware infrastructure and standards-based interfaces. This effort was started and restarted several times, and had a resurgence of interest a few years ago, when the Java Message Service was first introduced as a way of providing standard interfaces to a common messaging backbone. This manufacturing company had many "islands of integration" and departmental pockets of proprietary and third-party message buses, which had been installed and controlled at a departmental or business-unit level. The requirement was that all departments and business units be integrated with each other to form a more consistent environment in which to plug in applications.

Their IT organization was looking to JMS to provide a standardized interface and common behavioral semantics across all applications, across all departments, across all business units. While many of us in the JMS business were excited about this, the reality is that JMS alone can't meet that requirement. The company also needed integration broker functionality such as routing based on rules and data transformation, all based on an abstraction of loosely coupled shared service interfaces.

At the time, the manufacturing company was faced with a dilemma caused by several things. While JMS had been selected as part of the solution, not all of the messaging vendors supported it. The existing messaging vendors and integration broker hubs that were entrenched in the various business units couldn't support the highly distributed approach required to span across global business units in a reasonable and manageable way. Some of the newer messaging vendors had the right JMS support, as well as the right security, firewall traversal, and message broker clustering to support the distributed topologies required to bring the geographically dispersed business units of the company together. However, there was no model in place for a service abstraction layer upon which to build an SOA, nor did the rest of the integration-stack layers exist that were required to integrate all of those applications across the organization.

Some of the forward-thinking IT leaders in this manufacturing company started working with the forward-thinking JMS and MOM providers. Through the course of such work in this global company and in others like it, many of the details of what eventually grew into early blueprints for the ESB were fleshed out.

The need was identified for a loosely coupled design center of event-driven services that could be coordinated across a common middleware substrate. The solution was to define a stack of functionality that consisted of a standards-based integration backbone, making use of JMS, SOA, XML, transformation and routing, and adapters. This approach went a long way, but still couldn't solve the connectivity issues.

The IT architects at the company realized that they couldn't just make a mandate saying, "On this date, all applications will be required to support JMS." It just was not practical. The same can also be said for web services. IT staff is too busy just trying to keep up with their daily work to embark on a mission that takes every application across the organization and retrofits it into one particular connectivity style.

Common APIs and event-driven service interfaces are a core part of the design center of an ESB. However, diversity in connectivity options is critical to the adoption of an integration strategy. Another need that was identified was a way to bring the infrastructure to the applications, allowing the applications to plug into the infrastructure in whatever manner made sense for them and facilitating an incremental approach to adoption. This is how the requirement of multiple client types, connectivity protocols, application adapters, and MOM bridges became a core part of the definition of an ESB. The various IT departments across the business units needed to protect their investments in existing messaging and integration broker installations, and be able to reach the other corporate applications as shared services in a nonintrusive way.

Putting It to the Test

In an effort to provide customers, suppliers, and vendors with one unified view of their diversified business units, the manufacturing company embarked on a major strategic operations initiative. The goal of the initiative was to provide one-stop shopping for customer service, invoice and payment tracking, inventory management and ordering, and so on, as opposed to forcing constituents to deal with five different product units (Figure 3-2).

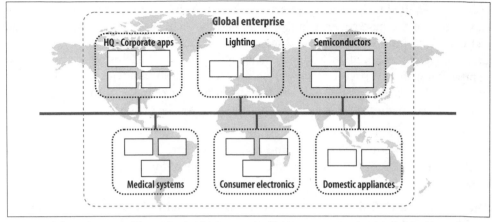

Figure 3-2. Loosely coupled, autonomous business units sharing a common integration backbone based on messaging and standard interfaces

The overall goal of the project was the creation of a single corporate IT backbone for integrating the payment processing applications across all the various product divisions worldwide.

The manufacturing company built its "payment automation" application on top of an early rendition of an ESB. This was the first test of the vision of a shared services network. The payment automation is based on an ESB-like implementation that serves as an enterprise-scale, centralized payment processing clearinghouse for all product divisions.

The payment automation backbone is a standard corporate payment service used by all divisions that allows the company to centrally manage, track, and clear orders for payment to vendors and suppliers worldwide. Because this project used an early ESB prototype, a corporate-wide payment service could be shared by all the business units, as a service plugged into the bus. Payment processing could now be routed through one shared business function, versus having to be cleared through a variety of geographically dispersed banks and banking systems.

Finding the Edge of the Extended Enterprise

For the past decade, through the era of EAI and the evolution of the Internet and application server technology, a clear dividing line has developed between the communications and application integration infrastructure within the four walls of a corporation, and the "external" communication with business partners, vendors, and customers.

This separation has been driven largely by the capabilities and limitations of the technology. To date, technology such as application server infrastructure has been specifically designed to make clear distinctions between what's inside the firewall and what's outside the firewall. This distinction is evidenced by completely separate architectural approaches, with different programming models required for building applications. In the J2EE application server architecture, for example, this is manifested as a web container versus an EJB container.

Hub-and-spoke EAI brokers could get as far as the corporate boundaries, but were not really built for scaling beyond that. Various bridging technologies were designed to bridge the gap at the "edge" of the network. In many legacy cases, this is "bolted on" as an afterthought. The majority of the work being done in the area of web services has also been focused on this "edge" of the network.

But just where exactly is this "edge" of the network anyhow? Before we get to that, let's explore another ancestor of the ESB, the e-Marketplace, also known as the e-Commerce Trading Hub.

e-Commerce Trading Hubs

In a trading network of business partners, there is the desire to move away from expensive EDI Value Added Networks (VANs) and use the public Internet as a means of communications wherever possible, and to lower the barrier of entry such that small to medium enterprises can afford to participate. This was the impetus behind the creation of e-Marketplaces and trading exchanges such as those powered by CommerceOne and GE Global eXchange Services (GXS).

A trading exchange acts as an intermediary, or semiprivate business portal, that facilitates electronic commerce between buyers and suppliers in a supply chain. The majority of the interactions within the "portal" are not browser-based—they are performed directly between specialized applications that require little or no human interaction. The interactions occur between applications residing in a trading partner, and backend applications residing in the trading hub. These backend trading hub applications provide value-added functions such as the dispersion of Requests For Quote (RFQs) between a buyer and multiple suppliers, or Availability To Promise (ATP) data from suppliers to buyers (Figure 3-3).

This environment introduced some rather challenging requirements, some of which seemed at odds with each other. For example, e-Marketplace deployment topology depicted in Figure 3-3 requires secure access between the applications at the partner sites and the applications in the trading partner hub, using the public Internet as the vehicle for communication. This scenario also requires reliable messaging, but the traditional MOM vendors did not have a MOM infrastructure that was capable of spanning across the public Internet in a scalable and secure fashion.

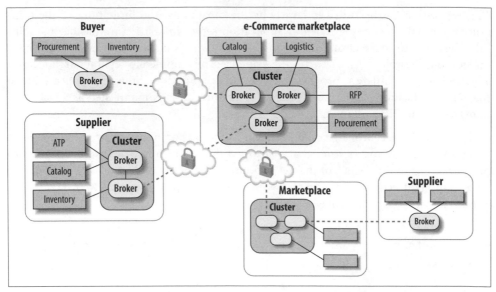

Figure 3-3. Deployment topologies of e-Commerce trading hubs encountered some interesting technical challenges

The suppliers communicating through the same trading hub are often fierce competitors with each other, so it is imperative that they not be able to see each other's data. This requires full authentication and access control between the trading partners and the trading hub. Functionality in the trading hub must be exposed to trading partners through a service interface. A supplier must also be able to freely share its data with the trading hub, and the trading hub applications must be able to selectively pass that data along to buyers, but not to other suppliers. A supplier must never be able to masquerade as another supplier and get access to its sensitive data.

An e-Marketplace community could potentially consist of thousands of trading partners, all communicating through the same trading hub. Trading partners need to be able to asynchronously communicate with the trading hub in a "fire-and-forget" mode using reliable messaging.

Some very important ESB capabilities were born out of these requirements. For example:

- Strict authentication and access control between the entities connecting to each other
- Scalable clustering of message servers (Figure 3-3) to handle large volumes of message traffic from potentially thousands of concurrently connected trading partners
- Complete segregation of data channels
- Selective control over which channels can be opened up between application endpoints, across intermediary hubs

- Selective access to shared service interfaces and endpoint destinations
- Coordination of the business-level message exchange between applications that are separated by physical network domains and geographical location
- Secure MOM communication through all the firewalls that exist between the trading hub and the suppliers and buyers

Another contributor to the vision of the ESB architecture was the requirement for a trading hub to do business with other industry-related vertical trading hubs. This means that segregated groups of applications (the trading hub backend apps) need to selectively expose and share their interfaces and data with groups of applications residing in other trading hubs. Each trading hub and each trading partner needed to be able to maintain their own autonomy and local integration environments while communicating in a larger e-Commerce network. This network of trading hubs and trading partners could potentially fan out ad infinitum.

The evolution of e-Marketplace infrastructure has significantly contributed to the emergence of ESB providers offering the underpinnings to support the requirements of e-Marketplaces. The vendors building trading exchanges looked at a variety of EAI brokers and application server technology, and turned to the messaging vendors for help. Some of the newer messaging vendors were already beginning to provide the required underpinnings for the routing, segregation, and fan-out deployment topology. This process of defining requirements, talking to vendors, and designing this infrastructure took more than a year. During this time, a number of messaging vendors and EAI broker vendors put a great deal of effort into ensuring that their next-generation products would be able to support the requirements of e-Marketplace vendors, and this helped to contribute to the emergence of the ESB concept.

The Extended Enterprise: The Ever-Changing Edge

Fast-forward a couple of years, and it turns out that the technology requirements of large-scale trading exchanges are the same requirements of corporations building out their own integration networks. While the e-Marketplace never really took hold as a business model, there remained a need to provide common shared services across departmental and corporate boundaries. This need expands well beyond supply chain scenarios.

Due to mergers and acquisitions, collaborating business partners, and globally distributed business units, varying modes of communication are based on the degree of trust between the business entities. This model represents the "extended enterprise." In the extended enterprise, the "edge" of the network is always changing—or perhaps there was never really a single outer edge to begin with. For example, in a global organization of semi-independent business units, there are many firewalls, but also a need to have a distributed integration backbone that transcends the underlying topology (Figure 3-4).

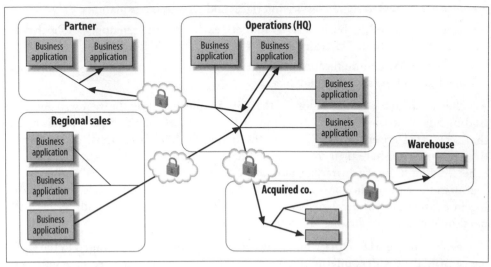

Figure 3-4. Corporate IT domains: intra-corporate requirements have technology challenges very similar to e-Marketplaces

There are different levels of trust when dealing with business partners. Reliable messaging requires that a piece of MOM software be installed on either side of the communication link. Sometimes it is acceptable business practice to tell a business partner, "If you want to do business with me, you must install this software at your site." In such a case, it's perfectly acceptable, from a technology point of view, to have an efficient, reliable MOM link between the two organizations. Chapter 5 will provide more information about MOM wire protocols, and new reliable SOAP protocols that can help (but not completely alleviate) the requirement to have MOM software installed on both sides of the wire. When your relationship with a business partner is not as close, you may instead need to supply clear instructions on how to send business documents over a secure HTTP link, and manage business message exchanges using a layered service that specializes in partner links.

Corralling the Ever-Changing Edge of the Network

The ESB provides the architecture that separates the higher-level SOA and integration fiber, which includes the management of physical destinations as abstract endpoints and the transformation and routing, from the details of the underlying protocols. This means that the network boundaries can change over time, and an ESB can support the changing of the underlying protocol (i.e., from MOM to SOAP-over-HTTP to WS-Rel*) without affecting the higher-level integration functions that sit above all of that. In the trading hub example, SOA, data transformation, and routing of messages based on context was the job of the value-added services that resided inside the hub. As we take the lessons learned and the concepts of trading hubs and apply them toward in-house IT integration, we can make those same concepts available as independently deployed services.

Standards-Based Integration

The maturity and adoption of relevant standards for integration have helped to foster the emergence of the ESB as a technology trend. The ESB makes full use of standards for integration wherever possible. The use of such standards can have significant effects on a business, as follows:

- Allows you to leverage existing IT staff, rather than specialist consultants. The amount of information available on XML and web services standards such as SOAP, WSDL, XSLT, XPath, and XQuery is expanding at an ever-increasing rate. There is an educational ecosystem in which information about standards (and budding specifications) becomes available as the standards evolve. The introduction of a popular specification creates a fertile ground for industry experts to write articles, tutorials, and O'Reilly books on the subject, which in turn allows IT professionals to learn more and stay current. This means that the average IT professional can readily attain the expertise he or she needs to become the in-house integration architect.

- Reduces proprietary vendor lock-in. With a proprietary integration stack, an organization can't simply say, "Well, vendor A wasn't what we expected, so let's try vendor B." This would result in an expensive restart and relearning. Adopting standards as part of an integration infrastructure means the ability to pick and choose best-of-breed implementations from different vendors and have them work together.

- Java standards. While the ESB concept can be Java-free, Java provides a set of specifications that don't exist elsewhere and that can standardize components and interfaces between those components. These standards define application interfaces, behavioral semantics of middleware and application adapters, and deployment models. Standards such as JMS, MessageDrivenBeans, and JCA can significantly increase the ability to interoperate between enterprise applications and J2EE application servers. J2EE application servers from various vendors have found their way into most, or perhaps even all, enterprise organizations.

- Increases the ability to integrate with business partners using standard interfaces and standard protocols.

- A JMS interface to an ESB is currently the only way that application servers from different vendors can talk asynchronously using reliable messaging in a common environment with an SOA. RMI-over-IIOP is (or was) the "blessed" method of application server interoperability, but it doesn't provide a model for loosely coupled interfaces or SOA, nor does it work outside of J2EE. While in theory any J2EE server can interoperate with any other J2EE server using JMS, in practice this doesn't really happen out of the box, nor is there any incentive to do so. An ESB can provide a neutral ground where application servers from multiple vendors can communicate with each other.

- J2EE Connector Architecture (JCA) can also provide the standard contract for application adapters, which can add to your arsenal of integration with any packaged applications that support Java interfaces. Entire suites of application adapters, available from multiple vendors, use JCA as the unified way of connecting between the adapter and the middleware infrastructure. Once an application is introduced into the ESB through a JCA adapter, its functionality is exposed as a standards-based, event-driven service. This gives you much greater flexibility and reuse than if it were plugged into a proprietary broker through a proprietary adapter.

WHAT ARE "STANDARDS," EXACTLY?

When talking about the use and adoption of standards, it is hard to tell just exactly what that word means. We live in a world of multiple overlapping efforts from different standards bodies to define standard specifications. Vendor alliances are producing web services specifications outside the domain of any standards body or consortium.

Every once in a while I am challenged on the use of a Java specification as a "standard." The argument is that because the Java Community Process (JCP) is owned by one vendor (Sun Microsystems), the specifications that come out of that process are not really *standards*—they are just specifications.

I tend to use the words "standards" and "specifications" interchangeably. As far as I'm concerned, any specification that has been through the JCP should be considered standard enough. That is, it has gone through a formal process in which it was jointly defined by a group of independent companies and/or individuals, and was posted for public review prior to ratification.

There are also "de facto standards" such as open source implementations, which either invented their own ways of doing things or conform to industry-accepted "standard" specifications. The Apache SOAP and Apache Axis toolkits are examples of such standards.

The evolving WS-* stack of specs from ad hoc vendor collaborations can also be considered de facto standards in that they represent the work and statement of direction for a meaningful constituency of the largest platform vendors. Some of these WS-* specifications have already been submitted to an official standards body, and the rest have been part of a program that involves public feedback sessions.

In short, the word "standard," in terms of standards-based integration, refers to either a specification or an implementation that has gained enough traction in the industry to have long-lasting staying power, and is open enough for multiple vendors to implement or repackage it.

An SOA built upon the combination of enterprise messaging with certain key technologies such as SOAP, WSDL, XPath, and XSLT, with interfaces to Java, .NET, and C++, collectively defines the means for a platform that allows cleaner solutions based on standards. The concept of standards-based integration allows developers to learn and build a valuable skill set that can be used across a variety of integration projects. Integration based on standards also provides IT managers with a larger talent pool of developer resources, and allows for repeatable success patterns that can be carried from project to project.

A major European food distribution network was an early adopter of an ESB, and successfully completed their first supply chain automation project in six weeks. One of their directors of IT strategy had this to say about the use of standards for integration in an ESB: "Now we no longer have to worry how long the next integration will take, or even if it is possible."

The New Economics of Integration

In the ESB, you deploy what you need, when and where you need it. The licensing model being put forth by vendors leading the charge in ESB technology reflects these physical deployment characteristics.

According to a Forrester Research report, license costs for integration brokers begin at $100,000 per project and have an average price of $400,000 to $750,000. In contrast, an ESB license can cost 10 to 15 times less than that. Does this mean that ESB vendors have an unrealistic licensing model that is incapable of sustaining a business? No. The ESB licensing trend is based on the philosophy that integration should be pervasive throughout the enterprise, and a high cost of licensing should not be a hindrance to adoption. This licensing philosophy reflects the technology model, which is to license only what you need on a per-project basis, while building toward the strategic goal of corporate-wide integration. So you can start wherever you need it most, and grow at your own pace without costly obstacles.

For integration brokers, you typically pay for consulting services that are four to five times the licensing costs. Because the ESB is based on standards, you can leverage in-house staff and avoid having to pay high fees for consultants who specialize in proprietary integration broker technology. By investing in the adoption of standards and educating your in-house IT staff on standards for integration, you are future-proofing your staff as well as your technology.

Driving Down the Cost of Technology

In his book *Loosely Coupled*, Doug Kaye illustrates his own version of a "technology adoption curve" in support of a discussion on how the cost of a particular technology decreases over time. As an example, he talks about the publishing of O'Reilly books on a particular subject as a significant event in the adoption of a technology, helping to drive down the cost of the technology by making knowledge about it more readily available. You are witnessing that now in terms of the ESB.

Case Study: Manufacturing

As an example of how ESB technology is changing the economics of integration in a real deployment scenario, let's take a look at how a building material manufacturer is using an ESB. We will pay special attention to how they are taking advantage of the selective deployment model of the ESB.

The manufacturer operates 50 plants in 15 countries. They distribute their products through large building supply retailers, such as Home Depot and Lowe's, as well as through a network of more than 60 independent distributors serving retail and wholesale customers in regional markets across the United States. Twenty-eight of their larger distributors are connected to their headquarters using an EDI VAN.

Connecting one supplier with 60 distributors is a simple challenge for an integration infrastructure that is capable of scaling out to thousands of diverse endpoints. However, the point of this case study is not the scale of the deployment, but the traits of the ESB that it utilizes. Its simplicity highlights yet another characteristic of the ESB—that it is capable of scaling up to large global integration networks, but is also well suited for small projects.

Building a Real-Time Business

To improve operations and optimize the distribution chain, this manufacturing company embarked on building an infrastructure that would enable direct distributor participation in inventory management and ATP as a means of achieving real-time order fulfillment.

Inventory management

The inventory management application allows the manufacturer to better anticipate the demand of its distributors by tracking each distributor's monthly inventory consumption and creating a recommended monthly order requisition for each distributor.

By deploying an ESB, the manufacturer can now analyze its distributors' order and sales histories, thus allowing inventory to be jointly managed. This was accomplished by implementing a message exchange that allows the manufacturer to anticipate a distributor's inventory requirements. In this scenario, distributors periodically send product activity data to the manufacturer, which uses that data to anticipate product consumption activity and determine when the distributors need to replenish the stock. They then generate a shipping schedule message indicating the products and quantities that the distributor should order to replenish its stock. The distributor will use this data to generate a purchase order back to the manufacturer.

This process allows the manufacturer to better manage inventory, reducing the quantity of on-hand product needed for the distributors and achieving more predictable production schedules and revenue forecasts.

Technical challenges

The manufacturer looked to integrate the 60 disparate ERP systems of their distributors with their own SAP R/3 inventory management and order processing systems. One of the challenges they faced was accommodating varying levels of technical sophistication among their broad range of distributors. They already had an EDI infrastructure for about half of the larger distributors, but that was a high-cost solution that would not be viable for the smaller distributors. Some of the larger distributors had the technical capability to communicate with them using SOAP and web services, but some of the smaller distributors didn't have the sophistication or technical know-how to do that. Most distributors had an ERP system locally, with the extent of their IT expertise limited to how to operate it. The manufacturer needed a simple solution that could be installed at each of the distributor sites, and configured and managed remotely by a central IT staff.

Availability To Promise (ATP)

The manufacturer has also deployed an ATP lookup for nonstock items. ATP is a common business function in supply chains that allows you to accurately predict the delivery of goods between multiple buyers and suppliers. This is particularly important when the immediate supplier does not have the item in on-hand inventory and needs to custom-build it, which could involve another level of special-order items from its own suppliers. Being able to plan and predict the timely delivery of nonstock items can significantly reduce the unnecessary cost overhead of carrying special inventory items to effectively meet the demands of customers and avoid lost business.

Flexible Partner Integration

The solution for both the inventory management and ATP issues was to deploy an ESB. For the inventory management function, they needed a remote integration solution that was easy to install, deploy, and integrate with the many disparate ERP systems at each distributor site. For the ATP solution, they decided to expose the ATP function as a service and use a direct web services link with the distributors.

The inventory management function is facilitated by an ESB-managed business process that controls the routing between the partners and the inventory management application, which is implemented in SAP. There are no integration brokers or application servers required at the remote sites. Still, the solution provides standards-based connectivity, reliable and secure messaging, and transformation and service orchestration between its own systems and the individual ERP systems utilized by the remote distributors. The "edge" of the ESB network is capable of supporting a variety of connectivity options as new distributors come on board. Even existing links with distributors can change their underlying protocol without affecting the higher-level business processes and XML message exchanges between the manufacturer and the distributors.

To manage the link between distributors and headquarters, the manufacturer chose to deploy an ESB service container at the remote distributor sites (Figure 3-5).

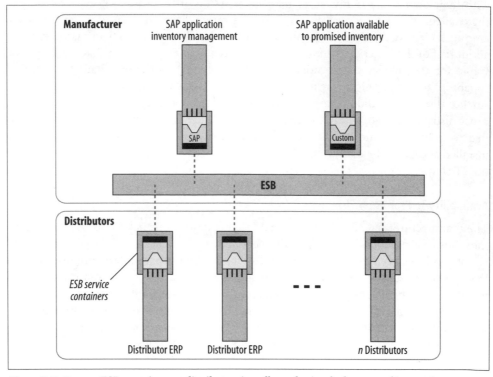

Figure 3-5. Remote ESB containers at distributor sites allow selective deployment of integration capabilities

Remote ESB containers located at the distributor sites allow selective deployment of integration capabilities when and where they are needed, with no integration brokers or application servers required. In addition, this approach provides both the manufacturer and their distributors the following advantages:

- A secure, authenticated channel between the distributor and headquarters
- Reliable delivery of messages, both synchronous and asynchronous, between the distributor and headquarters
- Simple integration at the partner site
- A managed environment, where deployment configuration and management can be handled remotely by the manufacturer's IT staff, without requiring any additional IT expertise at each partner site
- No need to license and install an integration broker, application server, or "partner server" at each distributor location

- A link to an EDI VAN, and transformation between EDI messages and XML messages
- Integration with SAP within the manufacturer's inventory management system

Within the ESB network at the manufacturer, data transformation between comma-separated ASCII (CSV) files, an internal canonical XML format based on Common Business Library (xCBL), and SAP's Intermediate Document (IDOC) format is accomplished as part of several orchestrated business processes facilitated by the ESB. More details on the virtues of a canonical XML format are discussed in Chapter 4. Chapter 8 will explore the more technical details of this deployment.

Summary

In this chapter, we saw that the ESB concept was developed out of necessity, and had many catalysts. We also explored the following:

- The ESB provides a pervasive, event-driven SOA, which is based on requirements of IT architects working together with vendors to build broad-scale integration networks using messaging, standard integration services, and standard interfaces.
- e-Marketplaces provided a fertile breeding ground for scalable and secure ESB infrastructure capable of supporting the needs of large trading hubs with potentially thousands of trading partners. Out of this environment, the requirements of sophistication routing across segregated data channels were identified.
- The proliferation and reasonable maturity of standards has provided the benefits of standards-based integration.
- Application servers have their place in IT infrastructure as containers for housing business logic. An ESB architecture can provide a loosely coupled integration fabric for integrating application servers with other application servers and cross-platform applications at large.
- Remote ESB service containers obviate the need to install integration brokers at every remote site to be integrated.

4

XML: The Foundation for Business Data Integration

This chapter will explore the use of XML as a means for providing the mediation between diverse data structures and formats as data is passed between applications. We will also examine how ESB-enabled data transformation and content-based routing services can support an XML data exchange architecture that insulates individual applications from wholesale changes in data structures.

The Language of Integration

XML, the eXtensible Markup Language, is accepted by the industry as the ideal vehicle for sharing structured data among applications and organizations. Putting aside for a moment the benefits of web services technologies such as SOAP and WSDL, there is much to be gained by simply adopting XML as the means for representing data that is shared between applications. XML has many benefits, including the following:

XML is becoming universally understood. XML has become a lingua franca for representing data and interfaces between applications. Many packaged-application vendors provide inputs and outputs in XML. Think about your own applications and how they could better integrate and share data if they accepted and emitted XML.

XML provides a richer data model. The power of XML to represent data is one reason that it's been adopted so broadly. XML lets you model hierarchies, lists, and complex types directly in the data structure. This is in contrast to an RDBMS, which requires table joins, special schema features, and mapping routines to achieve the same thing.

XML makes data self-describing. XML embeds metadata that describes the hierarchy and data element names. This is the basis for XML parser technology that can use the tags and associated schema to identify elements of data by name and datatype.

XML is dynamic. An XML document is loosely coupled with its schema, unlike data structures in relational tables, which are hard-wired to their schemas. This means that programs that extract data directly from the XML structure using standard

XML expressions such as XPath are independent of the schema and loosely coupled with the structure itself.

XML eliminates fixed formats. The order in which the data elements appear in a document doesn't need to be fixed. Each element can be of a variable length and can include a variable number of other fields.

When combined, these principles allow XML to encode the entire contents of a database—all its tables, columns, rows, and constraints—in a single XML file.

XML Is Human-Readable

Well, some would say that is up for debate, but it is certainly more human-readable than some of its predecessors, such as EDI. XML is generally readable by many tools. You can view XML documents in Microsoft Explorer, and most developer tools have viewers or editors for XML. XML is also writable. XML is well suited for integration tools that can visually create and manage sophisticated data mappings.

Any well-formed XML document is parseable by a variety of standard parsers. This contrasts starkly with most other data representations, such as EDI, which required specialized parsers based upon the type of data being represented.

Consider the following EDI fragment:

```
LOC+147+0090305::5'
MEA+WT++KGM:22500'
LOC+9+NLRTM'
LOC+11+SGSIN'
RFF+BM+933'
EQD+CN+ABCU2334536+2210+++5'
NAD+CA+ABC:172:20'
```

This is not very self-describing. It is also very fixed. In this case, we at least have an EDI standard that defines "LOC" and "NAD" as having special meaning, and the "+" operator has special syntactic meaning to something that is parsing and interpreting the data. However, many implementations of EDI emitters and consumers vary in interpretation, and are prone to interoperability issues.

When not using an EDI link, it is more common to have proprietary data formats that can be as simple as a comma-separated list of data:

```
0090305, 22500, NLRTM, SGSIN, 933, ABC
```

Inevitably, this data needs to be shared with other applications. It may be obtainable through some application-level interfaces, or it may be accessible only through an ETL type of dump and load. If you have some kind of schema to help recognize and parse the data, some custom data translation can be applied to get the data into an appropriate form for another application's consumption.

In contrast, data represented by XML is more readable and consumable. It is more easily read by humans, and easier to consume using parsing technology because it carries more *context*, or information about the nature of the content. Here is the XML equivalent of the previous EDI fragment:

```
<EDI_Message>
<Address>
    <AddressType>Stowage location</AddressType>
    <AddressLine>0090305</AddressLine>
    <CodeList>ISO</CodeList>
</Address>
<Quantity>
    <QuantityType>Weight</QuantityType>
    <QuantityNumber>22500</QuantityNumber>
    <QuantityUnits>KGM</QuantityUnits>
</Quantity>
<Address>
    <AddressType>Loading port</AddressType>
    <AddressLine>NLRTM</AddressLine>
    <Codelist>UNLOCODE</Codelist>
</Address>
 <Address>
    <AddressType>Discharging port</AddressType>
    <AddressLine>SGSIN</AddressLine>
    <Codelist>UNLOCODE</Codelist>
</Address>
<Documentation>
    <DocumentationType>Bill of Lading</DocumentationType>
    <DocumentationNumber>933</DocumentationNumber>
</Documentation>
<Address>
    <AddressType>Carrier</AddressType>
    <AddressLine>ABC</AddressLine>
    <CodeList>BIC</CodeList>
</Address>
</EDI_Message>
```

As we will see in the next section, individual XML elements can be identified and consumed independently from the rest of the XML document.

Applications Bend, but Don't Break

An application and its external data representation can be extended without breaking the links between it and the other applications it shares data with. XML is *extensible*, in that portions of an existing XML document can be modified or enhanced without affecting other portions of the document. For example, additional data elements and attributes can be added to a portion of an XML document, and only the application that will be accessing that new element needs to be modified. Other applications that don't require the extended data can continue to work without modification.

Let's explore this point by examining a scenario. Say you need to increase the operational efficiency of a supply chain. In a supply chain that moves billions of dollars of goods per year, even a nominal increase in operational efficiency, such as reducing the time from order placement to delivery of goods to receipt of payment, can have an impact of millions of dollars in savings per year. Improving the time it takes to fulfill the actual order can be a significant factor in reducing the overall cycle time in the supply chain process. In this scenario, improving the order fulfillment time involves adding more details to the shipping address. With XML, we can extend data without adversely affecting all the producing and consuming applications that need to exchange that data.

Consider the following XML fragment, which represents the body of message M_1:

```
<ShipInfo >
    <Address>
        <Street>...</Street>
        <City>...</City>
        <State>...</State>
        <PostalCode>...</PostalCode>
    </Address>
</ShipInfo>
```

XML is extensible in that a data element may have attributes added to it, such as serviceLevel="overnight" in the following listing:

```
<ShipInfo serviceLevel="overnight" >
    <Address>
        <Street>...</Street>
        <City>...</City>
        <State>...</State>
        <PostalCode>...</PostalCode>
    </Address>
</ShipInfo>
```

This attribute is additional information, but for applications that don't know about serviceLevel, its existence is unimportant. The structure didn't change, the values didn't change, so it's all good.

Another simple thing we can do to decrease the overall time of the order fulfillment process is to upgrade the shipping address data to make use of nine-digit postal codes instead of just the five-digit prefix. (The U.S. postal code routing system requires that a minimum five-digit postal code be used. An optional four-digit predicate allows the postal delivery service to more efficiently route the package to its destination.)

A simple business requirement such as this can be the driver for why applications need to change to produce and consume the new data formats. In our postal code example, this requirement is driven by the consuming applications, such as the ones responsible for the logistical processing (e.g., printing the shipping labels).

To support the full nine-digit postal code, we need to make changes to the data structures themselves. The following listing shows message M_2 with an additional Plus4 that represents the optional additional four digits:

```
<ShipInfo serviceLevel="overnight" >
    <Address>
        <Street>...</Street>
```

```
        <City>...</City>
        <State>...</State>
        <PostalCode>
            01730
            <Plus4>????</Plus4>
        </PostalCode>
    </Address>
</ShipInfo>
```

The process by which message M_1 becomes M_2 by adding the Plus4 element across all applications can be done incrementally. This is largely driven by the requirements of the receiving applications that need to consume the data with the enhanced format. In some cases, the Plus4 element may not be necessary. For example, the invoicing application that generates the itemized invoice containing the ShipTo address could do without the Plus4 information. Eventually, it may be nice to have it there for consistency's sake, but the urgency to upgrade that application is not as high as extending the application that prints the physical shipping label. XML thus reinforces the ESB philosophy of "leave and layer," allowing you to selectively upgrade interfaces and data structures as time permits.

To illustrate this point, let's consider a simple example of two applications, X_1 and Y_1, which exchange message M_1 (Figure 4-1).

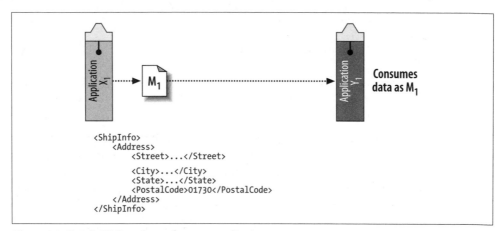

Figure 4-1. Simple XML exchange between applications

Now let's say that a new application, Y_2, needs to consume the new data as represented by message M_2, as illustrated in Figure 4-2.

Assume that a new business requirement is introduced where the receivers need to process the extended data, message M_2, which includes the Plus4 element. The new application, Y_2, needs to process the extended address data as represented by message M_2. The producing application, X_2, has been upgraded to send the new datatype, but one of the consuming applications can't be upgraded until there's room in the budget. This is

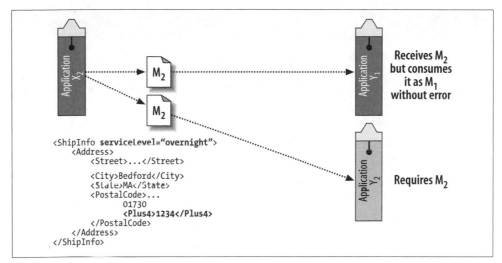

```
<ShipInfo serviceLevel="overnight">
    <Address>
        <Street>...</Street>

        <City>Bedford</City>
        <State>MA</State>
        <PostalCode>...
                01730
                <Plus4>1234</Plus4>
        </PostalCode>
    </Address>
</ShipInfo>
```

Figure 4-2. Modified XML can be read by old applications in some cases

OK, provided that the receiving application was written using XPath, DOM, or SAX parsers to extract the data.

If the application or the routing logic is using XPath to examine the contents, it doesn't matter whether the message is structured as M_1 or M_2. The XPath expression to access PostalCode is the same:

```
normalize-space(/ShipInfo/Address/PostalCode/text()) → 01730
```

But applications that know the extended structure of M_2 can access the additional element:

```
normalize-space(/ShipInfo/Address/PostalCode/Plus4/text())
```

To access the full element as 01730-1234, the following XPath expression can be used:

```
concat(normalize-space(/ShipInfo/Address/PostalCode/text()),'-',
    normalize-space(/ShipInfo/Address/PostalCode/Plus4/text()))"
```

The intrinsic extensibility of XML combined with best practices for extending an XML schema and for accessing the data in XML provides the ESB with a loosely coupled data model. This loosely coupled data model is a key aspect of the ESB, with significant benefits for development, deployment, and maintenance of the integration infrastructure.

Because of the extensibility of XML, producers and consumers of XML messages can be upgraded independently of one another to deal with the extended data structure. X_1 can begin to send message M_2 without any changes to either of the consumers; consumers Y_1 and Y_2 can be upgraded to process M_2 independently of each other and of the producers. This scenario will work even if all the producers are not updated in tandem with the consumers.

XPath is an expression language for accessing nodes in an XML document. It allows the use of XML element names separated by forward slashes (/) to delineate the hierarchy of XML elements. Regular-expression pattern matching is also possible to identify levels in the XML element hierarchy.

Consider the following XML fragment:

```
<?xml version="1.0"?>
<A>
 <B x="1">aa</B>
 <C x="2" y="3">bb</C>
 <C x="4" y="5" z="6">cc</C>
 <D y="7">
   <E z="8">dd</E>
 </D>
</A>
```

The following table shows the results of applying an XPath operator to that XML fragment:

Operator	XPath Expression	Result
/	/A/B	<B x="1">aa</B>
@	/A/B/@x	1
[ ]	/A/C[@x=4]/text()	cc
//	//@z	68
*	/A/*/@x	124
.	/A/C/@x[.=2]	2
..	/A/D/E/../@y	7

XPath also allows the use of inline scripting functions to perform runtime evaluation of XML items. For example:

```
normalize-space() - ignores whitespace such as newlines, tab characters, etc.
concat() - concatenates the results of XPath expressions.
text() - returns the content of an XML element as text.
```

Because XML parsing technology is largely event-driven and data-driven, a receiving application can be written such that the additional information (in this case, Plus4) will be processed only if the data in the XML message contains it. This means that if an element is not present, there is no error! Now, you might say that building a system in which missing data is not an error is bad design, and there is some truth to that. But the ESB will help you handle these business rules too.

There are cases in which incomplete data is acceptable, and should not generate a fatal error. The "business rules" surrounding the use of a postal code is a good example. The use of the Plus4 element of a postal code means that efficiency and expediency of delivery of the physical goods can be improved. However, if the application that receives message M can use only the five-digit postal code, it's not fatal to the application. The package will still get to its destination, just not as efficiently as it would using the nine-digit postal code.

Content-Based Routing and Transformation

So far, we have been focusing on the generic benefits of using XML as the means for exchanging data between applications. The generic benefits of data-driven parsing technology and XPath expressions for pattern matching can provide a certain degree of loose coupling between applications, and allow for some improvements in data structures over time without forcing a simultaneous upgrade of all the applications concerned.

XML can provide a great deal of resilience to changes in applications, as long as you're just adding data or enhancing structure, and not actually *changing* the structure. However, this can get you only so far. What's important to understand about the previous example is that the PostalCode field still has its original raw data, but now it also has additional element field names that help to structure PostalCode data for use separately. The structure changed—it got richer—but the ability to access the PostalCode field remains basically the same in both versions of the message.

We can improve upon this by applying some basic ESB concepts: a business process definition, content-based routing, and data transformation. All of these concepts are inherently part of the ESB.

A business process definition represents a series of steps in a flow between applications. For example, a purchase order document might follow these basic, logical steps: credit check, inventory check, order fulfillment, and invoice (Figure 4-3).

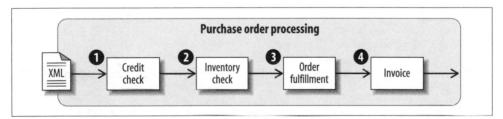

Figure 4-3. An ESB business process definition combines a series of logical steps

In the ESB, these steps may be mapped into service endpoints that represent physical applications. Using a business process definition, it is possible to administratively insert additional steps into that path of control flow, without modifying the applications directly.

What kinds of things might you insert into a business process? In the PostalCode example, the components would be specialized services that can alter the path or otherwise affect the content of the message. The path of execution, or the message flow, between the producers and the consumers can be augmented by adding a transformation service into the business process.

Let's assume that we have shut down Y_1, and Y_2 is the only version running (Figure 4-4). However, X_1 (the original application) must remain online for another year, waiting for the allocation of money and time to upgrade it. There needs to be a strategy for keeping X_1 working, and still satisfying the extended information needs of Y_2. This can be accomplished by inserting a transformation step into the message flow between X_1 and Y_2.

Transformation is performed using a stylesheet language called XSLT (eXtensible Stylesheet Language Transformation). XSLT can restructure XML documents from one format to another, as well as transforming or enhancing the content. By applying an XSLT transformation, application X_1 can still send document M_1, as long as the transformation from M_1 to M_2 is done before the data arrives at Y_2 (Figure 4-4).

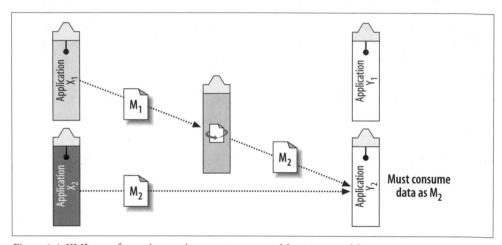

Figure 4-4. XML transformation service converts message M_1 to message M_2

In the future, when X_1 is upgraded to behave like X_2, this transformation won't be necessary.

For this XML transformation to work, it needs to make an external call to a database lookup using the street and city to obtain the extended Plus4 element. Advanced lookup capabilities using XQuery will be explored in later chapters.

What we've seen so far is that by combining the extensibility of XML and the transformation power of XSLT processing services that are inherently built into the fabric of the ESB, we can provide resilience to change in more complex situations. While this approach has its merits, it doesn't necessarily work well as the problem starts to scale up. The downside of this approach is that it requires direct knowledge of each point-to-point interaction between the various flavors of X and Y applications, and of when and

XSLT extensions can be used to make callouts to external code. Depending on the XSLT processor, calls can be made to Java, JavaScript, C#, or VBScript. A stylesheet can be used to supply the template for the PostalCode and Plus4 conversion, and scripting code can be written to do a table lookup or make a web service invocation. If the data being used to enrich the content is stored in an XML file, web service, or XML database, XQuery can be used as a replacement for XSLT. Depending on the maturity of the tools that are supplied with the ESB, the creation of the XSL Transforms and XQuery expressions can be supported through development tools that support these languages.

where message M_1 must be upgraded to M_2. What happens when message type M_3 is introduced?

This process can be further automated and generalized by introducing another ESB concept, Content-Based Routing (CBR). A CBR service can be plugged into the message flow between the producer X_1 and the consumer Y_1. This CBR service can be a lightweight process with the sole purpose of applying an XPath expression, such as the one used in our example, to determine whether the message conforms to the format of M_1 or M_2. If the message is of type M_1, it can be routed automatically to another special service that fills in the missing pieces of data (Figure 4-5).

This transformation service can apply some simple rules to convert the five-digit postal code to a nine-digit format. The method by which this is done depends on the implementation of the service. It can be done simply by writing code to do a table lookup based on some values stored in a database, or implemented as an XSLT transformation that applies a stylesheet to produce the desired result. It can even make a call to an external web service using an outbound SOAP request. Structured integration patterns for performing Validate, Enrich, Transform, (Route,) and Operate (VETO, VETRO) will be explained in Chapter 11.

Inserting the routing and transformation into the process between the producers and consumers of the postal code gives us an advantage that we didn't have with XML alone. Through a sequence of inspection, routing, and transformation combined with the use of XML documents, we can handle a wide array of complex integration tasks and add a great deal of resilience to changing data in the underlying applications. We can also think about these formats, routes, and transformations separately from the underlying applications.

The integration architect can use the ESB's process management and XML processing facilities to improve the message data without ever modifying the sending applications. Using this model, only the consuming applications need to be modified to support the improvement in data. And as we have seen, not all the consumers need to be upgraded either. For the ones that do, the upgrade can happen independently of the data

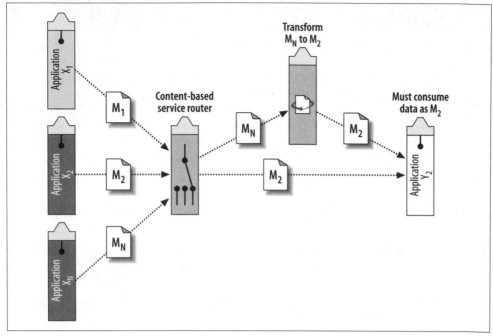

Figure 4-5. Content-based routing can identify the need for transformation

translation upgrades, allowing greater flexibility in the coordination of development timelines of the applications that are driving the requirement.

A Generic Data Exchange Architecture

The simple example in the previous section is a one-directional map: it flows from left to right. If we want a general-purpose architecture for the exchange of information, data will need to flow in multiple directions. Figure 4-6 expands on our routing and transformation concept by replicating the process on both sides of the communication, allowing the multiple forms of data to flow in all directions.

Data Translation to and from a Canonical Format

In the middle of this generic data exchange architecture is a canonical, application-independent version of the data. A best-practice strategy in integration is to decide on a set of canonical XML formats as the means for expressing data in messages as it flows through an enterprise across the ESB. Companies often use their already-established enterprise data models, or, alternatively, adopt industry-standard message formats as the basis for their own canonical representations. By doing so, companies standardize the definitions for common business entities such as addresses, purchase orders, and invoices.

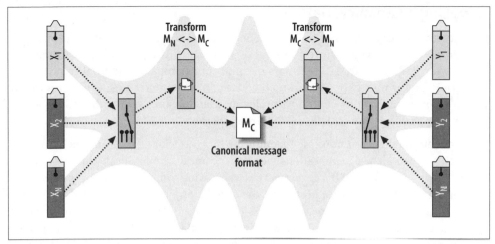

Figure 4-6. Generic data exchange architecture using a canonical message format

The integration architect then works with the owner of each individual application to transform any application content into and out of this canonical format. By having an independent representation of the data, all application teams can work in parallel and without requiring advanced agreement between them. When extensions to the canonical format are required, they can simply be added as extra XML attributes and elements, relying on the inherent flexibility of XML.

As the applications change, the impact is limited to the transformation into and out of the canonical format. In addition to XML's inherent flexibility, application owners have a great deal of freedom to enhance their applications and take advantage of new information within the canonical format.

There have been several attempts within the industry to provide a standardized representation of business data, and the results of these attempts have achieved various degrees of adoption. For example, in the heyday of electronic marketplaces, CommerceOne made popular the xCBL format, Ariba has promoted cbXML, and RosettaNet uses something called Partner Interface Processes (PiP). Some businesses have gone ahead and created their own proprietary XML formats. The level of "format" is at the business-object level; e.g., the definition of a purchase order or shipping address.

What this means to you, the integration architect, is that there are a number of XML dialects and overlapping conventions out there for representing business data in XML. Your business partners may have already standardized on one of these dialects, but you can probably safely assume that at least a few of your business partners haven't standardized on XML at all just yet. Most of your business partners are probably limited to some kind of fixed format for exchanging data. For example, in financial services you have come to rely on FIX and SWIFT; in healthcare, you probably rely on HIPPA and HL7. Furthermore, the partners that *have* standardized on XML probably haven't decided on the same dialect.

Adopting a Canonical Data Exchange

One scalable strategy that can be built upon is to use the routing and transformation technique that was explored previously and create a set of common XML formats for use in your ESB. These XML grammars become your company's internal standard and comprise "MyCompanyML," a markup language for data interchange within your company. Many organizations choose to build upon an existing standard, such as xCBL, rather than starting from scratch and inventing their own.

All applications that communicate through the bus can share data using these formats. Does this mean that all applications need to be modified to speak this new dialect immediately? No. The ESB can convert data flowing onto the bus or off the bus, depending on the formats supported by the specific applications that need to be integrated. The recommended approach that is being used today in many ESB integrations is to create transformation services that convert the data to and from the common XML format and the target data format of the application being plugged in, as illustrated in Figure 4-7.

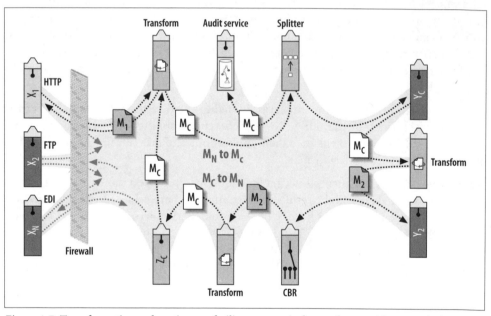

Figure 4-7. Transformation and routing can facilitate a generic data exchange with a canonical XML format as the native data type of the ESB

Figure 4-7 shows the series of steps that occur when a document flows through an enterprise using a canonical XML data exchange. The space in the middle between the applications and services is intentionally depicted as nebulous so that we can focus on the exchange concepts rather than the physical details of the underlying ESB. The details of what's in that center—the core architecture of the ESB—will be addressed in the next three chapters.

The following are the processing steps illustrated in Figure 4-7, beginning from the top left in a clockwise direction. Each step is treated as an event-driven service that receives a message asynchronously using reliable messaging, and forwards the resulting message on to the next step after processing.

1. An external partner sends an XML or SOAP message over the HTTP protocol. Once inside the firewall, the message is assigned to a business process that controls the steps through the ESB.

2. The message (M_1) is run through a transformation service. The transformation service converts the XML content from the data format used by the partner to the data format used as the canonical XML format. The resulting message (M_C) is then forwarded onto a "splitter" service.

3. The splitter service has the sole purpose of making a copy of the message and routing it to an audit service. The audit service may add additional information to the message, such as contextual information about the business process and a timestamp of when the message arrived. The audit service itself could be implemented as a native XML persistence engine that allows the direct storage and retrieval of XML documents. This subject will be covered in Chapter 7.

4. The original message is forwarded on to application Y_C, which *operates* on the message; that is, it consumes the message and processes it. Conveniently, this particular application already knows how to consume messages in the canonical data format.

5. As part of the business process, the message now needs to be forwarded to application Y_2, which understands only its own proprietary format. Therefore, before moving on Y_2, the M_C message is routed to a transformation service that converts it to M_2, which is the target data format required by application Y_2.

6. The transformation service sends the message M_2 to the application Y_2.

7. After being consumed and operated on by application Y_2, the message now needs to get routed to another business process. This other business process can be invoked in a variety of ways from a number of different places within the bus. The process can't ensure that the message is already in the canonical format. Therefore, it has a CBR service that examines its content and determines whether the message needs to be transformed.

8. In this case, the CBR service has identified the message as being in M_2 format, and routes the message to a transformation service to get converted to M_C format before getting delivered to application Z_C.

9. Application Z_C is responsible for generating an invoice and sending it asynchronously back to the partner.

10. Before doing this, however, the invoice needs to be converted into the format that the partner understands. Therefore, it is routed to another transformation service that converts it from message M_C to message M_1. In addition, this service constructs the SOAP envelope around the message (if required by that partner).

11. The invoice message is delivered to the partner asynchronously using the protocol that is appropriate for dealing with that partner.

Alternate Approaches

The individual steps in the previous section could have been implemented in a number of different ways. Steps 2 and 3 could be combined; the transformation service in Step 2 could have done the splitting up of the message without a separate splitter service. An XSLT stylesheet can be written so that a "splitter" or "fan-out" operation can be performed while the data transformation is occurring. For example, a single XSLT stylesheet can perform a transformation that converts a purchase order from cXML to xCBL, and also splits off the line-item details into separate messages for the supply chain applications that need to process them.

The dual transformation from M_C to M_2 for processing by application Y_2, and then back again into M_C, could have been done another way under different circumstances. The format of M_2 could have preserved the original message content in its M_C format, and appended the translated content to the end. That way, when the message moved on to the next step, it would still have its original M_C message content intact and would avoid the need for an additional translate step. However, this method doesn't work in this particular case. Here, the Y_2 application also needs to enrich the message with content that is required by the next application in the process.

The application Z_C, which generates the invoice, could have simply generated it in the target M_1 format that the partner expected. However, many partners have their own formats and protocols that they prefer to communicate with. Z_C is a generic invoicing application that needs to know only the canonical XML format. Specialized transformation services that know how to convert the canonical invoice message M_C to the specific targeted formats, such as EDI, PiP, or proprietary flat file format, can take on that responsibility separately. Even the management of the multiple partners and their protocols and formats can be separated into its own service.

At first glance, it may seem a bit exorbitant to require a transformation engine for each and every application that plugs into the ESB. However, in contrast with the point-to-point transformation solution, this method can reduce complexity over time, as the number of applications on the bus increases and as changes are introduced. When using specific point-to-point transformations between each application, the number of transformation instances increases exponentially with the number of applications. This is commonly referred to as the *N-squared* problem. With the canonical XML data exchange approach, the number of transformations increases much more linearly as new applications are brought into the integration.

Applying the canonical XML data exchange technique on a larger scale yields the following benefits:

- Each application needs to focus on only one type of transformation to and from a common format. This illustrates an important philosophy of the bus that will be reinforced throughout the book. If you are the owner of an individual application, your only concern is that you plug into the bus, you post data to the bus, and you receive data from the bus. The bus is responsible for getting the data where it needs to go, in the target data formats that it needs to be in, and using the protocols, adapters, and transformations necessary to get there.

- New applications being written to plug into the bus can use the canonical XML format directly. And multiple applications not anticipated today can tap into the flow of messages on the bus to create heretofore unimagined uses.

- ESB services such as the CBR and the splitter can be written to use the canonical XML format. As we will see in Chapter 7, a service type can be written once and then customized on a per-instance basis by supplying different XSLT stylesheets, endpoint definitions, and routing rules. Having an agreed-upon format for common things such as address tags and purchase order numbers can be a tremendous advantage here.

- Standard stylesheet templates and libraries can be created and reused throughout the organization.

Does it matter which XML dialect you choose for the native format of the ESB? That would depend on what the majority of the applications already speak. If much of your in-flight data is destined for a particular target format, and that target format is sufficient for generically representing all possible forms of your business data, go ahead and standardize on that XML format as the native datatype for the ESB. An example of such a format is xCBL. xCBL is a standard for describing things such as addresses, purchase orders, and so on, and was jointly developed by SAP and CommerceOne during the early days of dotcom and public exchanges. Like many other standards efforts, xCBL has not gone on to dominate the XML industry. However, because it was codeveloped by SAP, the message schema has a high degree of affinity to SAP's IDOC elements and terminology.

The only basic recommendation here is that the format be XML. As you now know, many advantages can be realized when XML is the native datatype for in-flight documents within the ESB. And there are many more advantages of using XML as the native datatype, as will be discussed throughout this book.

Summary

In this chapter we saw that there are tremendous advantages to using XML as the means of representing data that is shared between applications. We have also learned the following:

- XML allows applications to evolve more easily. It provides the flexibility to enhance data structures to handle the changes that businesses need to make. In doing so, XML allows you to upgrade your systems incrementally and continuously.

- XML provides a richer data model than relational databases and includes standards-based transformation grammars such as XSLT and XQuery.

- XML also supports best practices that enable resilient data access in evolving XML schema. This is accomplished through the proper use of XPath and XML data access APIs. It is expected that tools and methodologies will be developed that automate and validate these best practices.

- XML alone won't accommodate all the data exchange requirements of an enterprise that is dealing with legacy systems and partner interactions. With the help of intelligent content-based routing and targeted transformation services, ESB lays the groundwork for a generic data exchange architecture and the basis for more sophisticated business process management.

Message Oriented
Middleware (MOM)

5

Enterprise messaging is at the core of an ESB architecture. In this chapter we will explore Message Oriented Middleware (MOM) and what it contributes to an enterprise integration strategy. A MOM is a key part of the ESB architecture, as it provides the underpinnings of the network of virtual channels that an ESB uses to route messages throughout an extended enterprise and beyond.

Message Oriented Middleware is a concept that involves the passing of data between applications using a communication channel that carries self-contained units of information (messages). In a MOM-based communication environment, messages are usually sent and received asynchronously. Using message-based communications, applications are abstractly decoupled; senders and receivers are never aware of each other. Instead, they send and receive messages to and from the messaging system. It is the responsibility of the messaging system (MOM) to get the messages to their intended destinations.

In a messaging system, an application uses an API to communicate through a messaging client that is provided by the MOM vendor. The messaging client sends and receives messages through a messaging system, as illustrated in Figure 5-1.

The messaging system is responsible for managing the connection points between multiple messaging clients, and for managing multiple channels of communication between the connection points. The messaging system is usually implemented as a software process, which is commonly known as a *message server* or a *message broker*. Message servers are usually capable of being grouped together to form clusters that provide advanced capabilities such as load balancing, fault tolerance, and sophisticated routing using managed security domains. The "server" implementation is the most typical, although some messaging vendors offer alternate architectures where the "server" functionality is built into a more heavyweight client.

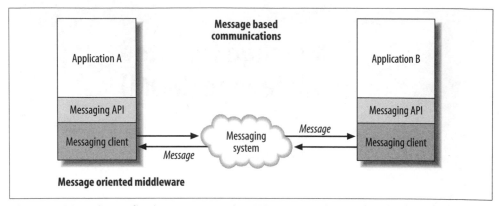

Figure 5-1. Messaging applications use a messaging API to communicate with each other through a messaging system

Tightly Coupled Versus Loosely Coupled Interfaces

Messaging enables a loosely coupled environment in which an application doesn't need to know the intimate details of how to reach and interface with other applications. In choosing a type of communication infrastructure, it is important to consider the tradeoffs between loosely coupled and tightly coupled interfaces, and asynchronous and synchronous interaction modes.

Remote Procedure Call (RPC)-Style Programming

Remote Procedure Call (RPC)-style programming has had reasonable adoption in the industry for a number of years. Technologies that predominantly use RPC-style communication include Common Object Request Broker Architecture (CORBA), Remote Method Invocation (RMI), DCOM, ActiveX, Sun-RPC, Java API for XML-RPC (JAX-RPC), and Simple Object Access Protocol (SOAP*) v1.0 and v1.1.

RPC-style interfaces have the advantages of a programming model where remote procedures are exposed in a way that mimics the underlying object architecture of the applications concerned, allowing a developer to make "normal"-looking method calls in the native language.

RPC-style communications tend to be synchronous in nature. By design, RPC-style programming mimics the serial thread of execution that a "normal" nondistributed application would use, where each statement is executed in sequence.

---

* SOAP 1.2 has moved to support asynchronous message-based exchange as well as synchronous RPC.

In RPC-style programming, an object and its methods (or a procedure and its parameters) are "remoted" such that an invocation of a procedure or method can happen across a network separation. An application uses a local proxy, commonly referred to as a "stub," that mimics the interface of the remote object and its methods. The application making the procedure calls is known as a "client," and the remote implementation is referred to as a "server" or "service." The client executes what looks like a local method invocation or procedure call, which is actually getting "marshaled" across the wire to the remote implementation. Likewise, the return values and output parameters are marshaled back to the caller.

A distributed synchronous RPC call provides the luxury of an immediate response indicating whether an operation was successful. However, in a distributed system, there are additional failure scenarios that a nondistributed program does not have to deal with. When performing a synchronous operation across multiple processes, the success of one RPC call depends on the success of all the downstream RPC calls that are part of the same synchronous request/response cycle. This makes the whole invocation an all-or-nothing proposition. If one operation is unable to complete for any reason, all other dependent operations will fail with it (Figure 5-2). If one of the processes is not available, the application initiating the request must somehow make note of the failure, try it again later, or take some other course of action—e.g., inform a human that they are simply out of luck and must try back later. To compensate for this, error handling and recovery logic must be built into every application that makes use of RPC-style programming.

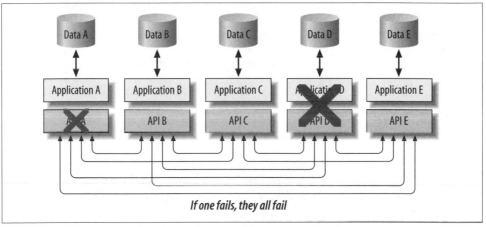

Figure 5-2. Synchronous RPC-based interactions consist of multiple point-to-point integrations that intrinsically depend on each other

Tightly Coupled Interfaces

In a tightly coupled RPC environment, each application needs to know the intimate details of how every other application wants to be communicated with—the number of methods it exposes and the details of the parameters that each method accepts. As the number of applications and services increases, the number of interfaces that need to be created and maintained quickly becomes unwieldy.

An interface represents the public methods that are exposed by a remote service or a remote object. If the number of interfaces of each object is exactly one, the number of connection points represents the number of interfaces. In practice, the number of interfaces on an individual object or service is more than one.

A simple formula that is often used for estimating the number of interfaces between applications is $n(n–1)/2$. If the number of applications is 5 $(n=5)$, as in Figure 5-3, the number of interfaces is 10. That doesn't sound too bad, does it? But if the number of applications is 13, as in Figure 5-4, the number of interfaces is 78. And if the number of applications is 100, the number of interfaces between them becomes 4,950. This formula makes two assumptions that you need to consider when factoring in your own potential situation. First, it assumes that each application endpoint has only one interface, and second, it assumes that every application needs to interact directly with every other application.

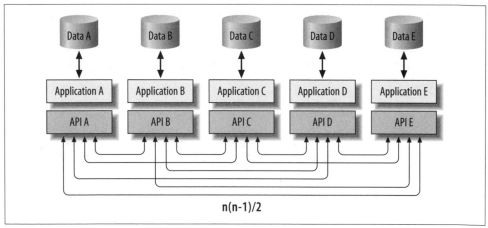

Figure 5-3. The conservative formula for calculating the minimum number of application interfaces is n(n–1)/2

In practice, each application will have much more than one interface, and not every applications will need to interface directly with every other application. For example, if each application has an average of four RPC-style interfaces, and each of your 100 applications needs to communicate with only 50% of the other applications, your total number of interfaces will be 200 * 199 / 2 = 19,900. If we were to use the statistics cited in Chapter 2 and assume only 15% of the 100 applications were actually connected to each

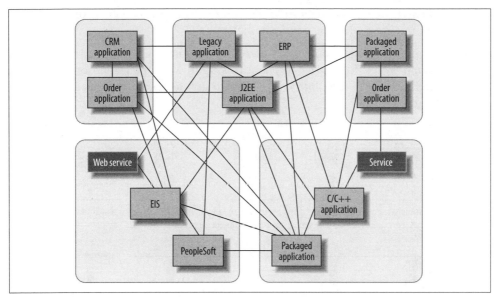

Figure 5-4. The number of tightly coupled point-to-point interfaces between applications can quickly become unwieldy

other, that would be 60 * 59 / 2 = 1770 interfaces. Still, that's a lot of interfaces to create and maintain over time.

Loosely Coupled Interactions

Asynchronous messaging allows each communication operation between two processes to be a self-contained, standalone unit of work. Each participant in a multistep business process flow need only be concerned with ensuring that it can send a message to the messaging system (Figure 5-5). The higher-level ESB built on top of the messaging system will get the data to the places that it needs to get to, in the target data format that it needs to be in. Asynchronous request/response patterns are also possible, as discussed later in this chapter. The application initiating the conversation need only be concerned with initiating the "request," knowing that it will eventually receive a "response" asynchronously. In a complex interaction across multiple processes and services, the response may not even go to the original requestor. Each response may actually be a new message being sent to a forwarding address. This is the basis of what has become known as itinerary-based routing in an ESB.

Loosely Coupled Interfaces

Asynchronous interactions are a key design pattern in loosely coupled interfaces. In an environment where multiple applications and services need to interact with each other, it is not practical that every application be required to know the details of every other application's myriad method calls and parameters.

An asynchronous message should be an autonomous unit of work that carries data and context around with it from place to place. It is up to each application or service that processes the message to look into its contents to get the data that it needs and to act upon that data.

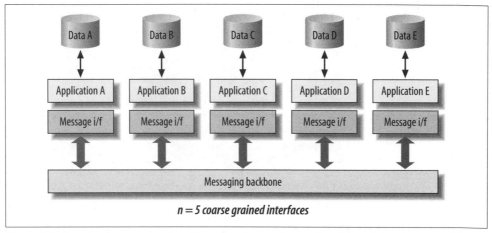

Figure 5-5. Asynchronous message-based interfaces are much more loosely coupled and manageable

In contrast to the $n(n–1)/2$ problem of tightly coupled RPC, using loosely coupled messaging reduces the number of interfaces to something more linear, where the number of interfaces is exactly the number of connection points. This view can also be a bit skewed in that all applications across an enterprise do not share exactly the same data. However, many applications can share common business messages even if they operate on different parts of it. A business message can carry enough information that it can be accessed, shared, manipulated, and updated by many different kinds of applications across an enterprise. For example, a purchase order document can contain the name and address of a buyer. The address could be divided into two distinct addresses for billing purposes and for shipping purposes. The invoicing applications will focus more on the billing address, while the shipping logistics application will focus more on the shipping address. A purchase order document can also contain individual line-item data for goods purchased, which can be used by the inventory and fulfillment applications. This document can be encapsulated in an XML message and passed around between all these applications as a single message.

Does this mean that messages are bigger than they need to be? Perhaps. However, performance and throughput in a reliable messaging system are by and large governed by the number, not the size, of messages traveling through the system. The size of the messages certainly matters, but it is a secondary issue. In Chapter 6 we will explore how an

ESB can help reduce the excess processing overhead that is caused by the verbosity of XML data.

Arguments regarding the N-squared versus N-linear formulas can be a bit subjective at times, but they are grounded in reality. Your mileage will certainly vary. The bottom line is that loosely coupled message-based interfaces significantly reduce the number of distinct interfaces that need to be created between applications and services.

N-Squared Data Formats: It's Really About the Data Transformations

Perhaps what's equally important is how the N-squared formula can also be applied to the number of data transformations that need to occur between applications in a system consisting of multiple point-to-point integrations. If every point-to-point link between every application has exactly one data transformation, the numbers are just as daunting as the numbers of point-to-point interfaces. In contrast, the generic data exchange architecture approach using a canonical XML format, as described in Chapter 4, allows a more linear ratio between the number of applications and the number of data transformations that need to be created and maintained. Applications that are plugged into the bus don't need to know how other applications represent data. Each application needs to be concerned only with how it converts to and from the canonical format.

Get on the Bus

The combination of loosely coupled interfaces and asynchronous interactions is a key concept of bus terminology. Think of hardware bus architecture, such as a PC motherboard, with multiple slots that any type of compatible card can be plugged into. The use of the term "bus" in ESB is analogous to that. There is a standard way that you plug into the bus, and whatever is being plugged into the bus is not concerned with how it communicates with anything else on the bus. Everything on the bus is accessible by anything else on the bus. If you are the owner of a service or an application domain, you need only be concerned with three operations: plugging into the bus, posting data to the bus, and receiving data from the bus. The bus then gets the data to the applications in the target data formats.

Loosely Coupled Web Services Standards

It's not only ESB proponents who recognize the need for loosely coupled interfaces. The many groups that are defining web services standards have recognized that loosely coupled asynchronous processing is a more appropriate model for describing interfaces and interactions between applications and services. For example, SOAP 1.2 and WSDL 2.0 have removed all dependencies on RPC-style invocations that were once heavily ingrained in their respective invocation models. The specifications still support it, but they don't promote it as the recommended means of interaction. Web service–based process modeling and choreography efforts such as WS-BPEL and WS-Choreography are also based on a loosely coupled asynchronous exchange of information. In the Java community, even JAX-RPC, the Java specification for performing RPC-style invocations, has decided to adopt asynchronous processing as a goal for Version 2.0 of the JAX-RPC specification.

MOM Concepts

MOM is a concept that has been around for two decades. Over the years, new ideas have been introduced, new vendors have moved into the MOM space, and new standards continue to evolve that are related to messaging and MOM concepts. While the messaging category of technology continually gets better, there is also a set of core concepts that will remain similar across many MOM implementations.

Abstract Decoupling

Messaging applications use a messaging client API to communicate with one another through a messaging system. When an application is communicating in this fashion, it is acting as either a *producer* or a *consumer*. Senders (producers) produce messages and receivers (consumers) consume messages. An application may be both a producer and a consumer at the same time.

Producers and consumers are loosely coupled in that they are not directly tied to each other; instead, they are abstractly connected to each other through virtual channels called publish-and-subscribe channels or point-to-point channels. These two distinct channel types are often referred to as *topics* and *queues*, respectively (Figure 5-6).

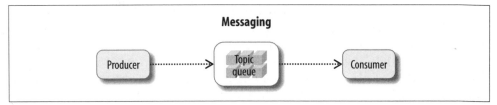

Figure 5-6. Producers and consumers are abstractly decoupled from each other using virtual channels known as publish-and-subscribe topics and point-to-point queues

The producer does not need to know which applications are receiving a message, or in some cases even how many are receiving it. Likewise, the consumer does not need to know which applications are sending the data; it only knows that it receives a message and acts upon it. If a response is required, that fact is encoded in the message via the presence of a "ReplyTo" destination to identify the channel on which to send a response.

Depending on the implementation, these virtual channel definitions are either coded into the application, or are described and configured administratively using a tool, with the details of the configuration stored in a directory service. Even if the details of channel configuration are stored in a directory service, the creation of the message channels needs to be coded into the application when using a basic MOM, rather than a higher-level ESB that is built on a MOM. With an ESB, the details of creating and managing the messaging channels are encapsulated in a container-managed environment that is configured instead of being written into application code.

Messaging Models: Publish-and-Subscribe and Point-to-Point

As shown in Figure 5-7, the publish-and-subscribe (pub/sub) domain is intended for a one-to-many broadcast of information, while the point-to-point domain is intended for a one-to-one communication between two specific applications.

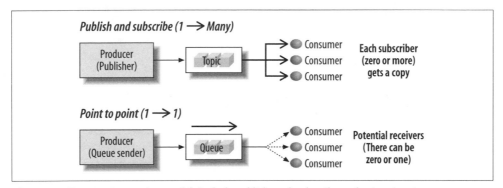

Figure 5-7. Common messaging models include publish-and-subscribe and point-to-point

In the pub/sub model, multiple consumers may register an interest with, or *subscribe* to, a topic. A producer sends a message on that channel by *publishing* on that topic. Each subscriber receives a copy of that message.

In the point-to-point model, only one consumer may receive a message that is sent to a queue. As shown in Figure 5-7, a point-to-point queue may have multiple consumers listening for the purposes of load-balancing or "hot backup"; however, only one receiver may consume each individual message. There may also be no receivers listening, in which case the message stays in the queue until a receiver attaches itself to the queue to retrieve messages. In the publish-and-subscribe model, messages not flagged as reliable can be discarded if no subscribers are registered to receive them at the time they are published.

The choice of which model to use can largely depend on how many consumers need to see duplicate copies of the same message. For example, in a supply chain, a supplier might want to broadcast special price reductions to its buyers in a one-to-many fashion using the pub/sub messaging model, with all buyers receiving the same information. However, if a particular buyer wants to react to that lower price by purchasing the goods being advertised, that will require a point-to-point conversation that involves only the two parties: the buyer and the seller.

Topic Hierarchies

Many MOM implementations allow publish-and-subscribe topics to be managed in a hierarchical tree structure, as illustrated in Figure 5-8.

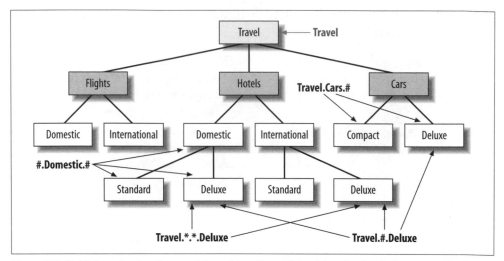

Figure 5-8. Publish-and-subscribe topic hierarchies allow wildcard-based subscriptions at any level

Using topic hierarchies, a message consumer may subscribe to any level of any branch within a topic tree. Wildcard substitution can be used to represent an entire subnode within a tree. For example, using the topic hierarchy represented by Figure 5-8, a subscriber who subscribes to the Travel.#.Deluxe topic will receive all messages addressed to the Travel.Hotels.Domestic.Deluxe, Travel.Hotels.International.Deluxe, and Travel.Cars.Deluxe topics. In this representative syntax, the # character matches any number of node levels in the topic tree that begin with Travel.

Another example of topic hierarchies, this time in the financial services industry, is the segregation of market data (Figure 5-9).

These examples both use the popular "." (dot) syntax to separate topic names. Industry efforts are underway to standardize hierarchical topic trees using XML syntax in the WS-Notification family of specifications. WS-Notification uses a subset of XPath for expression matching on individual branches and leaves in a tree, in addition to allowing for various proprietary dialects.

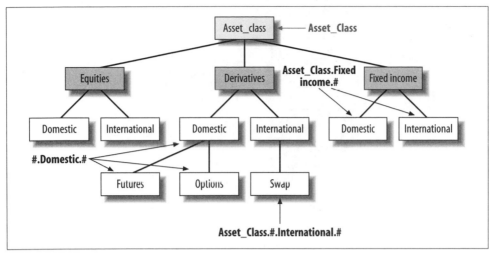

Figure 5-9. Segregation of data in a financial services topic hierarchy

Access Control Lists (ACLs)

A companion security feature may also be implemented to take advantage of hierarchical topic trees. Access Control List (ACL) mechanisms can allow administrators to grant access to different levels of the hierarchy using a similar wildcard approach to specify routes to a particular branch or leaf of a topic tree. Security realms can be implemented such that individuals or groups can be granted permissions, either positively or negatively, to individual branches or leaves within a tree-based namespace of messaging destinations. For example, you can administratively specify to "Grant this group of users all access to the graph of topics that match the expression Travel.#.Domestic.#, excluding these three users." If the point-to-point queue namespace has a similar form, the same pattern matching can occur.

In an ESB, this capability helps to enable the federated autonomy between departments and business units. Each ESB segment can reside in an individual business unit and have its own local control over ACLs.

What's in a Message?

A message is typically composed of three basic parts: the headers, the properties, and the message payload or body (Figure 5-10). The headers are used by both the messaging system and the application developer to provide information about things such as the destination, the reply-to destination, the message type, and the message expiration time.

The properties section may contain a set of application-defined name/value pairs. These properties are essentially parts of the message payload or body that get promoted to a special section of the message so that filtering can be applied to the message by consumers or specialized routers.

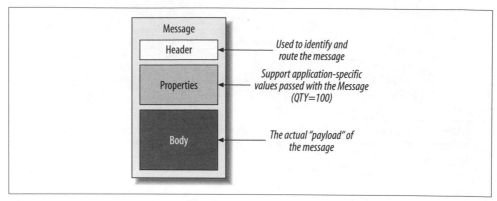

Figure 5-10. MOM messages consists of headers, properties, and the message body

 Note that not all MOM implementations support the notion of a property section. Instead, they merge the concept of headers and properties into a single space.

The format of the message payload can vary across messaging implementations. Most common formats are plain text, a raw stream of bytes for holding any type of binary data, or a special XML message type that allow the message payload to be accessed using any number of common XML parsing technologies.

Asynchronous Reliability

With asynchrony comes the need for reliability. When an application sends an asynchronous message, there often needs to be some sort of assurance that the message will get to where it needs to go. There are three key parts to reliable messaging: message autonomy, store and forward, and the underlying message acknowledgment semantics.

Message Autonomy

Messages are self-contained, autonomous entities that represent a business transaction. Once a message producer sends a message, its role is completed. If the message is properly designated for reliable delivery, the messaging system guarantees that it is received by any interested parties, and the ESB ensures that it arrives in the desired target data format. This contract between a sending client and the messaging system is much like the contract between a JDBC client and the database. Once the data is reliably delivered to the messaging server, it is considered "safe" and out of the hands of the client.

Store and Forward

MOM provides message queuing and guaranteed delivery semantics, which ensure that "unavailable" applications will get their data queued and delivered at a later time.

The message delivery semantics cover a range of delivery options, from *exactly-once* delivery to *at-least-once* delivery to *at-most-once* delivery. In the exactly-once (a.k.a. *once-and-only-once*) delivery mode, the messaging system guarantees that the message will arrive at the intended destination no matter what, and will never be sent more than once. Even in the pub/sub model, where multiple receivers may consume a copy of a broadcasted message, the rules still apply within the relative view of each consumer. Exactly-once delivery guarantee is accomplished in part by the use of a technique known as *store and forward* (see Figure 5-11).

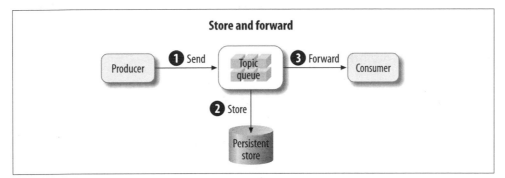

Figure 5-11. MOM uses a store-and-forward mechanism as part of the solution to guarantee once-and-only-once delivery of messages

There is much more to once-and-only-once delivery than what is illustrated in Figure 5-11. Store and forward is accompanied by a set of rules for governing message acknowledgments at the wire protocol level, and for handling transactional recovery if the application or the messaging system fails. This behavior will be explored momentarily.

At-most-once delivery is a less stringent Quality of Service (QoS) setting on a message, which means that the messaging system is allowed to occasionally lose a message in the event of a hardware, software, or network failure. There are valid business cases in which this is acceptable behavior. A common example is a stock feed application in which the system is set up to cycle through ticker symbols every few minutes. If the broadcast of a particular ticker symbol does not reach its intended destination, another one will be along shortly. Typically, the performance and throughput of messages using at-most-once delivery are much higher (up to 10 times the throughput) than with exactly-once.

In addition to guaranteed delivery mode, most messaging systems have options for message ordering guarantees. Message ordering means that messages are delivered to the receiver in the same order in which they are sent by the sender. A variety of things can affect the ordered delivery of messages. In cases of failure and recovery, for example, messages may be held in a queue and redelivered to an application at a later time than the messages that were sent while the system was unavailable. Typically there will be settings to control whether order is guaranteed globally across the entire system, guaranteed between two distinct endpoints, or not guaranteed at all.

Message Persistence

When messages are marked *persistent*, it is the responsibility of the messaging system to utilize a *store-and-forward* mechanism to fulfill its contract with the sender. The storage mechanism is used for persisting messages to disk to ensure that it can be recovered if there is a failure of either the messaging system or the consuming client. The forwarding mechanism is responsible for retrieving messages from storage, and subsequently routing and delivering them.

Message Acknowledgments

Message acknowledgment at the wire protocol level is a key factor in guaranteed messaging. The acknowledgment protocol allows the messaging system to monitor the progress of a message so that it knows whether the message was successfully produced and consumed. With this knowledge, the messaging system can manage the distribution of messages and guarantee their delivery.

In the loosely coupled asynchronous environment of MOM, senders and receivers (producers and consumers) are intentionally decoupled from each other. Hence, the roles and responsibilities are divided among the message producer, the message server, and the message consumer.

Reliable Messaging Models

A common misconception regarding publish-and-subscribe versus point-to-point messaging queuing is that pub/sub is for lightweight, unreliable messaging and point-to-point queuing is more heavyweight and reliable. That may have been true a decade ago, when there were really only two messaging vendors: one that supported lightweight pub/sub and one that supported heavyweight, reliable point-to-point queues. Since then, however, many new messaging vendors have come onto the market supporting both messaging models, each with its own full range of QoS options. In addition, these reliable messaging techniques can be utilized across some potentially sophisticated deployment topologies.

Reliable Publish-and-Subscribe

A pub/sub message can be delivered just as reliably as a point-to-point message can. A message delivered on a point-to-point queue can be delivered with little additional overhead if it is not marked as being *persistent*. A reliable pub/sub message is delivered using a combination of persistent messages and *durable subscriptions* (a common term in JMS parlance). When an application registers its interest in receiving messages on a particular topic, it can specify that the subscription is durable. A durable subscription will survive the failure of the subscribing client. This means that if the intended receiver of a message becomes unavailable for any reason, the message server will continue to store messages on behalf of the receiver until the receiver becomes available again. When the receiver reestablishes its subscription with the messaging system, the stored messages will be delivered.

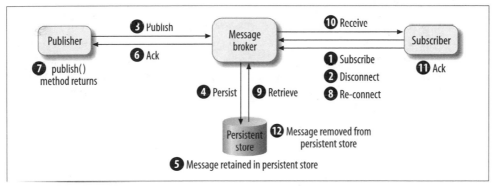

Figure 5-12. Reliable publish-and-subscribe involves message acknowledgments, message persistence, and durable subscriptions

Figure 5-12 shows the steps involved with delivering a pub/sub message using persistent messaging and a durable subscription.

1. The subscriber subscribes and indicates that the subscription is durable.
2. The subscriber disconnects from the message server, either through a graceful shutdown or through some kind of a failure.
3. The publisher sends the message using a publish( ) method. The publish( ) method will block and wait until it receives an acknowledgment from the message server.
4. The message server writes the message out to a reliable, persistent storage device.
5. The message is held reliably on disk.
6. An acknowledgment is sent back to the sender indicating that the message is now safe in the hands of the message server.
7. The publish( ) method returns.
8. The subscriber reconnects and reestablishes the subscription.
9. The message is retrieved from the persistent store.
10. The message is delivered to the subscriber.

11. The subscriber acknowledges to the message server that it has successfully received the message.

12. The message server removes the message from the persistent store.

Reliable Point-to-Point Queues

For point-to-point queues, messages are marked by the producer as either persistent or nonpersistent. If they are persistent, they are written to disk and subject to the same acknowledgment rules, failure conditions, and recovery as persistent messages in the publish/subscribe model.

From the receiver's perspective, the rules are somewhat simpler than with durable subscriptions because the receiver has no role in the durability aspect. With point-to-point queues, because only one consumer can receive a particular instance of a message, it's in the queue as either a persistent message or a nonpersistent message. A persistent message stays in the queue and on disk until it is delivered to a consumer or it expires. A nonpersistent message also stays in the queue until it is delivered or expired, but it is not guaranteed to survive a failure and recovery of the messaging server. The receipt of the message is also subject to the same acknowledgment rules and recovery from failure conditions as with the pub/sub model—once a persistent message is delivered to the consuming application and an acknowledgment is sent back to the message server, the message can be removed from persistent storage. If something fails during that process, the message will be redelivered during recovery.

Store-and-Forward Across Multiple Message Servers

In an ESB MOM core, the concept of store-and-forward should be capable of being repeated across multiple message servers that are chained together. In this scenario, each message server uses store-and-forward and message acknowledgments to get the message to the next server in the chain (Figure 5-13).

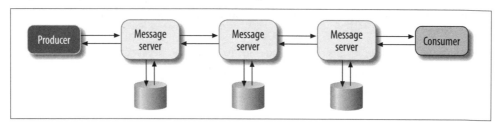

Figure 5-13. Reliable delivery across multiple message servers using store-and-forward and message acknowledgments

Each server-to-server handoff maintains the minimum reliability and QoS that were specified by the sender. This is all done in a fashion that is transparent to both the sender and the receiver.

The chain of message servers may not always form a straight line. Depending on the implementation, sophisticated and dynamic routing may be possible that directs each message to remote locations across a different path of servers based on routing information that is associated with the destination (Figure 5-14).

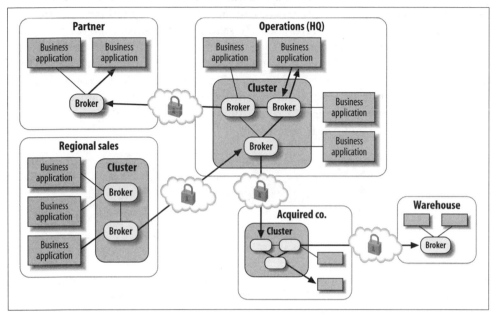

Figure 5-14. Dynamic routing of reliable messages across secure links

As illustrated in Figure 5-14, these links can be secure, authenticated, and capable of traversing safely through firewall boundaries using mutually authenticated channels with digital certificates on both sides of the communication link, ensuring that only the most secure link can be established through the corporate firewalls.

Transacted Messages

Having all producers and all consumers of messages participate in one global transaction would defeat the purpose of a loosely coupled asynchronous messaging environment. In a loosely coupled environment, applications need to hand off their messages to the messaging environment using local transactions, and go about their business. They don't need to be concerned about whether all the other interested parties are available to concurrently participate in a global transaction on the piece of data that the message represents.

Local Transactions

Within the context of an individual sender or an individual receiver, many MOM implementations have a model for grouping together multiple operations as a single transaction that is locally scoped to an individual sender or receiver. One such case is the grouping together of multiple messages in an all-or-nothing fashion. The transactions follow the convention of separating the send operations from the receive operations. Figure 5-15 shows a transactional send of a group of messages, in which either all of them or none of them will get to the message server. From the sender's perspective, the messages are held by the message server until a commit command is issued. If a failure occurs or if a rollback command is issued, the messages are discarded. Messages delivered to the message server in a transaction are not forwarded to the consumers until the producer commits the transaction.

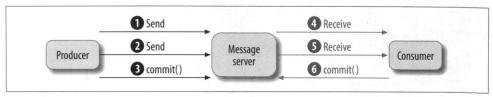

Figure 5-15. Transactional messages are sent in an all-or-nothing fashion

The message server will not start to deliver the messages to its consumers until the producer issues a commit command on the session. A message-based local transaction can include any number of messages.

There is also the notion of a transactional receive, in which a group of transacted messages are received by the consumer on an all-or-nothing basis (Figure 5-16). From the receiver's perspective, the messages are delivered as expeditiously as possible, but are held in a recoverable storage mechanism by the message server until the receiver issues a commit command. If a failure occurs or a rollback command is issued, the messaging system will attempt to redeliver all the messages.

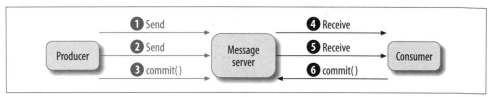

Figure 5-16. Transactional messages are received by a consumer in an all-or-nothing fashion

Local transactions can also be used to group receive and send operations (Figure 5-17). In this case, the client application is both a consumer and a producer. It may receive one message, modify its content, and send the new message along to another destination. By using the local transaction to group together the send and receive, a single commit operation will remove the message from the server's persistent storage and send it to its next destination.

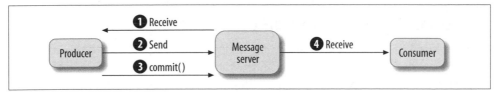

Figure 5-17. Receive and send operations can be grouped together in a single local transaction

Transactions with Multiple Resources

It is sometimes necessary to coordinate the sending or receiving of a local transaction with the update of another transactional resource, such as a database or a transactional EJB entity bean. This typically involves an underlying transaction manager that takes care of coordinating the prepare, commit, or rollback operations of each resource participating in the transaction. A MOM implementation may provide transaction interfaces for accomplishing this, allowing a message producer or consumer to participate in a transaction with any other resource that is compliant with the XOpen/XA two-phase-commit transaction protocol (Figure 5-18).

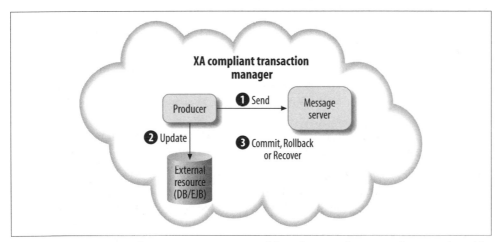

Figure 5-18. A message producer or consumer may participate in a two-phase-commit transaction with any XA-compliant resource, such as a database

Technically, this is a "distributed" transaction. However, from a MOM perspective, it is simply tying the message server interactions with the processing of a message that involves the use of another transactional resource. Multiple message clients would not participate in the same global transaction in a distributed manner, as this would defeat the purpose of a loosely coupled asynchronous environment. In an ESB, each participant in a message exchange needs to be able to rely on having transactional integrity with its interaction with the bus, and not with the other applications that are plugged into the system.

An ESB Removes the Low-Level Complexities

The usual way of using a MOM, whether it is JMS-based, SOAP-based, or something else, is to write code into an application client that manages things such as establishing a connection with the messaging server; creating publishers, subscribers, queue senders, and queue receivers; and managing the transactional demarcation and recovery from failure. An ESB removes this complexity by delegating that responsibility to the ESB service container.

An integration architect can use an administrative tool to configure an ESB service to send and receive messages using pub/sub, point-to-point queues, or other kinds of transport mechanisms simply by configuring the inputs and outputs of the service. The container takes care of the rest. It is even possible for an output channel to use pub/sub, which is eventually mapped onto an outbound web service invocation using SOAP. More details on service containers and their use of inbound and outbound channels can be found in Chapters 6, 7, and 8.

The Request/Reply Messaging Pattern

Communications across an ESB or a MOM are by and large intended to be asynchronous in nature. Applications and services send messages in a "fire-and-forget" mode, which allows an application to go about its business once a message is asynchronously delivered. This does not necessarily preclude the need to perform request/reply operations. Sometimes you need to perform a synchronous request/response operation, such as when you are trying to integrate with a web service client that blocks and waits for a synchronous response to return to it. Often the sender (requestor) can wait for the reply to happen at a later time (asynchronously).

Request/reply messaging patterns can be built on top of a MOM to perform synchronous request/reply or asynchronous request/reply. An ESB can further automate this process by managing the details of the request/reply in the ESB container invocation model. The request/reply pattern is introduced now, in the messaging chapter, as we will be referring to it in other discussions throughout the rest of the book. In Chapter 8, for example, we'll see how a synchronous request/response web service can be mapped onto an ESB simply by virtue of how the endpoints are created.

Figure 5-19 illustrates a request/reply pattern in its simplest form. Message channels are not bidirectional. To perform a request/reply operation, a requestor must use two channels: one for the request, and one for the response.

The key to this pattern is the use of a ReplyTo property that gets carried with the request message. The requestor needs to listen on a "reply" channel that will accept the reply

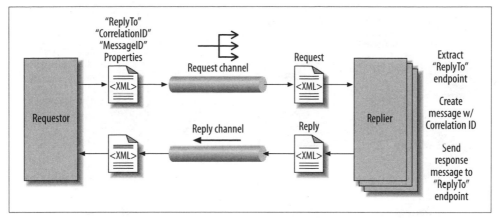

Figure 5-19. Request/reply pattern across asynchronous messaging channels using correlation

message. The request message that gets sent on the request channel needs to contain the identifier of the reply channel, along with a correlation ID that is used to correlate the request message with the response message. This is typically done using a message property, if the messaging system supports the notion of properties.

 The property name ReplyTo is simply an example of a common convention used in messaging environments. The actual name of the property could be anything, as long as it is consistent across all message requestors and repliers. If you are coding this pattern yourself, it is a good idea to establish a convention and stick with it. In the JMS specification, there is a special property named JMSReplyTo that is reserved for this purpose. In an ESB, these details are hidden by the service container invocation model.

Upon receipt of the request message, the replier extracts the identifier of the reply channel from the ReplyTo property, and uses that to identify the channel on which to send the reply. It also extracts the CorrelationID property and places that in the response message. In an asynchronous environment, multiple requests and responses may occur simultaneously. The requestor uses the correlation ID to match the response with the appropriate request.

The Reply-Forward Pattern

Sometimes, a reply does not need to be returned to the same service that initiated the request (Figure 5-20). An ESB uses a more elaborate request/reply model in which a reply from a service invocation can be another destination, or a forwarding address of where to send the message next. This is referred to as the *reply-forward* pattern.

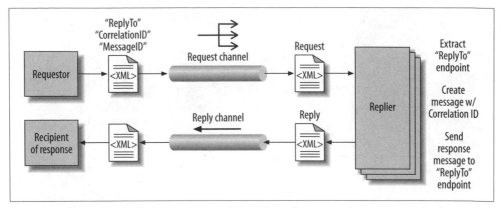

Figure 5-20. In a reply-forward pattern, the recipient of a reply message does not have to be the application or service that performed the request

Messaging Standards

There are a number of standards that continue to evolve in the area of MOM. One established standard is the Java Message Service, and others that are evolving are those based on SOAP and web services.

The Java Message Service (JMS)

The Java Message Service (JMS) is a messaging specification that has enjoyed widespread industry adoption since its introduction in 1998. JMS provides an API and a set of rules that govern message delivery semantics in a MOM environment for both reliable and unreliable messaging. The JMS specification defines rules for operational behavior of publish-and-subscribe and point-to-point queuing. There are also very rich and flexible definitions of what a message is composed of, and strict rules governing store-and-forward messaging, guaranteed delivery, message acknowledgments, transactions, and recovery from failures. JMS also provides the multiresource transaction model described in this chapter. The advantage of having specified behavioral rules is that you can rely on a base set of behavior in the messaging environment, regardless of the vendor implementation.

While largely intended as an asynchronous form of communication between applications, JMS also has a set of messaging patterns and helper interfaces to synchronously and asynchronously support the request/reply pattern using both the pub/sub and point-to-point messaging models.

JMS provides an optional interface for integrating with an application server. This allows a JMS provider from one vendor to integrate with an application server from another vendor. An ESB provider that supports a JMS interface should support the application server interfaces as well.

What about the "J" in JMS?

JMS most definitely has its roots in Java. However, you don't have to be a Java programmer to use a JMS-compliant messaging system if you are using an ESB.

While you could theoretically implement an ESB using a MOM that is not JMS-compliant, it's a better idea not to, for a number of reasons. Using an ESB that supports JMS message delivery semantics means that you can count on certain behavioral rules. Regardless of the vendor implementation, you can rely on the existence of capabilities such as durable subscriptions for pub/sub messaging, and transactional recovery from failure with either messaging model. You also reap the benefits of standards-based integration, as outlined in Chapter 3.

That said, even if you are not particularly wedded to Java, you can still take advantage of JMS if you are using an ESB. An ESB implementation that supports JMS can also provide non-Java client types for C++, VB, or C#. JMS defines an API that can be similarly implemented in Java, C++, or C# if you are coding messaging clients directly. If you are designing an ESB integration strategy that requires only plugging together application adapters and integration services without any specific client coding, JMS can add value by providing a consistent set of behavior rules for the underlying messaging system, regardless of the vendor providing the implementation.

Reliable Messaging with SOAP

One approach to achieving asynchronous reliability between web services is via a reliable protocol at the SOAP level. In this approach, message acknowledgments and delivery receipts are encoded in predefined SOAP envelope header constructs. Examples of this that are evolving today are WS-ReliableMessaging and WS-Reliability. ESBs are well suited for adopting these protocols as they mature and are implemented by more vendors. An ESB should be capable of supporting any number of reliable messaging transports and protocols.

Web Services Events and Notifications

Two nascent specifications, WS-Eventing and WS-Notification, describe how publish-and-subscribe should work across web services interfaces and protocols. A technical committee has been formed under OASIS under the auspice of WS-Notification to formalize a family of specifications detailing a publish-and-subscribe event notification model using web services and SOAP.

Summary

Messaging enables asynchrony and an interface style that is required for loosely coupled interfaces between applications.

Our discussion of enterprise-capable messaging has shown that producers and consumers have different perspectives on the messages they exchange. The producer has a contract with the message server that ensures that the message will be delivered as far as the server. The server has a contract with the consumer that the message will be delivered to the consumer. The separation of these two operations is a key benefit of asynchronous messaging. It is the role of the messaging system to ensure that messages get to where they are supposed to go, in accordance with the QoS settings associated with the message.

Through message acknowledgment, message persistence, and transactions, MOM provides a strong backbone that guarantees that your business-critical data will travel reliably throughout your global enterprise.

An ESB can abstract away the low-level details of using MOM by removing the dependencies of writing messaging behavior such as channel definitions and QoS options into the application code. With an ESB, these details are encapsulated in a container-managed environment that is configured through an administrative tool interface.

Service Containers and
Abstract Endpoints

6

In the next three chapters, we will examine the details of what makes an ESB. The ESB provides an architecture that brings together all the concepts described in previous chapters into an infrastructure that can span an extended enterprise and beyond. The base definition of an ESB provided by Gartner Inc. and discussed in Chapter 1, describes an ESB as consisting of four things: Message Oriented Middleware, web services, intelligent routing based on content, and XML data transformation.

Expanding on the definition from Gartner, we can go into more details of these key components:

- Message Oriented Middleware (MOM)
  - Robust, reliable transport
  - Efficient movement of data across abstract data channels
  - End-to-end reliability
- Web services
  - Service Oriented Architecture (SOA)
  - Abstract business services
- Intelligent routing
  - Message routing based on content and context
  - Message routing based on business process rules
  - Business process orchestration based on a rules language such as BPEL4WS (Business Process Execution Language for Web Services)
- XML transformation
  - Based on XSLT and independently deployed service types

The integration fabric that supports all of this requires an infrastructure, which includes the following:

- Highly distributed, scalable service containers
- Event-driven service invocation

- Centralized management of distributed integration configurations
- Diverse client connectivity and support for multiple protocols
- Seamless, dynamic routing of data across physical deployment boundaries
- Unified security and access control model
- Distributed configuration and caching of deployment resources, such as XSLT documents and routing rules
- Scriptable and declarative environment
- Changeable behavior of integration components based on configuration and rules, instead of compiling behavior into code

An ESB provides a loosely coupled, highly distributed approach to integration. It can integrate nicely with applications built with .NET, COM, C#, and legacy C/C++, and can utilize J2EE components such as the JMS, JCA, and J2EE web services APIs. XML standards such as XSLT, XPath, and XQuery provide data transformation, intelligent routing, and querying of "in-flight" data as it flows through the bus. These standards are used together to provide an open-ended, pluggable, service-oriented architecture. This architecture supports both industry-standard integration components as well as proprietary elements through the use of standardized interfaces.

So, just how are all these components tied together, and what makes the ESB approach unique? Perhaps the most distinguishing characteristic of the ESB is its ability to be highly distributed. Many things contribute to making the ESB highly distributed, but the three components that stand out the most are the use of abstract endpoints for representing remote services, Internet-capable MOM, and a distributed lightweight service container.

SOA Through Abstract Endpoints

The square boxes in Figure 6-1 represent the applications and services that need to connect to each other and share data through the bus. From the perspective of the integration architect who is assembling services to form a process flow, all applications and services are treated as abstract endpoints. What the endpoints actually represent can be very diverse. An endpoint may represent a discrete operation, such as a specialized service for calculating sales tax. The underlying implementation of the endpoint could represent a local binding to an application adapter, or a callout to an external web service.

This endpoint abstraction allows an integration architect to use higher-level tools to assemble service endpoints into process flows (Figure 6-2).

An endpoint may represent a single, monolithic application, such as a legacy payroll system. It may represent a suite of applications or an ERP system from an application vendor. It may represent an island of integration from a successful integration broker project. It may represent a whole department or business unit that has a microcosm of

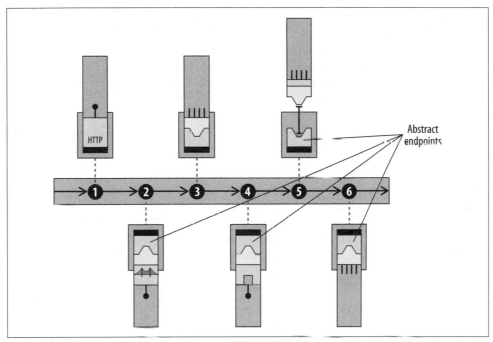

Figure 6-1. Everything that is connected into the bus is viewed as an abstract endpoint

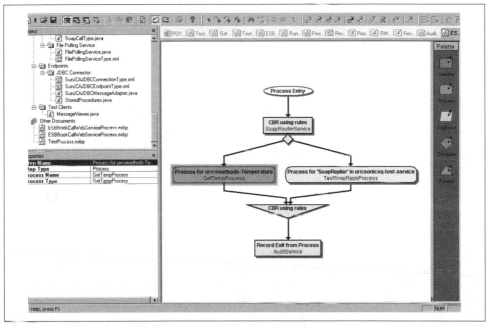

Figure 6-2. Integration architect's view of service endpoints in an SOA

its own, yet also needs to link into corporate information channels and share data. It may represent the interface to a business partner with completely separate IT systems.

All service endpoints in an ESB are equal participants in an event-driven SOA, whether the service represents a discrete operation or an interface to an entire ERP suite. From the point of view of the integration architect (you), service endpoints are just logical abstractions of services that are plugged into the bus. The task of building out an integration network involves tying together service endpoints and applying choreography, transformation, and routing rules into process flows between applications. The actual physical locations of the services can be anywhere that is accessible by the bus.

Messaging and Connectivity at the Core

In Figure 6-3, the series of connected rectangles in the center of the diagram represents the core of the ESB. A key component of this core is a highly scalable enterprise messaging backbone that is capable of asynchronously transporting data as messages in a secure and reliable fashion. The messaging backbone supports the asynchronous store-and-forward capability that was discussed in Chapter 5. This messaging core could represent a proprietary MOM, a MOM based on JMS, or a MOM based on WS-Reliability or WS-ReliableMessaging. Or, the messaging core could be a generic messaging engine that supports any combination of these.

The service endpoint provides an abstraction away from the underlying protocol (or MOM channel). The ESB allows the underlying protocol to vary depending on the deployment situation and the QoS requirements. The choice of protocol can vary, from proprietary MOM to unreliable HTTP, to WS-Rel*, depending on the criteria for that leg of the trip and the overall QoS requirements of a message flow. From the perspective of the integration architect who is weaving the fabric of integration, the task is to link together service endpoints into process flows. Using administrative tools supplied with the ESB, the technology behind the endpoint definition and the details of the underlying protocol can be dealt with separately, and can even change over time. It is the responsibility of the ESB to map the high-level process flows into individual service invocations across the designated transport.

Diverse Connection Choices

Figure 6-4 highlights some examples of client types and connection points, covering a broad range of options. The middleware at the core must be capable of supporting multiple connectivity choices. Providing a single JMS interface or a proprietary C-based interface is not enough. Diversity in connectivity is a core capability that is fundamental to making the ESB a realistic approach across a global enterprise.

Some large organizations that are in the process of integrating their enterprise have more than 1,000 distinct application types, with more than 10,000 actual instances of

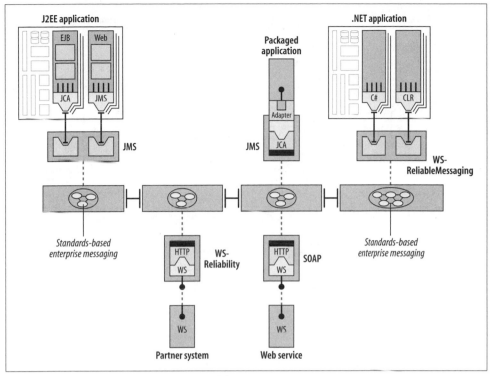

Figure 6-3. Enterprise messaging at the core of the ESB

applications behind those endpoints. (This is also one of the reasons you need an enterprise MOM at the core.) It is not reasonable to expect that all applications across the board resort to the same interface technology, whether it be web services–based, Java-based, or .NET-based, to participate in an integration environment.

IT departments have too many other things to worry about to go back and significantly retool all their legacy apps. An application that needs to be integrated may be capable only of dumping and loading flat files and transmitting them over FTP. The application may have never been intended to interface with anything, and perhaps was written in C or COBOL. The application may have exposed a low-level, network socket–level interface as part of a one of-a-kind point-to-point integration project, and can't otherwise be tampered with. Some of the applications that participate in the data exchange along the bus may reside at a business partner's site, and may therefore be able to interoperate with your applications only by using SOAP over HTTP. As we will see in Chapter 8, an ESB can even be used as an integration strategy to augment and replace EDI traffic. All of these situations are acceptable because the ESB provides connectivity options or "on-ramps" for each of these approaches.

Because the ESB can support multiple ways of connecting into it, applications don't require any drastic changes to "get on the bus." The motto for ESB adoption is "If you

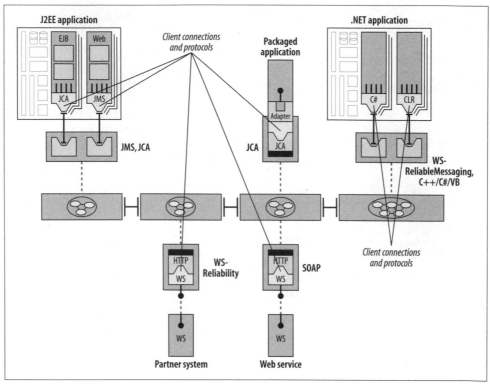

Figure 6-4. An ESB provides multiple client types, connection options, and protocols

can't bring the application to the bus, bring the bus to the application." This means that applications should be able to connect into the bus with as little modification as possible. It is the bus, not the applications, that provides the flexibility in connection technologies.

Diagramming Notations

Before going on to discuss the core components of an ESB, it is important to examine some new diagramming notations that are introduced in this chapter. This chapter describes in detail some key concepts of an ESB, and uses a set of glyphs to describe each one. (The Preface to the book goes into an explanation of the history of these glyphs and shows examples of all of them; Chapter 11 will show how these glyphs can be used together to form sketches for integration patterns.) Figure 6-5 depicts a generic ESB endpoint.

Throughout this book, an endpoint will always be shown as residing inside a service container, the details of which will be explained later in this chapter. There are different types of endpoints in an ESB, each with its own style of representative icon. Figure 6-6

TO J2EE, OR .NET TO BE

The scope of connectivity across an integration project is bigger than what can be solved with just Java technology or just .NET technology. I have yet to see an integration project in which the applications being integrated consisted of all Java or all .NET. You likely have some current projects underway that are using J2EE, and some that are using .NET. You may even work with organizations that consider themselves an "all-Microsoft shop" or an "all-Java shop," which means that they have chosen one platform for all new projects going forward. Now, you need to bring them into the fold of your existing applications and infrastructure, which is likely based on neither platform. The issue of J2EE versus .NET will not be going away anytime soon, but it will become much less of an issue when you're using an ESB to integrate. An ESB provides the common integration fabric that bridges the gap between these two technology platforms.

If an application is written in Java, it can use JMS to connect into the ESB. If it's written using a J2EE EJB server, a MessageDrivenBean (MDB) interface may be used. The .NET interface shown in Figure 6-5 depicts a .NET application that connects into the bus using a native .NET client, which connects directly into the MOM using the MOM's internal connection protocol. However, the application could just as well have been implemented using SOAP over HTTP, or WS-ReliableMessaging.

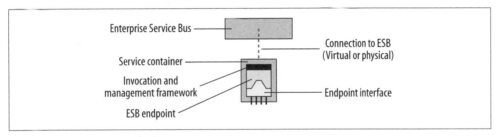

Figure 6-5. Generic ESB endpoint

shows how a SOAP or web services endpoint is visualized. Chapter 2 showed one of these in the "Refactoring to an ESB" section.

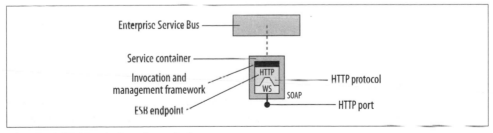

Figure 6-6. SOAP or web service endpoint

In Figure 6-6, the ESB endpoint that is labeled "HTTP" is an endpoint that uses the HTTP protocol. The HTTP endpoint either exposes a web service interface or acts as a client of a web services interface.

Figure 6-7 shows the icon for an ESB client API endpoint. The client interface exposes methods that an application or service would use to plug into the bus. For a Java client, the application interface would be JMS. For a C++ or C# client, the API would likely mimic the JMS API, but be implemented in either C++ or C#, respectively. For a custom ESB service, there can be a service API that exposes a DOM, SAX, or some other form of interface that treats a service invocation as an inbound SOAP message.

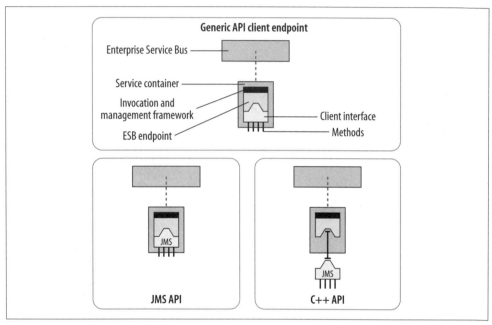

Figure 6-7. ESB client API endpoint

The dashed line between the ESB and the service container is a connection, usually a MOM connection. Note that the C++ client happens to be shown as slightly detached from the endpoint and the service container. This illustrates a separation between the physical implementation of the C++ client and the endpoint. For example, the ESB service container may be implemented in Java, and the C++ client may be hooked into the container using the Java Native Interface (JNI) or via a network layer. The client may also use the native on-the-wire protocol of the underlying MOM directly.

In practice, there may not be a physical container at all. For direct client API connections or protocol connections, the container may be more of an abstract concept than a physical implementation. The container is conceptually part of the bus, and therefore the dotted connection line is a virtual connection in the abstract sense. It may map to an underlying MOM connection in the physical implementation. The endpoint definition and the invocation and management framework could be transparently built into the bus fabric instead of being represented by a physically separate Java, C++, or C# process. These implementation details would also depend on the ESB vendor. The point is that these are representative forms of showing a service container with an endpoint. You, as the integration architect, have the flexibility to choose the appropriate rendition that most closely matches your perspective.

Figure 6-8 shows examples of the various connection types and protocols that an ESB should be able to support. They will be explained in more detail in the next section.

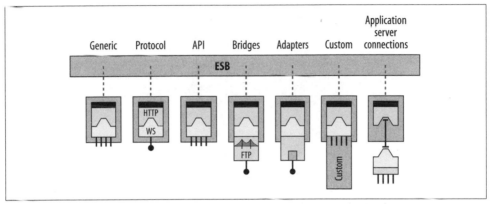

Figure 6-8. ESB endpoints with various client types and protocols associated with them

Independently Deployable Integration Services

Integration capabilities of the bus are implemented as separate services. Specialized integration services, which can be extended and augmented using a service interface, provide the integration capabilities that allow applications to easily interoperate (Figure 6-9). Examples of such services include:

- A specialized transformation service, with the sole responsibility of applying an XSLT stylesheet to convert an in-flight XML message from one dialect of XML to another
- A content-based routing service, which applies an XPath expression to look contextually into the nodes of the XML documents as they pass through the service and make determinations on where to send the message next
- An XML logging service, which extracts a copy of an XML message as it travels through a portion of a business process and logs it for auditing and tracking purposes

Chapter 8 explores more examples in a case study that uses custom services for EDI translators and SAP adapters.

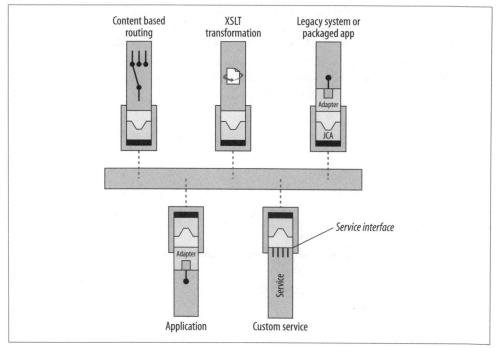

Figure 6-9. Integration capabilities of the bus can be augmented and extended through specialized integration services that use a common service interface

Because these integration capabilities are themselves implemented as services, they can be independently deployed anywhere within the network. The result is precise deployment of integration capabilities at specific locations, which can then be scaled independently as required. It also means that services can easily be upgraded, moved, replaced, or replicated without affecting the applications that they cooperate with.

The ESB Service Container

The highly distributed nature of the integration capabilities of the ESB is largely due to traits of the ESB service container. A service container is the physical manifestation of the abstract endpoint, and provides the implementation of the service interface. A service container is a remote process that can host software components. In that respect, it has some similarities to an application server container, but with the specific goal of hosting integration services.

A service container is simple and lightweight, but it can have many discrete functions. As illustrated in Figure 6-10, service containers take on different roles as they are deployed across an ESB.

Unlike its distant cousins, the J2EE application server container and the EAI broker, the ESB service container allows the selective deployment of integration broker

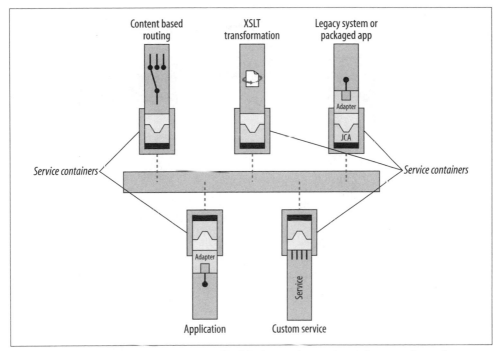

Figure 6-10. ESB service containers are specialized for integration services such as transformation, routing, and application adapters

functionality exactly when and where you need it, and nothing more than what you need. In its simplest state, a service container is an operating system process that can be managed by the ESB's invocation and management framework.

A service container can host a single service, or can combine multiple services in a single container environment, as illustrated in Figure 6-11.

An ESB service is also scalable in a fashion that is independent of all other ESB services. A service container may manage multiple instances of a service within a container. Several containers may also be distributed across multiple machines for the purposes of scaling up to handle increased message volume (Figure 6-12).

The Management Interface of the Service Container

An ESB service container should handle the inflow and outflow of management data such as configuration, auditing, and fault handling. Management interfaces should be implemented using the Java Management eXtensions (JMX) if the ESB implementation supports Java. A more detailed discussion on the use of JMX in an ESB can be found in Chapter 10.

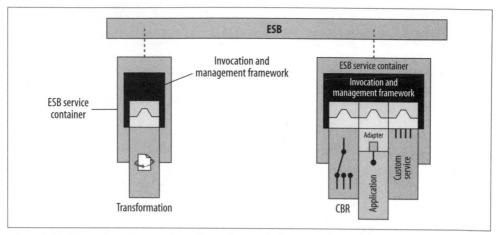

Figure 6-11. The ESB service container allows selective deployment of a single service, or can be combined with other services

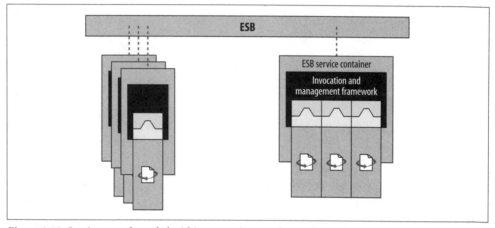

Figure 6-12. Services may be scaled within a container, and several containers may be scaled across multiple machines

As illustrated in Figure 6-13, an ESB service container supports the retrieval of configuration data from a directory service, and can also have a local cache of configuration data. This means that even if other parts of the ESB, including the directory service, become temporarily unavailable, the service container can continue to operate with its current set of configuration data.

Management input data can originate from a remote management console issuing commands such as start, stop, shut down, and refresh the cache. Management output data can consist of event tracking, such as notification that a message has successfully exited the service or that a failure has occurred. These inputs and outputs can be managed by a JMX management console or redirected to some other management tool using standard protocols such as the Simple Network Management Protocol (SNMP).

One of the most common observations regarding XML is its potential to consume computing resources due to its verbosity. An XML business document that represents an EDI document can range from 110 KB to more than 100 MB in size (often five times larger than the original EDI message), and can consume a great deal of CPU and memory while being parsed and translated. Deploying multiple instances of a particular XSLT transformation service across many machines can provide a very powerful and flexible scaling capability.

If the implementation of the service containers is portable across multiple platforms, you can also take advantage of existing hardware assets. Imagine having the flexibility to commandeer a set of Linux, AIX, and Win2K servers for the purpose of spreading out the load of a particular XML transformation. In addition, because the service containers are relatively lightweight, you can take advantage of less powerful machines that may be underutilized within your organization.

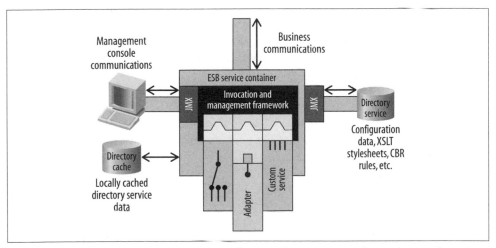

Figure 6-13. Service containers support inputs and outputs for management data such as configuration, auditing, and fault handling

The ESB Service Interface

The ESB container provides the message flow in and out of a service. It also handles a number of facilities, such as service lifecycle and itinerary management, that we will explore in a later section. As illustrated in Figure 6-14, the container manages an entry endpoint and an exit endpoint, which are used by the container to dispatch a message to and from the service.

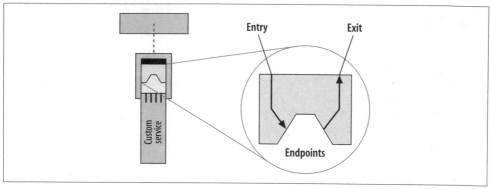

Figure 6-14. Message dispatch to a service uses the service's configured entry and exit endpoints

XML messages are received by the service from a configurable entry endpoint. Upon completion of its task, the service implementation simply places its output message in the exit endpoint to be carried to its next destination using the "request/reply" or "reply-forward" pattern discussed in Chapter 5. The output message may be the same message that it received. The service may modify the message before sending it to the exit endpoint. Or, the service may create a completely new message to serve as a "response" to the incoming message and send the new message in the exit endpoint. The following code example shows what a service implementation looks like:

```
public void service(ESBServiceContext ctx) throws ESBServiceException {
    // Get any runtime process parameters.
    Parameters params = ctx.getParameters();
    // Get the message.
    ESBEnvelope env = null;
    env = ctx.getNextIncoming();
    if (env != null) {
        ESBMessage msg = env.getMessage();
        ... // Operate on the message
    }
    // Put the message to the Exit Endpoint
    ctx.addOutgoing(env);
}
```

What is placed in the exit endpoint depends on the context of the situation and the message being processed. In the case of a CBR service, the message content will be unchanged, with new forwarding addresses set in the message header.

In more sophisticated cases, one input message can transform into many outputs, each with its own routing information. For example, a custom service can receive a purchase order document, split it up into multiple output messages, and send out the purchase order and its individual line items as separate messages to an inventory or order fulfillment service. The service implementation in this case does not have to be written using traditional coding practices; it can be implemented as a specialized transformation service that applies an XSLT stylesheet to the purchase order document to produce the multiple outputs (if the ESB has an XSLT extension to support multiple outputs).

Auditing, Logging, and Error Handling

Auditing and logging play an important business function within an integration strategy. Part of the reason you want to integrate across a common backbone is to gain real-time access to the business data that is flowing between departments in an organization. A reliable communications backbone will ensure that the data gets to its intended destinations. An auditing framework will allow you to track the data at a business level.

As part of its management capabilities, an ESB container provides an auditing and logging facility. This facility can have multiple sources for tracking data. System-level information about the health of the service itself and the flow of messages can be tracked and monitored. Application-level auditing, logging, and fault handling are accomplished through additional endpoints that are available to each service. As illustrated in Figure 6-15, the service implementation has three additional endpoints at its disposal: a tracking endpoint, a fault endpoint, and a rejected-message endpoint. A service can be created such that a message can be placed in the tracking endpoint in addition to its normal exit destination. A rejected-message endpoint can be used for system-level errors, such as a malformed XML document, or any case in which the service itself throws an exception. The fault endpoint can be used for any application-level errors, or faults, that can occur.

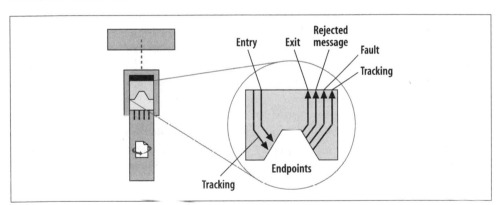

Figure 6-15. Additional tracking and fault handling endpoints are handled by the service container

There is an underlying philosophy behind the way tracking, system errors, and application faults are handled. In addition to a normal exit endpoint to handle the outgoing flow of a message, additional destinations are available to the service for auditing the message and for reporting errors. The service implementation has these endpoints available for its own use. From the service implementation's point of view, it simply places data into the tracking endpoint or fault endpoint, and the surrounding ESB framework takes care of managing the auditing, logging, and error reporting. A tracking endpoint can be configured to point to anything—a topic or queue destination, or even a call to an external web service. This approach provides a separation between the implementation of the service and the details surrounding the fault handling. The implementer of a service need only be concerned that it has a place to put such information, whether it is information concerning the successful processing of good data, or the reporting of errors and bad data.

Tracking can be handled at both the individual service level and the business process level. A business process may make use of different implementations of individual services over time. The tracking of a fault occurrence or the auditing of an individual message can be tied to the context of the greater business process that is utilizing the service at the time.

In Chapter 7, we will explore more about how auditing facilities are used. We will also see that the use of these endpoints is one way of doing auditing and logging with an ESB. Other approaches include placing a specialized XML persistence service in the path of a message in a process flow, which can be much less intrusive to each individual service implementation.

ESB Service Container Facilities

The container is an intrinsic part of the ESB distributed processing framework. In some sense, the container *is* the ESB—more so than the underlying middleware that connects the containers together. The container provides the care and feeding of the service. As illustrated in Figure 6-16, the ESB container provides a variety of facilities that a service implementation may have at its disposal. Facilities such as location, routing, service invocation, and management are taken care of by the container and its surrounding framework, so the implementation of a service does not have to be concerned with those things. The container also provides facilities for lifecycle management such as startup, shutdown, and resource cleanup. Thread pooling allows multiple instances of a service to be attached to multiple listeners within a single container. Connection management facilities provide the specifics of the binding to the underlying MOM, plus additional fault tolerance and retry logic.

QoP and QoS

Quality of Protection (QoP) and security, Quality of Service (QoS), and transaction services are also provided to the service via the ESB container. Some of these capabilities may be delegated by the service container to the underlying MOM that it is bound to. QoS options, such as exactly-once delivery of messages, are best delegated to a messaging infrastructure that is built for that. If the exactly-once delivery option is dependent

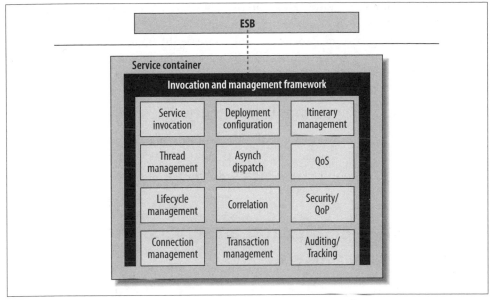

Figure 6-16. The ESB container provides many facilities for the service implementation

on an implementation of a reliable SOAP specification such as WS-Reliability or WS-ReliableMessaging, it would likely still be delegated to a SOAP processor that has MOM qualities such as message persistence, store-and-forward, and duplicate detection.

Administration of ESB facilities

All of these facilities of the ESB container are intrinsically tied to the administrative functions of the ESB, which means that even if you are writing your own custom service, these facilities are assumed to be there and don't have to be written into the service itself. Generally speaking, this type of "plumbing" is one of the reasons adopting a middleware infrastructure is so appealing. The ESB brings it to the next level by fully delegating this responsibility to the underlying "plumbing."

In most cases, the container facilities don't even need to be exposed to the implementation of the service itself. The container facilities by and large represent an agreement between the container and the underlying middleware. Each facility has its own configuration nuances that can be dealt with using an administrative tool that is part of the ESB offering. For example, a QoS setting for exactly-once delivery would be set as an administrative property of a service, not something a coder would do in the API. Of course, the individual capabilities within each of these facilities are likely to vary depending on the implementation from different vendors.

The method of administration of ESB facilities can range from a full-blown GUI to a command-line interface to an administrative API, depending on the implementation.

Don't assume that one administrative method is "better" than another when considering implementations; each has its purpose. A command-line interface can be a good approach for those accustomed to automating processes by building things into scripts. An API is useful when trying to build an ESB into a larger infrastructure that may already have its own set of user interface administrative tools.

Standardizing ESB Container Connectivity

Within the Java Community Process (JCP), the Java Business Integration (JBI) effort is underway to standardize the means by which components plug into an integration infrastructure. For an ESB, this will provide conformity across implementations. More details on JBI can be found in Chapter 10.

Service Containers, Application Servers, and Integration Brokers

I often get asked for clarification on just what the differences are between ESB service containers, an application server container, and an integration broker. This section will point out the main differences.

Adherence to Standards

You can think of the contrast of an ESB versus an integration broker as highly distributed and standards-based versus centralized, monolithic, and proprietary.

A hub-and-spoke integration broker engine includes four main pieces of functionality: application adapters, data transformation, routing rules, and connectivity (Figure 6-17). Today's integration brokers were built when few standards were available to exploit, and are therefore largely proprietary. Also, as illustrated in Figure 6-17, some integration brokers have bolted on some standard interface technology, such as web services.

An ESB makes prevalent use of standard interfaces and standard protocols throughout. Integration brokers have been largely proprietary, which, as discussed in Chapter 2, can carry a steep learning curve and result in vendor lock-in. Integration based on standards can provide a number of business benefits beyond just future-proofing your integration strategy. Chapter 3 discusses the benefits of adopting standards throughout your integration projects.

Centralized Hub-and-Spoke Processing

In a hub-and-spoke integration broker, the message payload must travel to the rules engine in the hub to perform data transformations and receive subsequent routing

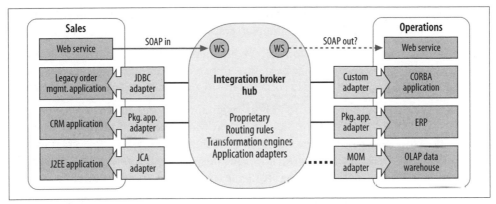

Figure 6-17. Hub-and-spoke integration brokers are centralized, monolithic, and largely proprietary; standard interfaces are an afterthought

instructions (Figure 6-18). Also, each link into the hub potentially runs over a different protocol and transport, limiting reliability to the weakest link.

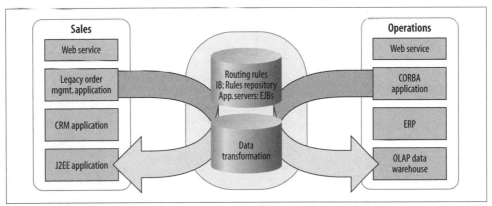

Figure 6-18. Hub-and-spoke integration brokers require that all messages return to the rules engine for further instruction after every step of processing

An ESB does not rely on any centralized processing engine, and lets the routing decisions occur at the remote nodes via itinerary-based routing. Hub-and-spoke has the advantage of centralized management and centralized control over routing and transformation rules. However, a good ESB should have a proper distributed management environment that allows remote containers to be updated with fresh information whenever necessary.

What's Hosted in the Container

To date, the main function of an application server has been to host business logic and to serve up web pages that are often based on dynamic content. Application server vendors trying to get into the integration business have been building integration broker capabilities on top of their application servers.

Both ESB containers and application server containers provide a managed environment for lifecycle issues, instance management, thread management, and timer services. Security and transaction services are also common in most application servers and ESBs.

An ESB service container is intended to host integration services and to execute business process flow logic, and host them only when and where you need them. For example, process flow logic can route an invoice to the proper financial system. Process flow logic can be specified declaratively or written as code in specialized services. Other examples of integration services include hosting an adapter or a content-based router.

Integration brokers, including those built upon an application server stack, require that the entire IB/appserver stack be installed everywhere you want integration broker functionality (Figure 6-19). Think of what it would mean to install an entire application server at a remote location simply so that it can host a JCA container, which hosts a JCA adapter, which acts as a conduit to an ERP system.

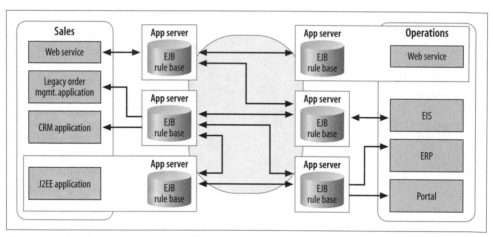

Figure 6-19. The "appservers everywhere" strategy

In contrast, with the ESB approach, integration broker capabilities are distributed across a more loosely coupled integration network as integration components that are independently deployed and managed (Figure 6-20). The only software component that needs to be installed at the remote location is the ESB service container. The ESB service container can act as a JCA container directly, without the rest of the appserver or integration broker stack, which in this scenario is just excess baggage. This is one of the business reasons why the ESB is changing the economics of integration. Licensing costs aside, the real cost of deploying application servers everywhere is in the installation, configuration, and ongoing operational overhead and cost of ownership over time.

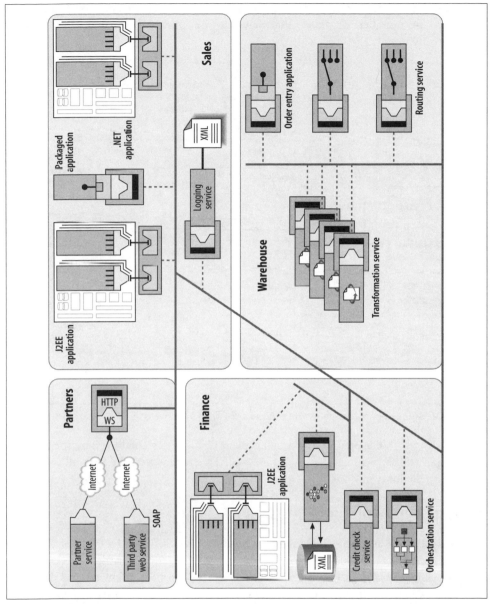

Figure 6-20. Distributed service containers provide selective deployment of integration services that are independently scalable

Management Substrate

Managing an application server, even when using JMX, requires a direct connection between the management console and the remote JMX agent for the application server.

In a highly distributed deployment, this separate management connection significantly increases the number of holes that have to be punched through the firewalls (Figure 6-21).

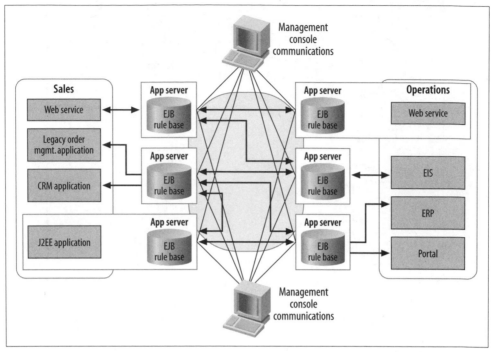

Figure 6-21. Managing application servers requires extra holes in firewalls

As we'll discuss in Chapter 10, ESB management traffic is designed to share the bus with application traffic, as illustrated in Figure 6-22. This means that the firewall configuration has to be done only once.

Compiled Class Files Versus Declarative Rules

The main benefit of using XML standards (XPath, XSLT, XML DOM, and SAX) for transformation is that it makes the deployed processes much less brittle. For example, as shown in Figure 6-23, an ESB transformation service can be configured and deployed, merely by supplying it with the scripts and parameters it needs to use, as XML documents that are read in from a directory cache. Once deployed, the implementation is remarkably resilient to change in the XML schema. In many cases, changes in the XML schema will not invalidate the XPath selections within the XSLT, and new attributes and elements are carried along by the existing XSL templates. Even if the XSL script does change, it is easily redeployed. More information on service reuse and redeployment can be found in Chapter 7.

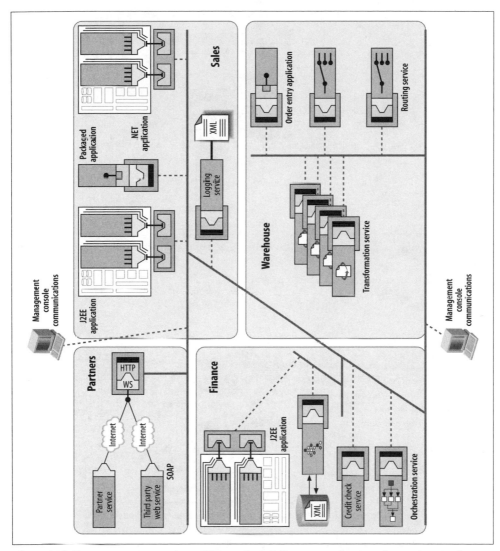

Figure 6-22. Remote management in an ESB requires no direct connection to each container, and no additional holes in the firewalls

In contrast, compiled classes such as XML beans introduce a dependency on the XML schema that obviates adaptation to change. As shown in Figure 6-24, the use of the schema to generate Java code sets in motion a chain of dependencies that must then be retraced every time the schema is modified. This is because schema elements must be bound to Java objects. The problem is further compounded if the transform in question is deployed in multiple locations.

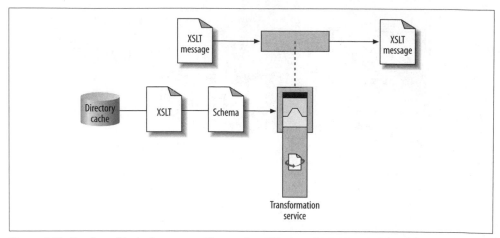

Figure 6-23. Configurable deployment artifacts such as XPath and XSLT are insulated from changes in XML schema

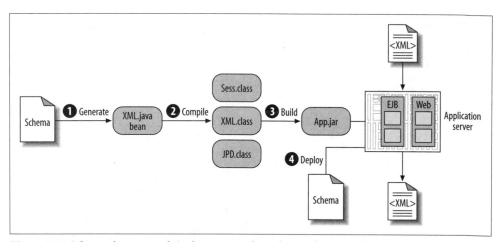

Figure 6-24. Schema changes result in downstream dependencies that must then be retraced whenever the schema is modified

Table 6-1 summarizes the comparison between compiled code in an application server and the declarative functions that are inherent in an ESB.

Table 6-1. Compiled code in ESB and J2EE appserver

	J2EE appserver	ESB
Web client proxy	Session bean*	HTTP endpoint**
Process definition	Compiled class (JPD)*	Process/itinerary**
Deployment parameters	Bean descriptor**	DS config params**
Routing rules	Message bean*	Routing rules**
Web service call	WS proxy class*	WS endpoint**

Table 6-1. Compiled code in ESB and J2EE appserver (continued)

	J2EE appserver	ESB
Aggregation service	Custom service*	Process JOIN**
Logging service	Entity bean*	XML service**
Transformation	XML bean*	Transform service**
Custom service	EJBean*	ESB service*

* Compiled code
** Declarative artifact

A key point to note is that the use of dynamically configured parameters, declarative scripts, and other runtime artifacts serves to reduce the amount of compiled code in the system, as illustrated in Table 6-1. The end result is a more flexible, loosely coupled deployment.

Abandon Application Servers?

You shouldn't take this negatively if you are an adopter of J2EE application server technology. Application servers are an important part of an IT organization, and an ESB is designed to integrate with them very well. In Chapter 11, we'll see a portal application design pattern in which application servers are used for both the frontend web container display logic and the backend business logic. The ESB is used in the middle to connect the two, providing an integration weave into the rest of the corporate fabric that is not application server–based.

Summary

In this chapter we explored the following:

- How an ESB supports an SOA across a series of abstract endpoints. Endpoints can represent applications and services of any size and scope. An integration architect connects endpoints into process flows.
- The details of an ESB container as a managed environment for services, and why it is a key component of an ESB architecture.
- The comparisons between an ESB container and an application server container.

The next chapter will discuss the concept of *itinerary-based routing* and the role it plays in enabling a highly distributed SOA across independently deployed services. We will also discuss service reusability and examine some core ESB services, such as content-based routing and XSLT transformation, as well as some advanced ESB capabilities, such as an XML persistence service and an orchestration service.

7
ESB Service Invocations, Routing, and SOA

In this chapter we will learn about the service invocation model, i.e., the underlying framework that provides the SOA in an ESB. We will discuss multiple forms of process routing, including the concept of *itinerary-based routing* and the role it plays in enabling a highly distributed SOA across independently deployed services.

We will also discuss some fundamental ESB services, such as content-based routing and XSLT transformation, and examine how service types can be defined and then reused for different purposes using configurable options that are declaratively specified rather than coded.

We will then explore some advanced ESB services, such as an XML persistence service and an orchestration service.

Find, Bind, and Invoke

One of the places where the ESB adds incremental value over a typical SOA is in the find/bind/invoke operations that ordinarily occur. To date, SOAs have typically been implemented using a client-server model. In an SOA that follows the client-server model, whether via web services or a predecessor, service clients contact other services through a process known as find, bind, and invoke. The find/bind/invoke model assumes that there is a registry or directory that stores the location and possibly other metadata about a service implementation. In the "find" operation, the service client does a lookup in the registry for the service, using certain criteria that may include names or characteristics such as "color dual sided." The next step is the "bind" operation, which for a web services request could simply mean doing an HTTP connect; and finally, the "invoke" operation, which means sending a message or invoking a remote procedure. With a web services approach to SOA, the bind and invoke are in the same operation.

The problem with the find/bind/invoke approach is that it requires writing the routing and flow logic into the applications that need to be connected. Each service client needs to write code that does a lookup of the service; we saw the downside of that in Chapter 2. While it is certainly possible to do this, and it is even appropriate under certain circumstances within an ESB environment, it is not intended to be the norm. The basic design center of the ESB is that a service is not invoked directly by another service, but rather is part of a larger event-driven process flow.

ESB Service Invocation

Like its predecessor, the client-server SOA, an ESB has the concept of a registry or directory service in which information about service endpoints is stored. An inherent find/bind/invoke operation occurs as part of the ESB mechanics, but it is separated out from the business logic. In an asynchronous ESB environment, the find/bind/invoke set of operations may actually map to sending an XML message to a queue or a publish-and-subscribe topic destination, and processing the reply. In the discussion of service containers in Chapter 6, we saw that the implementation of a service simply deals with an entry/exit endpoint metaphor. The service code focuses only on the implementation logic of a service. XML messages are received by the service from an entry endpoint that is managed by the service container. Upon conclusion of its task, the service implementation simply places its output message in the exit endpoint to be carried to its next destination. The output of the service is the reply, which the ESB routes to the next step (using the reply-forward pattern), or back to the requestor (using the request/reply pattern). The output message may be the same message that was received; the service may augment or modify parts of the message, or create a whole new "response" message. The operation of identifying and locating the next service in the chain, the binding to it, and the invocation of it is a set of tasks carried out by the ESB itself. The means by which the find/bind/invoke operations are defined is not through written code, but through configuration and deployment tools.

Itinerary-Based Routing: Highly Distributed SOA

The key importance of the ESB approach to SOA is that the service definition is separated from the mechanism for locating and invoking services. The role of the integration architect is to administratively define a composite business process flow by plugging services together into a *message itinerary*. The itinerary represents a set of discrete message routing operations, such as the basic steps introduced in Chapter 4 (see Figure 7-1).

Message itineraries are key to enabling a highly distributed SOA across an ESB. The details of the itinerary are stored as XML metadata and carried with the message as it travels across the bus from one service container to the next. An itinerary can begin with any entry point or event that can happen on the bus, including the creation and posting

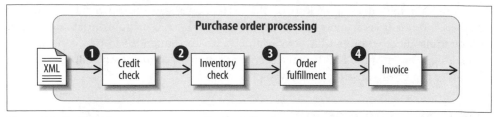

Figure 7-1. An ESB itinerary represents a distributed business process

of a message, initiated by any service that is accessible on the bus. An itinerary can even be attached to an inbound message as it arrives into the domain of the ESB. This could be an external event, such as the receipt of a SOAP message from an external business partner.

The logical steps of an itinerary can represent service endpoints in an SOA that are physically spread out across geographic locations and accessible from anywhere on the bus, as illustrated in Figure 7-2.

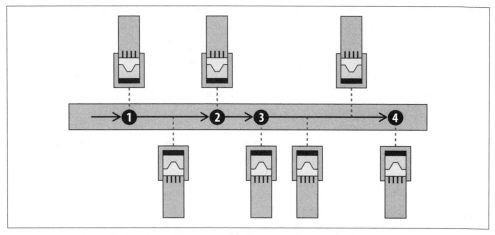

Figure 7-2. Service endpoints in an SOA, accessible from anywhere on the bus, are represented as logical steps in an itinerary

Gartner has used the term "microflow" to indicate a short-lived, transient process segment. The ESB itinerary process is well suited for such microflows. Message itineraries are very handy for a discrete set of operations in which simple branching decisions can be made, and where the separation of time between service invocations is not a significant factor. For simple branching, an itinerary may also support the notion of a subprocess. Figure 7-3 shows the flow of control whereby a parent process can temporarily be suspended to invoke a subprocess, and then resumed when the subprocess returns.

A message itinerary contains metadata that describes how to route the message, including a list of forwarding addresses described as abstract endpoints or as rules to evaluate along the way. The ESB container is a "smart" container, meaning that it knows how to

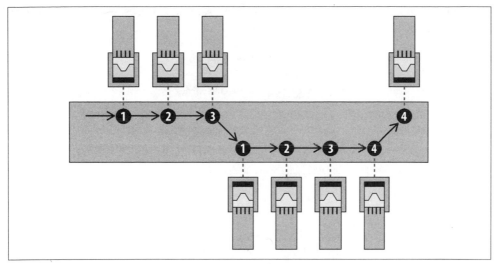

Figure 7-3. Flow of control in an itinerary subprocess

evaluate the itinerary of a message based on the metadata that gets carried with the message, combined with configuration knowledge that is cached locally at each container. This makes for a highly distributed routing network that doesn't rely on a centralized rules engine.

A message itinerary is analogous to a travel itinerary that you carry when going on a trip. Your travel itinerary tells you where to proceed at each step of a journey: your flight information, rental car, hotel, etc. Imagine that, instead of carrying an itinerary, you would stop and call your travel agent at each step of the way: "OK, I'm off the plane…what's my rental car agency?…OK, I have the car…what hotel am I staying at?" That would be the equivalent of a centralized hub-and-spoke routing engine.

The fact that there is no single "travel agent" to refer back to is a key differentiator that helps make the ESB approach highly distributed. It means that different parts of the ESB network can operate independently of one another without relying on any centralized routing engine that could potentially be a single point of failure. The management capabilities that are inherent in an ESB make it simple to remotely manage the distributed containers to push out changes in itinerary configurations. Since the message carries the itinerary and process state with it, only new messages entering the business process will get the newly configured instructions. Older messages already in process will not be affected.

Content-Based Routing (CBR)

Chapter 4 discussed a generic data exchange architecture and introduced the concept of a Content-Based Routing (CBR) service. An ESB CBR service may support scripting. The "validate" step could be implemented as a CBR service, and written using some simple JavaScript. The JavaScript code snippet in Example 7-1 uses XPath expressions to validate whether an XML document is a PurchaseOrder.

Example 7-1. Validating that a document is a PurchaseOrder

```
//
// Function returns "true" if this contains a PurchaseOrder document.
//
function isPO(){
    // Get the elements that would be at: /Envelope/Body/PurchaseOrder.
    nodeSet = getXPath("*/*/test:PurchaseOrder",
        "xmlns:test='http://www.sample.com/PO'");
    if (nodeSet == null || nodeSet.getCount() < 1){
        return false;
    }
    return true;
}
```

This snippet uses a JavaScript helper function, getXPath( ), to match a specific named element within the document that has the name PurchaseOrder, is the third level down from the root element, and uses the XML namespace identifier test='http://www. sample.com/PO'.

There are other approaches as well; for example, you could use the SAX interface, which would be more event-driven and positionally independent, or you could use an XML pull-parser. Other, more fundamental tests could have been used prior to this, such as simply validating that the document contains a SOAP envelope. XML schema could be used for validation, and other scripting languages or validating engines may also be plugged in. Different parts of an ESB can use different approaches, as appropriate.

This particular routing service relies on the invocation of a rule( ) method to perform the routing logic. The code snippet in Example 7-2 shows some simple JavaScript to implement the rule( ) method that invokes the isPO( ) method.

Example 7-2. A simple rule( ) function used by a CBR service

```
function rule()
{
    // Test if SOAP
    if (!isSoap()) {
        java.lang.System.out.println(" <Message NOT Soap>");
        throw new
            java.lang.Exception("[SoapRouterService] Non-SOAP message.");
    }
    java.lang.System.out.println(" <Message is Soap>");

    // Is this a SOAP Fault?
    if (isSoapFault()){
        java.lang.System.out.println(" <Message is Soap Fault>");
        return getEndpoint("ESBFaultEndpoint");
    }
```

Example 7-2. A simple rule( ) function used by a CBR service (continued)

```
    // Is this a PO?
    if (isPO( )){
        java.lang.System.out.println(" <Message is a PO>");
        return getService("POXformService");
    }
    java.lang.System.out.println(" <Message is not a PO>");

    // All other messages will be recorded in the audit file
    //(i.e. routed to the sample AuditService.)
    return getService("AuditService");
}
```

Note the implications of what happens when this function succeeds or fails. Returning a named endpoint from the service invocation causes the next destination in the itinerary to be automatically invoked by the surrounding ESB routing framework (Figure 7-4). A destination may be another service, another process itinerary, a MOM endpoint, or an external web service. The CBR rule may even return a valid endpoint destination that is outside of an itinerary, in which case the message exits the ESB process and is on its own.

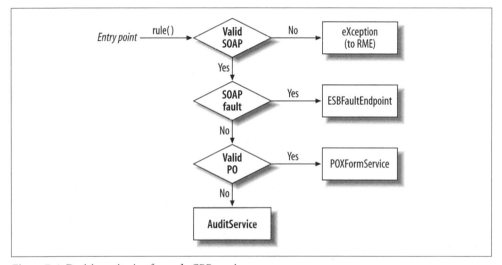

Figure 7-4. Decision criteria of sample CBR service

In addition to having the scripting code explicitly throw an exception, some other processing component such as the XPath parser could throw an exception at any point during the execution of the CBR service. In this case the surrounding ESB process will be aborted, and the message will be routed to a special destination known as a Rejected Message Endpoint (RME). The RME itself can be handled by an error-handling service; it can be incorporated into an auditing and logging scheme, or have custom logic applied to the message based on more business rules.

There are many other ways a CBR service could be implemented. For example, decision criteria could be configured using a GUI interface that specifies declarative rules that act on message properties, as illustrated in Figure 7-5.

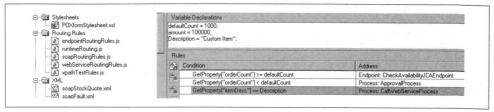

Figure 7-5. Declarative rules in content-based routing

Or you could use a GUI drag-and-drop interface, as illustrated in Figure 7-6.

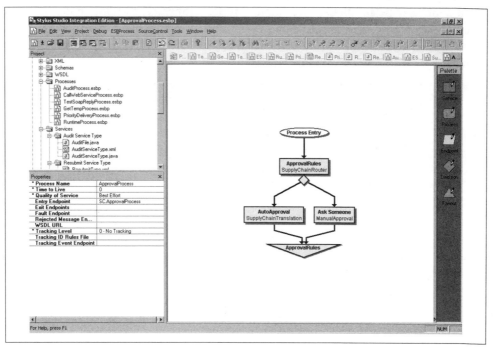

Figure 7-6. Routing rules using a GUI drag-and-drop interface

An alternative to coding JavaScript is to use XML to express decision criteria, as shown in Example 7-3.

Example 7-3. XML representation of declarative routing rules

```
<?xml version="1.0"?>
<rule:ruleSpec xmlns:rule="http://www.sonicsw.com/rule">
    <rule:helperFile url="dsdata:///jsHelperFunctions.js"/>
    <rule:declarations>defaultCount = 100;</rule:declarations>
```

Example 7-3. XML representation of declarative routing rules (continued)

```
<rule:declarations>defaultCount = 100;</rule:declarations>
<rule:declarations>Description = "Custom Item";</rule:declarations>

<rule:routingRule>
    <rule:condition>GetProperty("itemDesc")
            = Description</rule:condition>
    <rule:process endpoint_ref="CallWebServiceProcess"
            type="PROCESS"/>
</rule:routingRule>

<rule:routingRule>
    <rule:condition>GetProperty("orderCount")
            &gt;= defaultCount</rule:condition>
    <rule:endpoint endpoint_ref="CheckAvailabilityJCAEndpoint"

            type="ENDPOINT"/>
</rule:routingRule>

<rule:routingRule>
    <rule:condition>GetProperty("orderCount")
            &lt; defaultCount</rule:condition>
    <rule:process endpoint_ref="ApprovalProcess" type="PROCESS"/
</rule:routingRule>
</rule:ruleSpec>
```

Note the use of the `<rule:routingRule>` element, which declares that a `GetProperty( )` method be used to access a named message property at runtime. The following excerpt specifies that the `CheckAvailabilityEndpoint` value be used based on the test of whether the value of the `orderCount` property of the message is greater than or equal to the value of `defaultCount`:

```
<rule:routingRule>
    <rule:condition>GetProperty("orderCount")
            &gt;= defaultCount</rule:condition>
    <rule:endpoint endpoint_ref="CheckAvailabilityJCAEndpoint"
            type="ENDPOINT"/>
</rule:routingRule>
```

The method of specifying the branches of the routing and the means for defining the decision rules are details that will vary between vendor implementations. The important point is that the metadata describing the possible branches and the rules for the CBR decisions are evaluated at the remote container, *not* by a centralized rules engine. That is one of the discriminating qualifiers for whether something can be categorized as an ESB as opposed to being a centralized hub-and-spoke EAI broker. In an ESB, there is no centralized rules engine that can become a performance bottleneck or a single point of failure. The CBR service, like any other ESB service, holds its own operating instructions in its service container, and is completely capable of executing those instructions without needing to refer to anything else externally. The implication is that any part of the ESB network may shut down and become temporarily unavailable without affecting the integration network as a whole.

The service container may obtain its configuration information from a centralized or regionalized place, such as a directory service. If the service container is capable of caching its configuration data locally, it can continue to operate should the directory service become unavailable.

Other characteristics about this CBR service that are distinguishing traits of an ESB are its selective use of only the processing technology (XML parser, JavaScript interpreter) that is needed to get its task accomplished, and the ability to support multiple processing technologies transparently.

Conditional Routing Using BPEL4WS

The same branching conditions that were described using JavaScript code or an XML rules file could also be described using BPEL4WS, as shown in Example 7-4.

Example 7-4. CBR rules described using BPEL4WS

```
...

<variables>
    <variable name="purchaseOrder" messageType="sns:POMessage">
</variables>

...

<!-- wait for and receive a PO submission
     use createInstance to start the process -->
<receive partnerLink="customer"
        portType="sns:purchasingServicePT"
     operation="submitPO"
     variable="purchaseOrder"
     createInstance="yes">
</receive>


<!-- use a 'flow' element to enable concurrent execution of each rule -->
<flow>
    <switch>
        <case condition=
            "bpws:getVariableProperty(purchaseOrder, 'itemDesc')
             = 'Custom Item'">
        <!-- Found a custom item, so invoke the processOrder operation
             of the process identified by the "process" partner link -->
        <invoke partnerLink="process"
                portType="sns:processPT"
             operation="processOrder"
             inputVariable="purchaseOrder"
        </invoke>
        </case>
    </switch>
</flow>
```

Example 7-4. CBR rules described using BPEL4WS (continued)

```
<switch>
    <case condition=
        "bpws:getVariableProperty(purchaseOrder, 'orderCount')
            > 100 ">
    <!-- Order count is > 100, so check the availability using the
        availability partner link -->n
    <invoke partnerLink="availability"
            portType="sns:availabilityServicePT"
        operation="checkAvailability"
        inputVariable="purchaseOrder"
    </invoke>
    </case>

</switch>

<switch>
    <case condition=
        "bpws:getVariableProperty(purchaseOrder, 'orderCount')
          < 100 ">
    <!-- order count is less than 100, so process this order -->
    <invoke partnerLink="approval"
            portType="sns:approvalServicePT"
        operation="processOrder"
        inputVariable="purchascOrder"
    </invoke>
    </case>
</switch>
</flow>
```

...

BPEL4WS allows scripting of abstract processes that can handle more complex situations than itineraries can. Processing these complex relationships requires a specialized orchestration service, as described later in "Specialized Services of the ESB."

Service Reusability

One primary value of an SOA is the reusability of services. In an ESB, services are meant to be reusable. An ESB service is an instance of a service type. Reusability can be accomplished by instantiating a particular type of service and applying variable data and conditions through parameterization and configuration. Examples of variable conditions that can affect the behavior of a service are the use of different XSLT stylesheets, different rules for CBR, and different endpoint locations.

Parameterization and Configuration

Let's look at a practical-use example. Say an organization creates a business policy dictating that all services that provide data transformation functionality will create an audit trail by logging data to a known location using a specific algorithm for uniquely identifying the message being transformed. A service type can be established for all XSLT-based transformations that always writes audit information in accordance with the established rules. This service type is written once, and instantiations of this new service type can be reused in any number of situations by specifying the XSLT stylesheet and the entry/exit endpoint destinations as configurable parameters.

In the transformation service illustrated in Figure 7-7, all the endpoints are configurable, including the entry, exit, fault location, tracking, and rejected message endpoints. The nature of the transform can be determined by the documents that get fed into the service (by configuring the entry endpoint) and the XSLT stylesheet that is supplied (through the directory service).

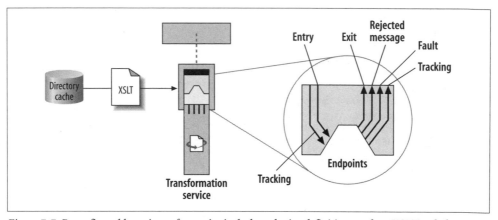

Figure 7-7. Reconfigurable options of a service include endpoint definitions and an XSLT stylesheet

This new auditing capability of the service may even be introduced as a new requirement after the transformation services are already in production. The new functionality can be introduced in the service type definition and redeployed to service containers using the ESB management framework. If the ESB's management framework supports live redeployment, this can be done without even taking down the container.

Figure 7-8 shows a similar example of the various things that can be parameterized and configured administratively for a CBR service type.

Here, the list of possible choices for exit endpoints is configurable. The routing rules definition, whether XML-based or script-based, and the "helper" functions are also fed into the service as configurable parameters. The isPO( ) and getXPath( ) functions from our previous CBR discussion (Example 7-2) are examples of things that would be implemented in a helper function and reused by multiple routing rule( ) implementations. The exit endpoint can also be dynamically determined from a list of supplied endpoint destinations by logic in the rule( ) implementation.

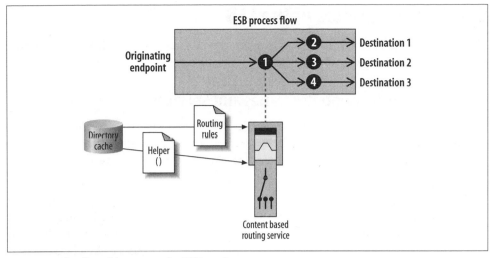

Figure 7-8. Configurable aspects of a CBR service

Reuse via Composition

Services can also be reused through composition; specialized services may be connected to form a composite business process. For example, rather than building the auditing function into the translation service type directly, auditing reuse can also be accomplished by creating a separate auditing service, as illustrated in Figure 7-9.

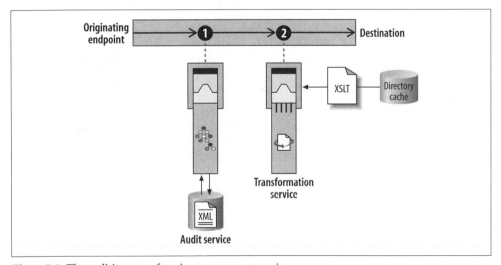

Figure 7-9. The auditing reuse function as a separate service

Specialized Services of the ESB

There are ways to enhance an ESB with specialized value-added services that can help solve some of the more complex integration problems.

Routing Patterns Using Itineraries and Services

One of the attractive characteristics of an ESB is the way in which services can be constructed together to solve common integration problems in ways that are profoundly simple. This section will examine some of the common patterns that are used in ESB integration solutions.

Multi-itinerary splitter pattern. Sometimes you need a more sophisticated means of controlling process flow. More complex business processes might involve multiple paths of execution to happen in parallel. These multiple paths can be handled through a combination of process itineraries and special services by placing a fan-out service within an itinerary that splits the process into two parallel subprocesses (Figure 7-10).

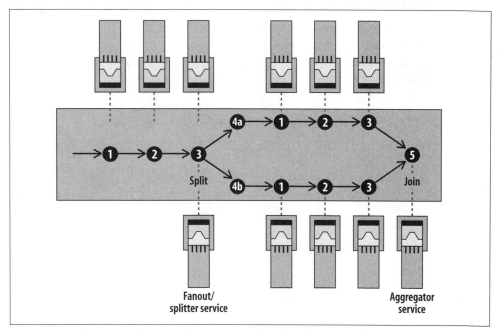

Figure 7-10. In the multi-itinerary splitter pattern, a fan-out/splitter service routes messages to parallel execution paths of multiple itineraries

Performing a simple join operation using itineraries means waiting for specific messages to arrive at a service. In this simple case, you can use an *aggregator* service along with some special design patterns that may require coding techniques. An example of this is discussed in Chapter 11 in the "Federated Query Patterns" section. Figure 7-11 shows a pattern sketch of this multi-itinerary splitter pattern.

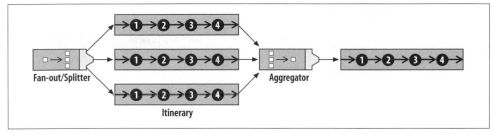

Figure 7-11. Pattern sketch of parallel execution paths using a combination of itineraries and splitter/ aggregator services

Multi-itinerary CBR pattern. A CBR service may need to choose between multiple possible paths, and at some point these parallel paths may need to converge. This is commonly known as a *join* operation, where a business process blocks and waits for one or more conditions to be satisfied before proceeding to the next step (Figure 7-12). This is also accomplished by some coding techniques in an aggregator service.

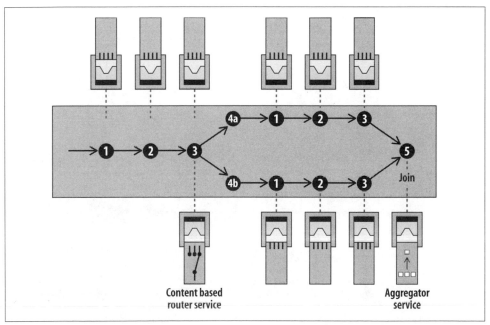

Figure 7-12. In a multi-itinerary CBR pattern, a CBR service chooses between multiple possibilities of itinerary paths

Figure 7-13 shows a pattern sketch of the multi-itinerary CBR pattern.

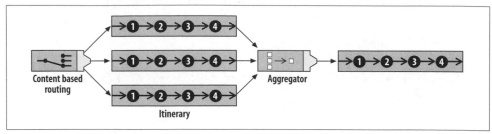

Figure 7-13. Pattern sketch of the multi-itinerary CBR pattern

Sophisticated Process Flow Using an Orchestration Service (BPEL4WS)

There are join conditions under which simply blocking and waiting for one or more responses to arrive at a service is not enough. For more sophisticated process management situations, you need a specialized ESB capability known as an *orchestration service*. An orchestration service is a special processing engine that can be plugged into the bus to coordinate other services that are on the bus, such as a BPEL4WS engine (Figure 7-14).

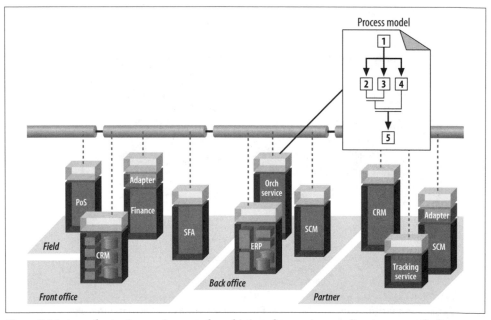

Figure 7-14. An orchestration service controls sophisticated processing coordination across the bus

An orchestration service can manage stateful information about a business process that spans a length of time. For example, a step in a business process may require human interaction, such as manual approval of a purchase order. Itineraries can carry state, and recover from failure if the messages carrying the itineraries are being transported over reliable messaging. However, if a message is traveling through an itinerary and there are no failures, the business process simply runs its course and finishes to completion. There is no automatic way to temporarily suspend an itinerary-based process and have it wait for an external event to occur. If a stateful conversation will be carried out over a long duration, with pauses and resumes that are separated by time and triggered by external events, then an orchestration service is a better choice than a process itinerary.

Figure 7-15 shows an illustration of multiple states being managed by an orchestration service, represented by four distinct state transitions. An orchestration service can work in conjunction with an XML persistence service to keep track of process state between state transitions.

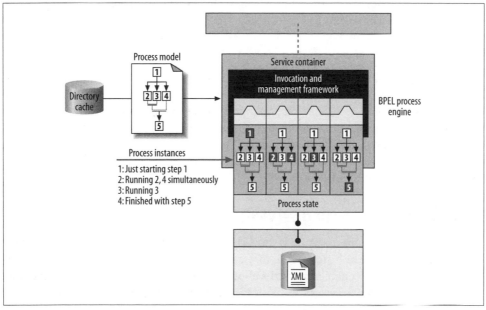

Figure 7-15. An orchestration service can manage sophisticated branching and stateful transitions between steps in a process

Even if no conditional joins of multiple processes occur, a business process can be set up to remain blocked until a certain transition condition is met. A transition condition blocks the process flow until a state variable in the process reaches a certain value or a Boolean expression evaluates to true. The release of a transition condition can be triggered by an event resulting from a person clicking an Approve button, or by the arrival of a message that the process is waiting for.

Recovery of process state

An orchestration service can better manage the scenarios of failure and recovery of stateful long-duration conversations. An example of stateful information could be the current values of join conditions themselves. If a join is waiting for multiple conditions to be satisfied, the current state of the process is that two out of three of those conditions have already been met. If the service goes down, the knowledge that two of the three transition conditions have been met will be restored upon recovery.

Correlation of asynchronous conversations

In a long-duration conversation that involves asynchronous requests and responses, the responses can arrive in any order over an extended period of time. An orchestration service can manage multiple conversations by correlating the requests with the appropriate responses. If using itineraries alone, it is conceivable that long-duration processes could be managed by letting messages build up in a queue, and then removing them from the queue when the join condition is met. However, it's not easy to take things out of a queue in any arbitrary order.

BPEL4WS for scripting of orchestration services

BPEL4WS is intended to be a portable way of abstractly describing a business process. An orchestration server may support BPEL4WS as the scripting language for describing the process definition, as well as supporting other scripting languages that are proprietary. It is expected that initial adopters of BPEL4WS will provide import/export capabilities into their existing BPM tools, but still use something proprietary as an internal representation. Microsoft BizTalk 4.0 takes this approach, for example. More details on BPEL4WS can be found in Chapter 12.

XML Storage and Caching Services

Another type of specialized service is an XML storage service. An XML storage service can be used to capture and store XML messages as they travel through the bus between services. This can help enable the retrieval of real-time data as it flows across the bus. Specialized aggregation services can be strategically arranged across the bus as a means of capturing important business data. Data can be collected regularly and retrieved using XQuery, and then used in reporting scenarios where meaningful data about the state of a business is reported and analyzed (Figure 7-16). For example, a common retail function is to collect and retrieve the details of the on-hand inventory in the warehouse, in the stores, and even in transit. This data can then be accessed via in-store kiosks to quickly locate out-of-stock items.

Data caching

Chapter 11 discusses the use of an XML persistence service for use in the *forward cache* and *federated query* patterns. In the forward cache pattern, data is proactively pushed

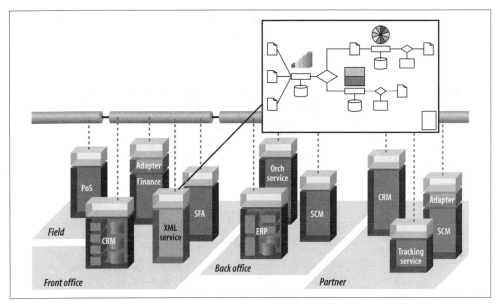

Figure 7-16. An XML persistence service performs caching, aggregation, and reporting functions to enable real-time insight into live business data

out from backend data sources across the ESB to be held in a cache that is coresident with the application that needs to access the data. In the federated query pattern, an XML cache is used to collect asynchronous responses from multiple messages that are fired off at different backend data sources to gather data.

Aggregation and reporting

An XML persistence service can be used to collect data from multiple data sources, making the data much more valuable than it is when lying dormant in its constituent parts. This can enable BAM functionality by collecting data that can be fed into visual reporting tools. Aggregated data can have XSLT transformations applied to it, which can make it more meaningful to a business analyst.

The implication is that applications can participate in providing BAM-like functionality without any modifications. Existing applications can continue to post the same bits and pieces of data as usual, and that data can be routed through business processes, transformed, and sent to an XML aggregation service to be fed into reporting infrastructures.

Implementation choices

An XML persistence service could potentially be implemented using a relational database, with some XML to relational mapping technology built on top of it. This involves a process known as "shredding" and "unshredding" an XML document into rows and columns to meet the requirements of a relational database table structure.

An XML storage service is best implemented as a native XML database that knows how to store and retrieve XML as an in-memory parsed representation. This allows the use of XQuery to access individual nodes of an XML document without running the entire document through a parser just to access an individual element.

If the XML is managed by the XML persistence service as a preparsed XML document, then multiple processing steps that access the same XML document can be coresident within the service and linked together. These multiple steps can be a series of XQuery statements that are executed sequentially as related actions, forming an *XML processing pipeline*. Figure 7-17 shows a series of operations on a shared XML document, which is accessible across multiple steps in a single service container and is shared between multiple service containers.

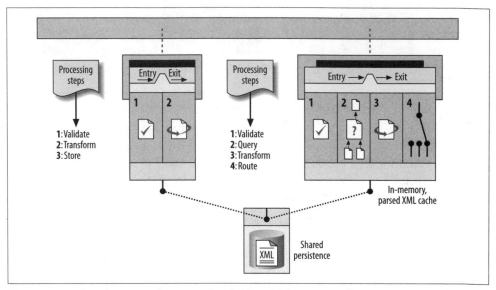

Figure 7-17. A shared XML persistence service avoids multiple parse-serialize-parse operations between steps in a process

The advantage of this is that you can optimize for multiple steps operating on the same instance of an XML document that is stored in the same XML persistence service. The shared XML document is parsed only once, as opposed to being parsed, serialized, and reparsed between each step in the process. If the process spans physical service containers, a message containing a token, or a key representing the shared XML document that is managed by the XML persistence service, is sent to the next container through the bus. This is called an XML pass-by-reference model.

The XML persistence service manages the transactional integrity of the document while changes are made to it during the XML pipelining process.

Convergence in Process Modeling

In this chapter we have examined three different ways of managing the steps in a business process: itinerary-based routing, sophisticated process orchestration using an orchestration service that is layered on top of the ESB, and the XML processing pipeline in an XML persistence service, also a layered service on top of the ESB. Each method has its merits and its optimizations, and each should be used in the situation that it is best suited for. Table 7-1 shows a summary of the advantages of each approach.

Table 7-1. Summary of advantages of each business process definition approach

	Highly distributed, metadata-driven	Conditional splits and joins	Optimized for XML parsing
Itinerary-based routing	X		
Process orchestration		X	
XML processing pipeline			X

The disparity in the underlying processing techniques can be converged in a unified view of a process model. Regardless of the form you use for a given situation, the means for expressing the business process should be the same. An ESB can provide a single visual tool interface for describing processes. Using a visual drag-and-drop tool that visualizes business processes using UML diagramming techniques, the business process can be defined. The tool itself can generate BPEL4WS as the scripting language to describe the abstract process. Ideally, the visual tool and the runtime infrastructure of the ESB can make the optimal choice of underlying implementation, whether it is based upon itineraries, process orchestrations, or XML processing pipelines.

Summary

In this chapter we explored the following:

- We discussed the concept of *itinerary-based routing*, and the role it plays in enabling a highly distributed SOA across independently deployed services.

- We discussed some core ESB services, such as content-based routing and XSLT transformation. Service reusability was also examined.

- We examined two integration patterns that combine itineraries with special services.

- We learned about some advanced ESB capabilities such as an XML persistence service and an orchestration service.

- We discussed the idea of a unified view of a process model, which makes optimal choices between the underlying process model options.

In the next chapter we will explore protocols, messaging, and custom ESB services using a case study from a live ESB deployment in a manufacturing supply chain.

8

Protocols, Messaging, Custom Adapters, and Services

This chapter will explore how the ESB can extend its MOM core to create the flexibility in protocols necessary to connect to applications in an adaptable and nonintrusive way, through protocol handlers and messaging patterns. This includes an explanation of how XML and SOAP messaging can be integral parts of an ESB strategy, yet also be flexible enough to carry other data formats such as EDI X12 messages. This chapter also shows the details of a partner integration using an ESB, and examines the use of third-party adapters and custom integration services for integrating with backend systems such as SAP.

The ESB MOM Core

At the core of the ESB communications layer is a MOM infrastructure that is capable of supporting a variety of industry-standard access mechanisms and protocols (Figure 8-1). Think of the MOM as a multiprotocol messaging bus that supports asynchronous delivery of messages with configurable QoS options ranging from *exactly-once* delivery with transactional integrity through high-performance, low-latency *best-effort* delivery (a.k.a. at-most-once delivery). The MOM support underneath an ESB should support scalable clustering that is capable of being deployed across the various types of geographical layouts that have been discussed throughout this book.

The physical topology of the underlying messaging layer is completely independent of the service-oriented view of an ESB process flow. An ESB must be capable of spanning geographic locations and of traversing firewall security using full certificate-based authentication. An ESB must also be capable of delivering messages reliably using message persistence and a store-and-forward capability. As illustrated in Figure 8-2, these capabilities are delegated to the underlying MOM layer.

The messaging layer should have the ability to cluster message servers into a gridlike infrastructure, where all message traffic can be routed seamlessly between message servers without exposing the underlying routing details to the application level or the ESB process level.

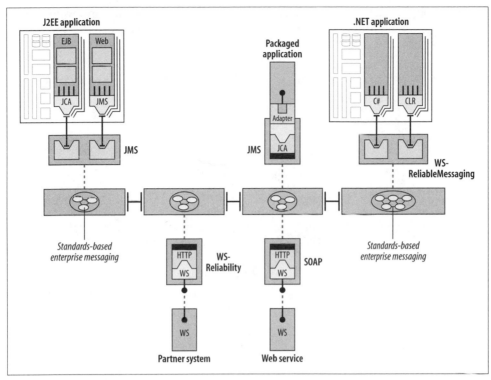

Figure 8-1. An enterprise MOM at the core of the ESB architecture

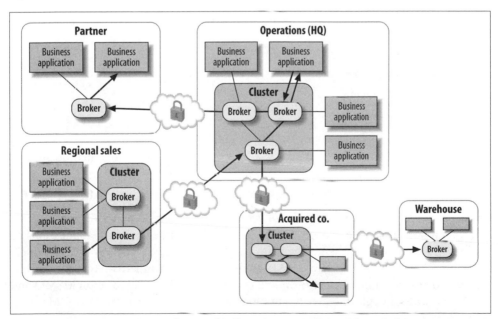

Figure 8-2. Clustering, security, and geographic dispersion are qualities of the underlying MOM

As illustrated in Figure 8-3, an ESB needs to be capable of connecting and transporting messages across multiple transports and protocols such as JMS, proprietary MOM, HTTP/S, SOAP, WS-Rel*, FTP, and SMTP (email).

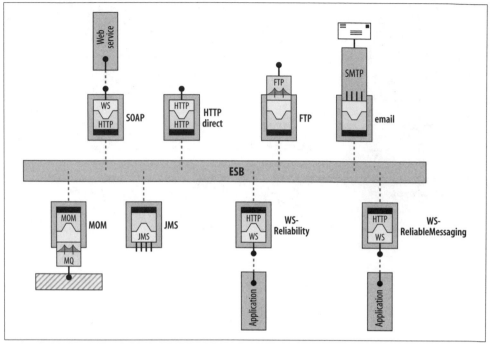

Figure 8-3. The ESB supports multiple transports and protocols as "on-ramps" and "off-ramps"

A variety of protocols can be bus-enabled:

- Direct support in a messaging broker (HTTP direct)
- WS-ReliableMessaging
- WS-Reliability
- A bridge or gateway to the MOM core
- As a custom ESB service that acts as a bridge to another interface method such as RMI, CORBA, or File Access
- As an alternative to the MOM core, e.g., SonicESB over WebSphereMQ

These protocols are primarily a means of getting into and out of the ESB. The main reason for supporting these protocols is so that the ESB can integrate with applications or business partners that use them. The main trunk line of an ESB is always MOM-based. Ideally the MOM is compliant with JMS in order to be as standards-based as possible, but even that is not a requirement; An ESB could conceivably be built upon MSMQ and Indigo. Advanced deployment configurations of an ESB might support MOMs from multiple vendors.

The MOM, along with the ESB containers, is deployed in as many places as you have control over. This is because the MOM provides scalability through clustering of message servers, a unified view of security, and asynchronous reliable delivery of messages using the store-and-forward capabilities discussed in Chapter 5.

MOM Interoperability

When using a MOM, the sender and receiver need a piece of client software supplied by the MOM vendor in order to participate in a messaging conversation. JMS is the only adopted standard for MOM, but it does not define an interoperable on-the-wire format and therefore does not alleviate this situation. The reason for this is that the internals of the wire protocol are part of a MOM vendor's proprietary implementation for providing highly efficient, reliable delivery of messages. This is not about UDP versus TCP/IP versus something else; it's about the next protocol level above that—the message transport layer—which has to do with what governs the behavior of things such as message-level acknowledgments and retries.

JMS does dictate that messages must be interoperable between vendors. This means that a JMS message must be capable of being received from a topic or queue from one JMS vendor implementation, and placed on a topic or queue of another without modification. Most JMS vendors (and ESBs) provide bridge technology to allow this.

WS-Reliability and WS-ReliableMessaging (collectively referred to as WS-Rel*) are industry efforts that define an open interoperable wire protocol for reliable messaging based on the SOAP protocol. It is conceivable, even probable, that a MOM implementation could be based entirely on one of these WS-Rel* specifications. However, it would still require a piece of MOM infrastructure on both sides of the wire to handle behavior such as acknowledgment of receipt, message persistence, and recovery from failure. From that perspective, having an open protocol means that the MOM piece of software on either side of the conversation can be provided by different vendors. Unfortunately, it also means that you have less room to innovate on efficiencies of acknowledgments at the message transport layer.

The 80/20 Rule of MOM Backbone Versus External Protocols

There's an 80/20 rule to be considered when you're talking about MOM backbones versus external protocols. For the most part, you aren't mixing MOM implementations on a regular basis unless you are bridging together a new project with an old one, or if you are connecting different departments, business units, or business partners with roots in one implementation or another. Therefore, for the 80% of normal cases, you are using one MOM vendor for a particular project, so the internal protocol between the pieces of the MOM software shouldn't matter any more than whether there was an open standard for how a DBMS writes and manages storage on disk. However, for the 20% of cases, you'll be mixing MOM vendors via bridging technology or WS-Rel* endpoint implementations.

In some organizations and deployment situations, the ratio is 90/10 or even higher. To determine the ratio for your own situation, consider all the applications that are spread out across your company that could benefit by being integrated together. These are best integrated using the MOM core of the ESB as the underlying transport. Compare that with how many instances of integration you need to do with outside entities where you have no control over what software gets installed. In these cases, you would need to have an open, reliable protocol such as WS-Rel*.

As interoperable standards for messaging such as WS-Rel* and process definition language specifications such as BPEL4WS become more prevalent, this will allow even more cross-vendor interoperability, and the 80/20 ratio will decrease even more.

IS JMS A PROTOCOL?

An ESB relies on a MOM, which can be JMS-based, to carry XML-formatted messages over message channels. Some people view JMS simply as a common API for connecting into a MOM. It is certainly that, but in addition to being an API, JMS also provides a set of rules for defining the semantic behavior of message delivery. Such behavior includes asynchrony, exactly-once delivery, and transactional recovery due to failure of the messaging provider or of the sending and receiving applications. In addition, JMS provides a clear set of definitions for structuring message content and headers.

When transporting messages across an ESB, JMS can be thought of as a protocol in the sense that a MOM channel or JMS queue is treated as a transport for carrying XML messages. In that sense, the terms "protocol" and "transport" are treated synonymously; i.e., JMS, HTTP, and WS-ReliableMessaging are all treated equally, even though they are all at different levels on the protocol stack. SOAP-over-HTTP can also be considered a "protocol" as far as the ESB is concerned.

This treatment of JMS is also occurring in the open source Apache Web Services project, Apache Axis. In Axis, JMS is allowed as a pluggable transport for web services invocations, as an alternative to HTTP.

A Generic Message Invocation Framework

Figure 8-4 shows some examples of protocol stacks that can be used for transporting messages across an ESB. These protocol stacks include SOAP-over-HTTP/S, WS-Rel* SOAP, MOM/JMS, SOAP-over-JMS-over-HTTP/S, and JMS-over-SSL.

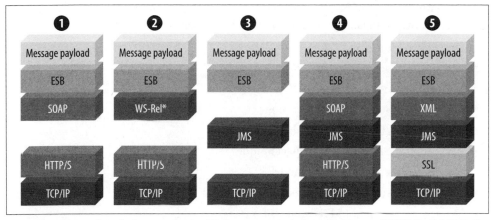

Figure 8-4. Protocol stacks for transporting XML messages include 1) SOAP-over-HTTP/S; 2) WS-Rel*; 3) MOM/JMS; 4) SOAP-over-JMS-over-HTTP/S; and 5) JMS-over-SSL

Here are brief descriptions of these protocol stacks:

SOAP-over-HTTP/S
> The standard means of carrying a SOAP message over an HTTP or HTTP/S transport.

WS-Rel*
> Using WS-Reliability or WS-ReliableMessaging as a transport. (Although not shown here, WS-Security, WS-SecureConversation, etc., can be used to secure SOAP over HTTP messages.)

MOM/JMS
> Using a MOM channel, JMS-based or otherwise, to transport messages.

SOAP-over-JMS-over-HTTP/S
> Using JMS to carry SOAP messages, combined with tunneling of a JMS connection through a firewall using the HTTP or HTTP/S protocol. This can be done between a JMS client and a message server, or between two JMS servers. This usually involves mutual authentication using x509 digital certificates.

JMS-over-SSL
> The act of tunneling a JMS connection through a firewall using the SSL protocol. This can be done between a JMS client and a message server, or between two JMS servers. This usually involves mutual authentication using x509 digital certificates.

SOAP is not a prerequisite for an ESB, although it is fairly common for ESB channels to carry SOAP messages. In some cases, the ESB may even strip off the SOAP envelope and just use the remaining XML payload information as the message that gets passed between services.

Quality of Service (QoS) levels can vary depending on which protocol is chosen to carry a message. This is another reason why there is a unified MOM at the core of the ESB. In fact, the enumeration of benefits to having a MOM at the core of the ESB is almost the antithesis of the disadvantages of the accidental architecture:

- Consistent QoS levels
- Consistent management
- Metrics and monitoring
- Consistent troubleshooting techniques
- Consistent scalability methodology
- Consistent performance tuning techniques
- Consistent security and ACL model
- Publish-and-subscribe broadcast of information
- Message persistence and reliability of message delivery

Protocol Bridging

Bridging is one way to attach a legacy protocol such as FTP or SMTP (email) into an ESB. As illustrated in Figure 8-5, an FTP or SMTP bridge is implemented as a specialized messaging client, which converts data from one protocol to and from the MOM channel.

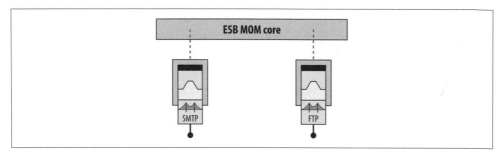

Figure 8-5. A protocol bridge converts between an "external" protocol and the ESB MOM channel

You could write the protocol bridge yourself, but most messaging vendors supply them for you. Later in this chapter ("Removing the Dependency on the EDI VAN") we will explore how a custom file-drop ESB service performs a similar bridge function.

What you gain by using a protocol bridge is a common backbone for transporting data across the enterprise. This pushes the unreliable FTP out to the outermost edge of your integration network, and in many cases completely eliminates its use by removing the dependency on FTP for transporting bytes across the network, and simply retaining the file-based interface between an application and an ESB. Chapter 9 will explore this scenario in more detail.

MOM Bridging

An ESB also provides a bridge across MOM implementations. Many corporations, especially larger ones that have been through a few acquisitions, have multiple installations of MOM from different vendors across their organization. A new installation of an ESB can link with these existing MOM installations using a MOM bridge. For example, you might have SonicMQ as a MOM core of an ESB, which links into WebsphereMQ and TIBCO RV, as illustrated in Figure 8-6.

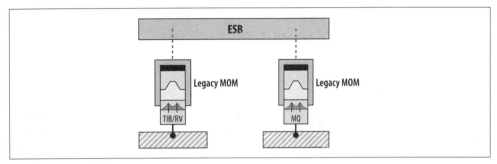

Figure 8-6. Bridging between two different MOM vendors

Recall the concept of "leave and layer" as introduced in Chapter 1. Bridging between MOM vendors accomplishes this goal, allowing an ESB to extend its reach into an existing MOM-based integration infrastructure without needing to tear it out and replace it.

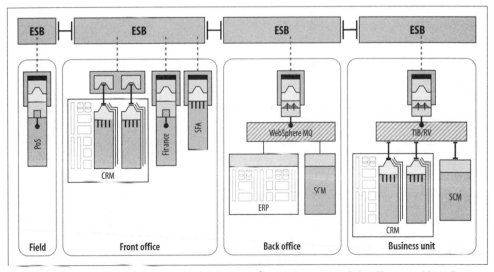

Figure 8-7. Bridging an ESB into an existing MOM infrastructure accomplishes "leave and layer"

Figure 8-7 represents a bridge layer sitting between the message channels of the ESB's native MOM core and the message channels of an existing MOM infrastructure. As standards for connectivity and messaging integration mature and are implemented by messaging and ESB vendors, the ESB may be able to treat "foreign" message channels directly as endpoints. Examples of these specifications are the Java Business Integration (JBI, JSR-208) effort that is underway within the JCP, and Reliable SOAP specifications such as WS-Reliability and WS-ReliableMessaging (WS-Rel*). Figure 8-8 shows an ESB infrastructure that directly interfaces with MOM endpoints from SonicMQ, WebSphereMQ, and E4JMS.

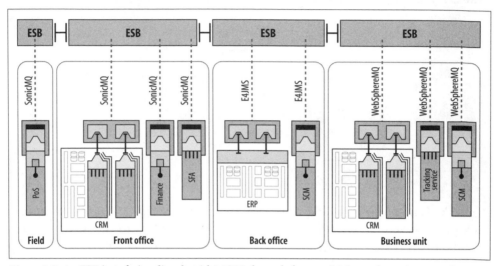

Figure 8-8. An ESB interfacing directly with MOM channels from multiple vendors using emerging specifications such as JBI and WS-Rel*

Direct Protocol Handlers

One form of integrating an ESB MOM core with another protocol is through direct support for that protocol within the MOM's message broker. In this scenario, the message broker itself provides the bridging, or mapping, between the external protocol and the internal MOM channel—for example, a mapping between SOAP-over-HTTP and SOAP-over-JMS. Figure 8-9 shows the kinds of protocols that are typically supported in this fashion.

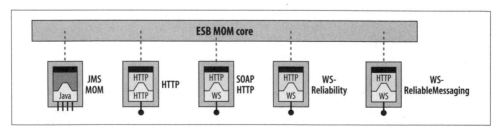

Figure 8-9. Direct protocol support in the MOM's message broker

The ability to process HTTP requests, both inbound and outbound, is a critical component that enables two of the four basic parts of an ESB as described by Gartner: MOM and web services. Providing the HTTP protocol support directly in a message broker allows the configuration and management of server clustering, fault tolerance, and high availability from a single vantage point without additional external processes. The servers in the cluster may act as one logical server, which can communicate on multiple protocol channels that send and receive MOM messages, SOAP messages, or non-SOAP HTTP requests. This means there are no additional moving parts or additional processes, such as web servers, servlet engines, or ISAPI filters, that can become bottlenecks or points of failure.

Synchronous request/reply: invoking an ESB service via HTTP

An ESB should provide an invocation framework that allows an ESB service to be invoked as a result of an external HTTP request. A single HTTP request, whether SOAP-based or otherwise, may even trigger the kickoff of an entire business process. The interface to the ESB service or business process can be described using WSDL and exposed to the outside world as a first-class web service endpoint. While an ESB is by and large intended for asynchronous processing, it should also be able to process a synchronous request/reply. Figure 8-10 shows the ESB processing components involved in making a simple inbound synchronous request/reply service invocation.

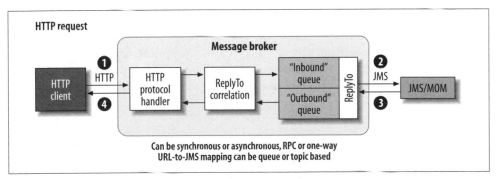

Figure 8-10. HTTP invocation from an "external" client can trigger an ESB service or an entire ESB process to be invoked

Figure 8-11 shows one of the many possible interaction patterns. An ESB should be capable of interacting with HTTP requests, both synchronous and asynchronous, and inbound and outbound. This introduces the concept of an HTTP protocol handler, which allows an ESB message broker to listen for inbound HTTP or SOAP requests, much like a web server or application server would. The protocol handler performs a mapping of the HTTP content into a JMS message and places the JMS message into a queue or a pub/sub topic destination. In an asynchronous messaging environment, a request/reply is accomplished by setting up two messaging channels: one for the request and one for the reply. The channels may be either pub/sub-based or point-to-point queue–based. The service handler on the other end of the queue or topic will invoke the service, correlate the reply with the request, and place the reply on another "outbound" queue to be sent back to the HTTP protocol handler using the ReplyTo pattern. Figure 8-11 shows the interaction in more detail.

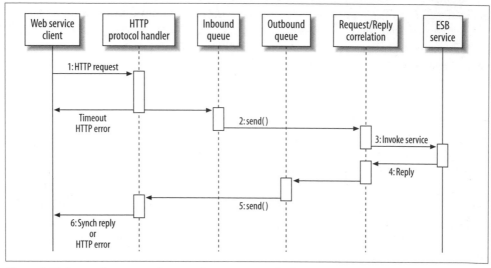

Figure 8-11. Interaction pattern for a synchronous request/reply

In the event that the service or part of the business process is temporarily unavailable, the HTTP protocol handler can generate an error back to the sender if the response time exceeds a configurable timeout period, as noted in Figure 8-11. If the service invocation generates an error, then that error will also be propagated back to the caller.

Asynchronous request/reply

Interactions between an HTTP request and an ESB process or service often need more than the requisite subsecond response time required to satisfy a synchronous request/ reply. This could be due to a number of reasons:

- The service represents an interface to an application with regularly scheduled downtime for maintenance purposes.
- The service represents an interface to an application, or a portion of your business that still relies on nightly batch processing and has not yet been fully brought into a real-time integration with the ESB. Therefore, the data required to fulfill the request will not be available until the next batch integration process.
- The process involves some human interaction, which could cause delay in getting the information needed.

In these cases, you'll need to utilize asynchronous request/reply. Figure 8-12 shows the interaction patterns for an asynchronous request/reply.

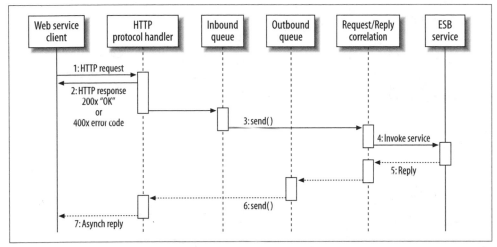

Figure 8-12. Interaction pattern for an asynchronous request/reply

This is a slight variation on synchronous request/reply. The main difference is Step 2, which sends an HTTP reply back to the sender immediately. The reply can be any valid HTTP response code to indicate success or failure. This response code indicates the success or failure of the HTTP request; it is not an indication of the actual service invocation. The "reply" to the service invocation will come at a later time (asynchronously).

The implication is that the sender has asynchronous capabilities as well. The inbound request must contain a URI indicating where to send the reply, which should map to a web service endpoint that the requestor uses to listen for the reply.

SOAP Protocol Handler

The previous discussion on request/reply was intended to be as simple as possible, and left out the details of processing the SOAP envelope and mapping it onto a JMS message and back again. Figure 8-13 illustrates the same architecture using a protocol handler that understands SOAP.

This is a slight variation on the HTTP direct example. The main difference is the presence of a SOAP handler that can understand a SOAP envelope, and can therefore validate it and generate SOAP faults under error conditions. Figure 8-14 shows the interaction patterns using a SOAP protocol handler.

Note the subtle differences between the SOAP inbound processing and the previous HTTP direct example. In Step 2, validation is performed to verify that the content of the inbound request is indeed a SOAP envelope, and in Step 3, a SOAP fault is generated if the validation fails. In the case of a synchronous request/reply, a SOAP fault would also be returned if the request could not be fulfilled for some reason.

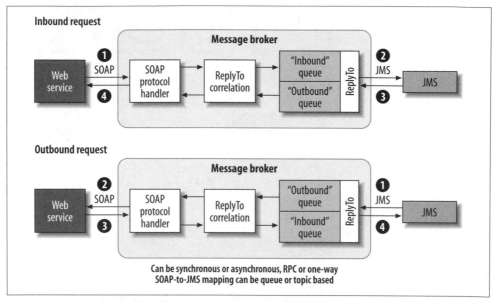

Figure 8-13. SOAP protocol handler processing inbound and outbound SOAP requests

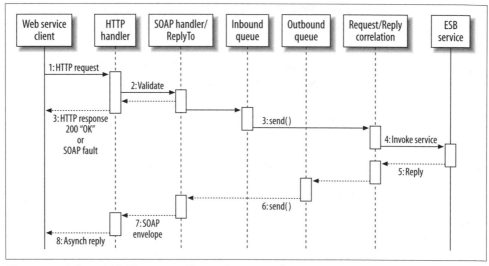

Figure 8-14. Inbound SOAP request with asynchronous reply

Where Do Asynchronous Errors Go?

If an outbound request cannot be satisfied because a web service invocation is unavailable, the message still exists on the outbound queue. A service can be set up to retry, or to fail over to another URL if a particular web service is unavailable. If the MOM supports the notion of a centralized error location, sometimes referred to as a Rejected

The Java Business Integration (JBI) specification can help provide a greater degree of protocol independence. If the ESB supports JBI, there will be a JBI-compliant binding component between the ESB and the service container. This binding component represents a contract between two vendor-supplied pieces of software: the MOM interface and the service container. JBI will normalize the message as it passes through to the service container, so it doesn't really matter how the message is packaged as long as it is supported by the binding component. More information on JBI can be found in Chapter 10.

Message Endpoint (RME) or Dead Message Queue (DMQ), then the failed message can be placed there (Figure 8-15).

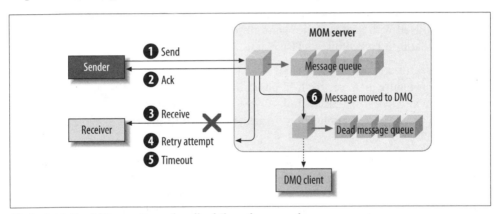

Figure 8-15. Dead Message Queue handles failures from asynchronous requests

The choice of whether the message goes to an RME or a DMQ can vary depending on the ESB or the MOM implementation. The ESB may have its own higher-level RME that's independent of the underlying MOM implementation, or it could delegate that responsibility to the MOM. Most MOMs have a DMQ concept; SonicMQ has something specifically referred to as a DMQ, and WebsphereMQ and MSMQ have something called a Dead Letter Queue. What's important is that there is a place to put errors that occur as the result of failed asynchronous requests, and that the messages are kept fully intact with a reason code explaining why they got there. The result of such failures can also vary depending on the implementation. An alert can be raised to an administration and management framework, which could cause something to happen in an administrative console.

The DMQ is a queue just like any other queue. A custom error-handling service could be written using familiar queue-based APIs that are native to the MOM; this service would peel messages off of the DMQ, analyze them, and decide what to do based on individual business rules. For example, if the message contains an address header, such as a WS-Addressing header, that specifies a fault location where all SOAP faults are to be sent, the administrative application could be written to route all messages to that location. Or better yet, the ESB could be configured to automatically examine the WS-Addressing header and route messages there.

This behavior of centralized error reporting and error handling is not unique to SOAP requests; it is inherent in all message processing across the ESB. This is yet another reason why a MOM is core to the ESB architecture: issues such as those addressed by a DMQ have already been solved and have infrastructure built around them.

Case Study: Partner Integration

Let's now take some of these concepts and put them to practical use by examining the details of a partner integration in the manufacturing supply chain area. This is a continuation of the case study introduced in Chapter 3, in which a manufacturer deploys an ESB to link itself with its distributors and implement improved inventory management and an Availability To Promise (ATP) system.

This manufacturer chose to deploy ESB service containers at the remote partner sites. As illustrated in Figure 8-16, secure JMS-based MOM links connect the partners with the main supplier. The secure MOM link carries xCBL-formatted XML documents across the ESB to the inventory application, which is linked into the ESB using an SAP business connector.

The manufacturer chose to use xCBL (Common Business Library) as an internal standard canonical format for representing XML as it flows across the bus. The benefits of establishing a common XML dialect within and across the ESB are discussed in Chapter 4. xCBL is a standard for describing things such as addresses, purchase orders, and so on, and was jointly developed by SAP and CommerceOne during the days of dotcom and public exchanges. Like many other standards efforts, xCBL has not dominated the XML industry. However, because it was codeveloped by SAP, the message schema has a high degree of affinity to SAP's IDOC (Intermediate Document) elements and terminology. For this reason, xCBL was a good choice for them to make, as it simplified the writing of custom adapters.

Secure DMZ Deployment

The secure MOM link is enabled by deploying a clustered ESB message broker in the DMZ (De-Militarized Zone). As illustrated in Figure 8-17, the ESB message broker is securely deployed between an "external" firewall and an "internal" firewall. The external firewall allows only SSL connections into the ESB message broker, which are mutually authenticated between the remote ESB containers and the ESB broker using digital certificates on both ends.

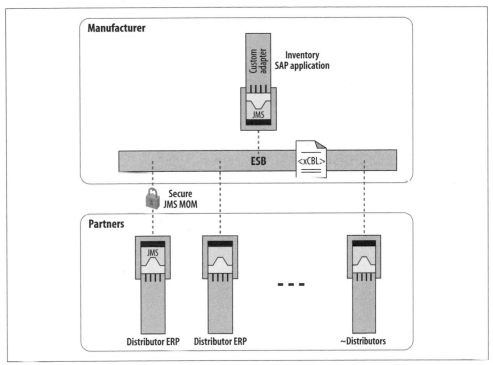

Figure 8-16. A secure JMS MOM link carries xCBL-formatted XML data across the ESB to an SAP adapter

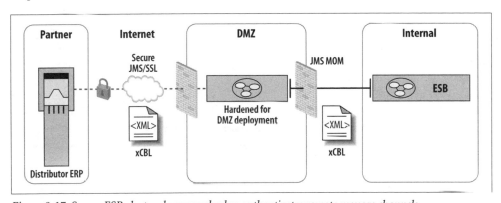

Figure 8-17. Secure ESB clustered message broker authenticates remote message channels

The internal firewall is configured to allow traffic only between the ESB message broker in the DMZ and the ESB message broker behind the firewall of the manufacturer. This link can be either another authenticated SSL channel or a plain TCP connection listening on a preconfigured port. This depends entirely on individual security policies and comfort levels on a per-organization basis.

The message channels are restricted by ACLs, which allow only authenticated partners to read and write designated message queues and topics.

Because the brokers are clustered together, they automatically route messages between the brokers as necessary to get the message to where it needs to go. This configuration is transparent to the level of coordination that occurs at the ESB endpoints. An ESB business process coordinates the routing of messages between the partner and the ESB endpoint that represents the SAP adapter.

Availability To Promise (ATP)

Meanwhile, implementing the ATP function as a separate project, the manufacturer. decided to use a direct web services link between itself and its distributors (Figure 8-18).

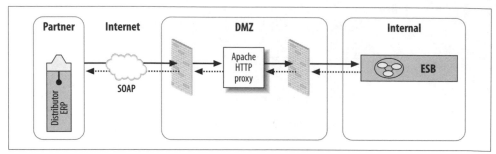

Figure 8-18. The ATP function uses a SOAP-over-HTTP direct link to carry xCBL-formatted XML documents

The distributor applications send a SOAP message containing an xCBL Availability-CheckRequest document as a payload in an HTTP POST request to a proxy server that is sitting in the manufacturer's DMZ. According to the proxy's rules, that request is forwarded to an "HTTP direct" listener on the internal ESB message broker that has been configured to place incoming messages onto a message queue. The message queue transport provides a special XML message type that allows it to carry SOAP messages, or multipart-MIME messages that can carry XML along with other types of opaque binary data. On the other side of that message queue is a custom ESB service that serves as an adapter to the SAP application that performs the ATP lookup.

In this case the incoming HTTP listener is set up to perform a synchronous request/reply. While the ESB is by and large intended to be asynchronous in nature, it is also capable of carrying synchronous request/reply messages from an HTTP request, across a MOM queue (or pub/sub topic), through an adapter, and back again with a reply.

The SAP Adapter: A Custom ESB Service

At the other end of the ATP queue is a custom ESB service, written in Java, which acts as an adapter into the SAP system. This is an alternative approach to the adapter strategy that was used in the inventory scenario. Here, the ESB service receives a message that is delivered as an xCBL-formatted XML document.

The service is configured with multiple listeners, each on its own separate listener thread. The service happens to use Castor for the Java<->XML binding, which is used to unmarshal the document in preparation for invoking an SAP Remote Function Call (RFC). The service uses the SAP Java Connector (also known as JCo) library to do the RFC invocation (Figure 8-19).

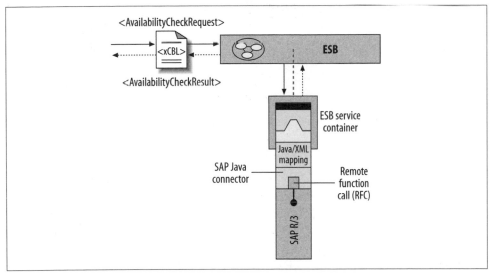

Figure 8-19. A custom SAP adapter uses Java-to-XML mapping objects and a third-party SAP Java Connector

With the help of the JCo library, the ESB service manages an SAP connection pool. The ESB container thread ID becomes the SAP connection poolname. The SAP connection parameters are configured administratively as ESB container initialization parameters.

The service invokes the appropriate SAP RFC to perform the AvailabilityToPromise request, and waits for a synchronous reply to occur. To create the reply to the ATP query, an xCBL 3.5 AvailabilityCheckResult document is retrieved from the ESB directory service. Using the results of the SAP RFC call, the AvailabilityCheckResult document is populated using the setter methods on the Castor object that represents it. The Castor object is then marshaled to the ESB container's outgoing exit endpoint, which is configured to use a default ReplyTo endpoint. The ReplyTo endpoint is in turn routed back to the HTTP direct listener, and back to the distributor system as an HTTP reply to the POST. Figure 8-20 illustrates the round-trip process end to end.

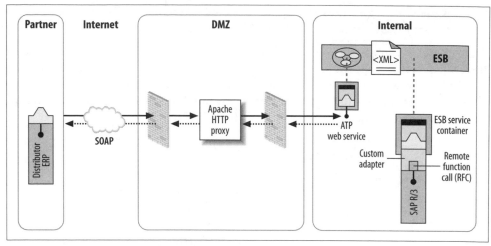

Figure 8-20. ATP round-trip request through to SAP RFC and back to HTTP reply

EDI Transportation and Transformation

A fair number of the manufacturer's partners are already accustomed to communicating using EDI. In order to continue to provide the same EDI interface with the partners in a nondisruptive fashion yet still migrate toward an ESB enablement, the manufacturer chose to continue using the EDI VAN between the partners and headquarters (for now). Once inside the manufacturer's headquarters, the EDI messages are placed onto the bus using a custom ESB service that acts as an EDI gateway (Figure 8-21).

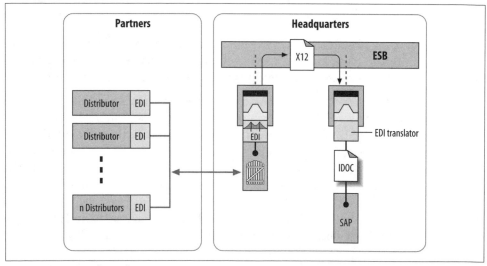

Figure 8-21. EDI Gateway is a custom service on the ESB

The custom service places an EDI X12 document onto a reliable message queue, which then gets routed to another ESB service that has been set up for the purpose of interfacing with an EDI translator. In this case it is using a third-party EDI translator called Inovis Trusted Link Enterprise (TLE). TLE converts the X12 message to an SAP IDOC message, which then gets sent on to the SAP application for processing.

Removing the Dependency on the EDI VAN

Over time, the use of the EDI VAN can be eliminated completely by using a remote ESB container directly at the partner site; this container can be used to transfer the EDI data over a secure, reliable ESB channel. In Figure 8-22, the partner system has an EDI translator linked to its JD Edwards application. Using a custom ESB service type that acts as an EDI gateway, EDI documents are placed onto a JMS queue to be transported securely and reliably through the ESB to headquarters.

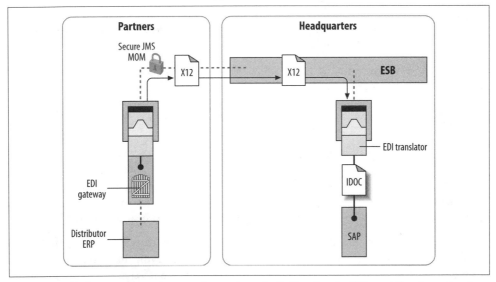

Figure 8-22. EDI messages are transported securely and reliably using the ESB, avoiding the cost and overhead of VAN

The EDI gateway at the partner site is a custom ESB file-drop service. This service knows how to read and write files to and from a filesystem directory that is shared by the file-drop service and the ERP system's EDI interface, as illustrated in Figure 8-23.

The JD Edwards application at the partner site doesn't need to know that it has just joined into an ESB infrastructure; it simply continues to interface with the EDI translator that it is linked to. The EDI translator, which has a filesystem interface built into it, doesn't need to know either. It simply reads and writes EDI messages from and to a filesystem directory. The ESB picks up the EDI message from the deposited file and places

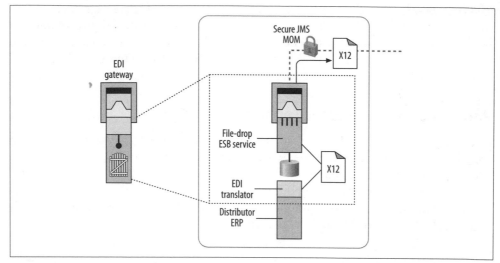

Figure 8-23. EDI gateway service is implemented as an ESB file-drop service that shares a filesystem directory with an ERP system's EDI interface

it on a reliable message queue to be delivered to one or more destinations within the manufacturer's headquarters.

Looking Ahead

With all of the connection options, data formats, and adapters into SAP, the manufacturer could benefit tremendously by adopting a generic data-exchange architecture, as described in Chapter 4. They are already partially there by having adopted xCBL as the data format for much of the data that travels through the bus. In some cases, such as the EDI interface, the data remains in the X12 format throughout its journey.

So far, we have examined two ways of exchanging data with partners (a remote ESB container and web services), two different formats for carrying information from the source to the destination (xCBL and X12), and three different ways of linking into SAP, all of which were done using a custom ESB service (SAP business connector, Castor/JCo/RFC connector, and Inovis TLE).

Since the ESB also supports a pure web services–based SOAP listener, they could have had a deployment that looks more like Figure 8-17 (the secure message broker in the DMZ). This has the clustered broker in the DMZ enabled as an HTTP direct listener, which speaks cross-cluster to another broker inside the firewall.

The interface to SAP and JD Edwards applications happened to use a combination of simple custom solutions, but it could have used a third-party adapter designed for a more general-purpose integration into those respective ERP systems.

This highlights one of the strong points of the ESB—the flexibility to connect and send data across the bus using the best means for the particular situation, instead of trying to build a one-size-fits-all solution. In addition, the manufacturer now has a set of generic approaches and ESB service types that can be mixed and matched to suit their needs.

Summary

In this chapter, we examined the following concepts:

- A MOM core is key to an ESB architecture, and provides the necessary underpinnings upon which to build a higher-level SOA. Reliable messaging and asynchronous processing are key components in a loosely coupled integration environment.

- XML and SOAP messaging can be an integral part of an ESB strategy. However, an ESB also allows the flexibility to carry other data formats such as EDI X12 messages.

- Flexibility in protocols, as an extension of the underlying MOM, is key to providing the necessary reach required to connect to applications in an adaptable and nonintrusive way.

- ESB containers provide flexibility and simplicity of integration at remote sites, and can also reduce the requirement of deploying an entire integration broker, or partner server, at partner sites.

- ESB containers can serve as application adapters that use simple approaches to address simple needs. ESB containers can also host third-party application adapters that are designed to provide a broader, more general-purpose integration into a particular packaged application.

9

Batch Transfer Latency

This chapter will examine the most common form of integration being done today: the practice of performing bulk data transfer and batch updating using Extract, Transform, and Load (ETL) techniques. We will discuss the business impact of the latency and reliability issues associated with this method of integration, and examine prescriptive steps for migrating toward real-time integration using an ESB in the context of a case study using pattern sketches.

Chapter 2 presented statistical data showing that enterprises aren't as integrated as you might think. Another stark reality is that most organizations don't have a good snapshot of their critical data at any given point in time. Amazon.com is well known for being completely automated, with instant access to all aspects of information in their supply chain, but this is the extreme exception to the norm.

Due to the latency of batch updates and rekeying information from "sneakernet" integration, and the margins of error associated with those common practices, there is always some latency between business events and the processing and recording of the associated data. In a supply chain, this can result in not knowing what's in inventory at any given time. The business impact from this method of integration can cause large amounts of business capital to be unnecessarily tied up.

ETL integration generally consists of a complex maze of applications, scripts, manual processes, and FTP file transfers. The process of an "overnight" batch transfer usually involves an application exporting its data to a common neutral format, such as an intermediary database or a flat file with some kind of delimiter to separate the data. The source representation is likely in a different format than the target; for example, the sending application may write all the data in plain text, and the receiver may expect the data in XML. The source data is run through a process to be transformed into the target format; the intermediary file is then transferred to another application using FTP, and imported into the other application using a merge-and-purge process (Figure 9-1).

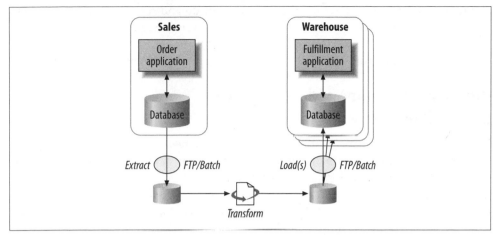

Figure 9-1. Extract, Transform, and Load is the most popular form of "integration"

Drawbacks of ETL

Although popular, this method of transferring data is also the most prone to problems. It is subject to these major drawbacks: unreliable transfer of data, lack of data validity, undesired downtime, and the overall latency of data gathering.

ETL Reliability and Data Validity

The process of merging and eliminating duplicate records is not an exact science. Checking for completeness and data integrity can be a manual process. If a file transfer fails, the process may just need to be restarted. If the file transfer succeeds, but the import fails, a lengthy reconciliation may need to occur to deal with a partial import.

In a global organization, not every country or region has reliable networking links. There may be slow dial-up lines, and WANs over satellite links that can be susceptible to connection problems as well. According to a CIO from a global manufacturing company that I recently interviewed, the solution to this problem often involves adding more IT staff.

If an "overnight" dump-and-load batch job takes several hours to complete, compensating for failures in this process can be even more costly in terms of time. The time needed to reconcile the resulting problems may even overlap the time when the next nightly batch transfer is set to begin. This can result in a bad situation that is difficult to recover from.

And there is a deeper, more fundamental problem, even when everything works as it's supposed to: the inherent latency of batch processing. In a global economy, there is no such thing as "overnight" anymore. Any business that has regional offices, business units, or remote storefronts can't really afford to just "power down" once a day in order to synchronize all of its data. The applications in question are ones that affect your ability to generate revenue, so any time they are not up and running could be costly to your organization. What's really needed is a move toward near real-time processing of information. As we will see in this chapter's case study, today's solutions often incur the overhead of missed business opportunities and unnecessary lockup of excess capital.

Undesired Downtime and the Logistics of Data Synchronization

In a case study of another global manufacturing company that is currently adopting an ESB, the entire end-to-end integration process along the supply chain was being done using batch file transfers. Some of the applications were able to do a complete dump-and-load replace of data within a two-hour window, but the application had to go offline in order for this to occur. In other companies, a complete dump and load wasn't possible; they required a more complicated merge-and-purge process, which usually took eight hours to complete. The application involved was too important to take down every day for eight hours, so they compromised by taking the application offline once a week for a merge-and-purge operation.

Overall Latency of Data Gathering

The biggest problem of ETL is that even when all systems are running smoothly and all exports and imports of data are happening successfully, there is still *at least* a 24-hour delay in getting access to real information. And this is the best-case scenario—as we have seen, the delay in getting data transferred and synchronized can take up to a week. This problem is often further magnified by the number of times the data is transferred between systems (Figure 9-2).

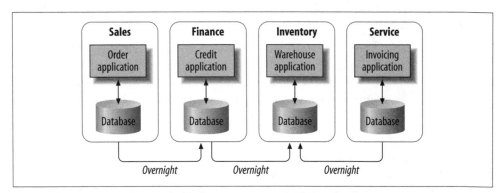

Figure 9-2. The latency of overnight batch processing is magnified across departments

With the latency of overnight batch processing, it's difficult to determine the real on-hand inventory, which could result in false backorder situations or overpromised delivery of goods. Companies have traditionally been forced to overbloat inventory (described in the next section) in order to compensate for not having an accurate snapshot of their supply line at any given moment in time.

To see how latency can hurt your business, let's walk through an example of a large-quantity order with a return, using a 24-hour delay as the latency period. Figure 9-3 shows the three applications involved in this process: Order Management, Inventory Management, and Shipping/Fulfillment Processing. Each night, the sales order, inventory, and customer service applications synchronize their data using an ETL process. As illustrated in the figure, the order management updates the master inventory application, and the shipping/fulfillment application also provides information about the goods returned, restocked, and reshipped (for replacement inventory). The consolidated data with a newly calculated on-hand inventory is then synchronized from the master inventory back to the order management and the shipping/fulfillment processing.

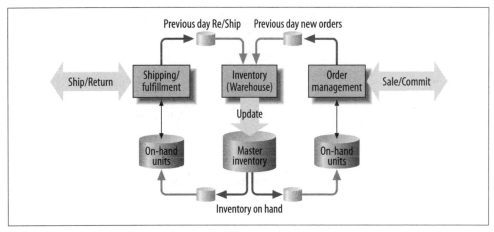

Figure 9-3. Nightly batch transfers of on-hand inventory data between applications

The manufacturing company has Service-Level Agreements (SLAs) in place with their buyers that specify that they must reply within 2 hours of receiving a request for an order. Let's say that on day 1, after a successful nightly batch transfer, Customer A orders 400K units, as illustrated in Figure 9-4. All applications are showing a consistent representation of 500K units in stock; therefore, the order is confirmed within the timeframe mandated by the SLA.

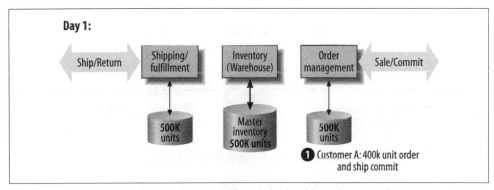

Figure 9-4. Latency due to overnight batch transfers can lead to false indications of inventory

On day 2, after another successful nightly batch transfer, all applications reflect the deducted inventory and show an on-hand supply of 100K units. As illustrated in Figure 9-5, Customer B now returns 300K units, replenishing the stock back to 400K, and Customer C places an order for 400K units. But because the on-hand inventory amount has not been updated, the sales order application thinks there are still only 100K units in inventory. Because the SLA requires that a firm commitment to deliver be issued within 2 hours, the order request can't be fulfilled, resulting in lost business.

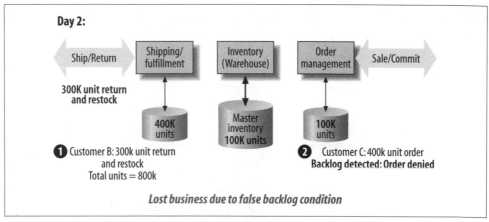

Figure 9-5. False backlog condition due to latency of batch transfer and update

Another variation on this problem is the violation of the SLA based on overpromising goods. As in the previous example, this too is based on not having a real-time snapshot of on-hand inventory. Again, we start out with a 500K supply of on-hand inventory, 400K of which is purchased by Customer A. At the same time, Customer B returns the 300K units because they were defective. The problem is that Customer B has an SLA specifying that the defective units must be replaced immediately. As illustrated in Figure 9-6, this condition results in an overpromise of 200K units over the available inventory.

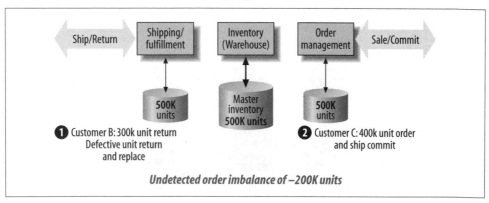

Figure 9-6. Negative inventory balance due to latency of batch transfer of data

The SLAs with both buyers also carry stiff fines when the orders cannot be fulfilled as promised. The buyer needs these kinds of SLAs because if it can't get its supplies, it places its own revenue-generating opportunities at risk. And the latency problems don't end there—in this case, the supplier doesn't even know that a problem has occurred until the next successful batch update!

The Typical Solution: Overbloat the Inventory

Losing out on revenue due to lost opportunities and dealing with SLA penalties for unfulfilled orders can be costly to any business. The common way to avoid these problems is to add an excess buffer of inventory at all times. This number will vary, but can be reasonably predicted based on the typical range of error that can be measured historically. For this example, let's assume that the supplier has determined that 500K units is a reasonable number to keep in excess supply. This solution works, but it can add dramatic costs to running the business. At $25 per unit * 500K units, that's $12.5 million in idle capital. And even at a low interest rate of 5%, it's a more than $52,000 per month carrying cost for that excess inventory, not to mention the costs of warehousing all this extra inventory while it sits idle and becomes obsolete. Of course, your individual mileage may vary depending on the size and nature of your business. In a manufacturing company the size of Philips, GE, or NCR, or a retail chain the size of Wal-Mart, overbloating the inventory can lead to millions of dollars in lost revenue per year.

Despite those drawbacks, this is the way most companies have handled the situation for years. The issue at hand is to understand how to reduce the margins for error, reduce excess inventory, and free up that cash. Industries such as manufacturing and retail work from such high volumes and low margins that even a small percentage of bloat or cost savings in the overall distribution chain can amount to millions of dollars in either direction.

Case Study: Migrating Toward Real-Time Integration

The accidental architecture has a certain technological brittleness that makes it difficult to migrate away from. This architectural brittleness also has organizational consequences. Making vast changes to the underlying integration infrastructure can be a daunting task.

Organizational and departmental coordination can be just as difficult to implement as any technological solutions. In an integration environment consisting of tightly coupled, point-to-point interfaces or time-dependent batch-transfer operations, getting all of the individual owners of the applications to agree upon and coordinate the changes required to move to a new integration infrastructure can be difficult and time consuming. And even if you can get the application owners in the same room and make them agree to all the details, the coordination of development schedules and deployment of upgrades to each individual application can be next to impossible.

An ESB allows you to migrate away from the accidental architecture incrementally, and in a fashion that fits the pace of each application's development group. In Chapter 4, we saw an example of how XML, CBR, and data transformation can provide a platform for independent migration. Here we will further explore how asynchronous communication and custom ESB service containers can provide a means for migrating away from the accidental architecture. We will do this by examining a case study of a company with a rather extreme accidental architecture.

VCR Corporation is a manufacturing company that relies exclusively on ETL for its end-to-end supply chain and logistics processing, and, predictably, suffers from all of the reliability, downtime, and overall latency problems just described. As illustrated in Figure 9-7, the Product Master application and the Master Product Index database are synchronized each night with the data across a number of its key applications, including Inventory, Shipping, Distribution Logistics, Supply Chain, CRM/SFA, Accounting/GL, and Order Management. Each night the data is gathered into the Product Master application and redistributed to all the other applications using an ETL process similar to the one described earlier.

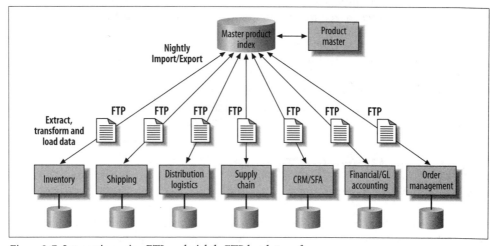

Figure 9-7. Integration using ETL and nightly FTP batch transfers

Once gathered into the Master Product Index, a database export is performed to produce a number of flat files. Through a series of scripts and programs, the data is transformed and filtered for each target application. The flat files are delivered to the application using an FTP file transfer. Figure 9-8 shows the pattern sketch for this part of the process. Often the data is transferred to the destination, and transformed and filtered there.

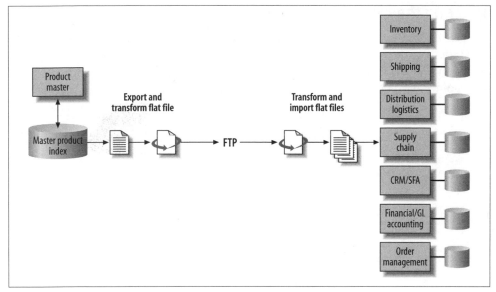

Figure 9-8. ETL using FTP file transfer

Migrating away from this scenario toward an integration using an ESB can provide the following benefits:

- Data sharing in real time.
- Broadcast of data to multiple targets using a publish/subscribe messaging model.
- Data skimming of messages to support new Business Activity Monitoring (BAM) applications.
- SOA that allows each application to be viewed through an abstract event-driven service endpoint and to be referenced by choreography and process modeling tools.
- Selective filtering of data using message channels and message filters. (This allows the routing of business data to be controlled by the ESB, instead of being hard-coded into each application or hand-coded into batch scripts.)
- Reliable delivery of data using asynchronous store-and-forward features inherent in the ESB (minimizing the need for lengthy reconciliation).
- Secured access using ACLs.
- Centralized management facilities: administrative configuration control over data channels and ACL security using a management tool instead of coding into applications and ETL scripts.

During the normal course of work, each application will be able to keep the Product Master and other interested applications up to date in real time by posting its data to the bus as updates occur, instead of waiting for a nightly batch operation. Each application will also be able to selectively receive data as it is posted to the bus by other applications.

Inserting the ESB

The process by which VCR Corp. can migrate away from its existing means of file-based integration and toward a real-time exchange of business data begins by putting an ESB in the place of the FTP file transfer (Figure 9-9). Services will read and write data at file drop points in order to mimic FTP behavior.

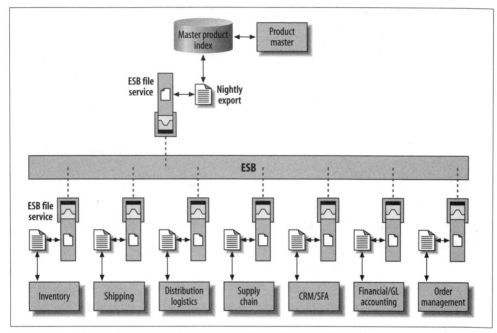

Figure 9-9. Replace FTP transfer with ESB message-based data transfer, preserving flat file interface

Figure 9-10 shows the pattern sketch of this process. The ESB acts as an intermediary that performs the nightly data transfer instead of using the FTP link. The nightly export from the Master Product Index database will still need to occur while in this intermediate migration phase. The data can be fed into the ESB by having an ESB file-drop service read from the flat file that was produced by the export. The flat file data is then transferred across the bus using reliable messaging to each of the other applications, and is deposited as flat files in their respective FTP destination directories.

At the receiving endpoints, another file service receives the message as an asynchronous event and writes the file onto disk in the FTP directory. The application is set up to poll a directory periodically to look for newly deposited files.

This provides the underpinnings for migrating toward a real-time exchange of live business data between all applications. So far, no changes have been required for any of the applications. The applications themselves are unaware that anything has changed, as they continue to read, write, and process the flat files the same way they always have.

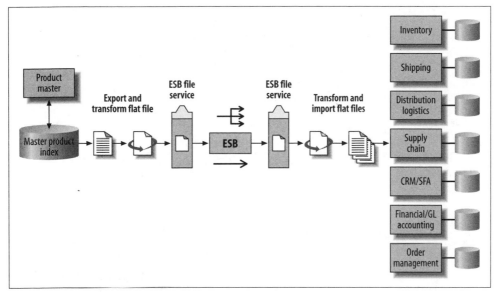

Figure 9-10. ESB file-drop service replaces FTP file transfer

There are also immediate benefits to making this change. It has removed one of the four main problems of the ETL solution: the unreliable FTP link. Now that the data is being transferred over message channels through the ESB, it is the responsibility of the ESB to get the data to where it needs to go, ensuring reliability and transactional integrity using the store-and-forward techniques discussed in Chapter 5.

Transforming and Routing the Data

In order to put the ESB to use, data channels, data transformations, and process flows need to be established.

Structured message channels

Once the ESB is inserted, you can start setting up structured data channels for each application. Not all of the applications need to see all of the data. In the pre-ESB stage, there may have been some data filtering during the export process via some SQL queries, or some filtering on the exported datafile via handwritten scripts. Now that the applications are plugged into the bus, data can be selectively dispatched through distinct routing paths to just the applications that need to see it. Initially, this can be done simply by routing the data over reliable publish-and-subscribe and point-to-point message channels (Figure 9-11).

Through the underlying MOM, the data can be broadcast to the other interested applications using a publish-and-subscribe messaging model. Using unique subscription

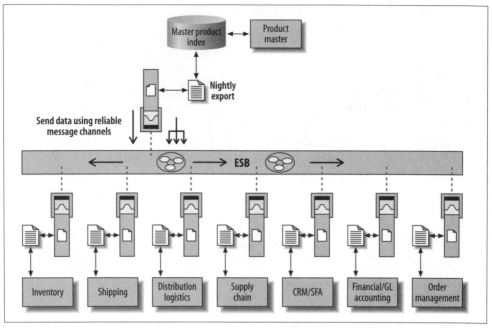

Figure 9-11. Dispatching of data using reliable messaging channels over pub/sub or point-to-point queues

channels and filtering via message selectors, data can be segregated and distributed so that each application receives only the data that it wants to see.

One of the many benefits of having a MOM as a core part of the ESB is that you can take advantage of the routing capabilities that are built into the messaging layer. A major advantage of using an ESB rather than just a message bus to do this is that the definitions of the publish-and-subscribe and point-to-point channels and the ACL security can all be configured in the ESB service using administrative tools, instead of being coded into the applications themselves.

Assigning process definitions

The next step in the migration toward real-time integration is to create specific ESB process definitions. This allows more selective control of business process flow across applications and services. As part of this step, the batch-scripted transformation and filtering is converted to use specialized ESB transformation services. Figure 9-12 shows the pattern sketch of this stage in the migration.

Considerations

As you migrate toward a real-time integration using an ESB, there are important things to consider regarding how you structure and transfer data.

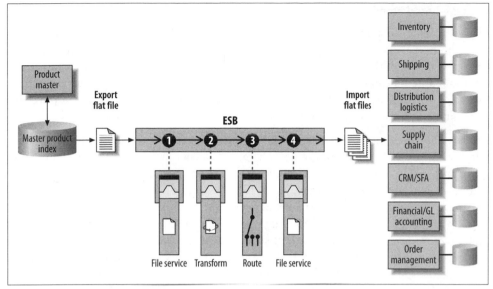

Figure 9-12. ESB process definition with transformation and routing as services on the bus

Streamlined data flow

As data exchange moves toward a near real-time occurrence, the way in which data is routed may change. In the batch processing model, data was overcommunicated. The Master Product Index needed to broadcast as much information as it possibly could in one shot because of the 24-hour interval between data exchanges. This forced a model in which data was disseminated more than it needed to be. With the introduction of the ESB, multiple applications can work on the same message data in an ordered process flow. Each application can process the message data as soon as it arrives, and pass it along to the next step in the process in a timely fashion. Therefore, it is not necessary to broadcast all information to all applications. A single message can carry the entire context of a particular business transaction, and it may travel from one place to the next along an ordered process flow.

As the FTP links are eventually removed and replaced with a more direct integration into the ESB container, the message itineraries and underlying message channels can be modified to meet the requirements of the new streamlined processing model.

Migrating to XML

Although not shown in these examples, part of the migration path can be the insertion of transformation services that convert the data from its current fixed format to structured XML data that is in a canonical form. This allows the benefits of common, reusable service definitions as described in Chapters 4 and 6.

Message-based atomicity

In an ESB-enabled application, data is posted directly from the application to the bus in the form of a message. The application can construct a fairly rich XML document that encompasses all of the known state information about the current business transaction. XML documents can be structured and hierarchical, and can therefore represent relationships and subcomponents that describe a business transaction, such as a purchase order and all its line items, its billing information, and so on.

An asynchronous message that represents a business transaction should be an atomic, self-contained, and self-describing unit of work. The data in the message should include any transient context information that is relevant to the current unit of work underway. This transient state can be carried with the message, or held by ESB-enabled state machines for as long as the transient state is relevant—which is the lifetime of the message or the lifetime of the business transaction. Once the business transaction is complete, you no longer need the transient state (except for audit trail purposes, but that's another story). In Chapters 6 and 7, we explored cases in which this transient state can be tracked as part of managing asynchronous conversation and choreography, and where XML messages themselves can be stored in their native form for tracking, auditing, and logging purposes.

Think asynch

As a general rule, moving toward message-based atomicity also requires asynchronous processing. The philosophy and merits of asynchronous processing are discussed in detail in Chapter 5. In short, message-style communications require an integration architect to "think asynch" and treat applications accordingly. The ramification of this is that when an application makes a request of another application, it should almost never expect to get an immediate response, if a response is even warranted. Asynchronous messages are intended to get to their destinations "eventually." In practice, the definition of "eventually" could be measured in nanoseconds, but the applications should be prepared for a more significant amount of time between the sending of a message from one application to the receipt of the message by another.

Because we are migrating away from a purely post-processing flat-file scenario, asynchrony is expected. The applications processing the data are already expecting to receive it sometime after a particular event has happened—sometimes up to a week later.

Achieving message-based atomicity requires you to think about how the data that is currently in the monolithic flat file can be broken up into individual records that represent atomic business transactions. Once this is achieved, the applications are ready to exchange data directly with each other in a real-time fashion. As the message exchange is more fully integrated into the applications, the messages can get smarter by carrying a more transient context that is known only by the application.

Removing the file interface

At any point along the way, you can begin replacing the file-drop service interface with a more direct interface into the applications using standard adapters that are ESB-enabled. As illustrated in Figure 9-13, the Product Master interface has been moved away from the database import/export process, and directly into the application using a JCA-compliant application adapter. Some of the other applications have been converted to use either adapters or a web service interface. ESB services for content-based routing, data transformation, auditing, and caching are inserted into the business processes.

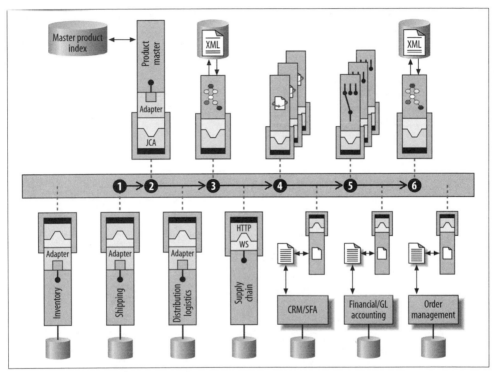

Figure 9-13. Full migration to an ESB using application adapters, process definitions, web service interfaces, and file-drop service interfaces

A few of the applications are still using the file-drop service interface; this is perfectly fine. The nice thing about this approach is that the migration can stop at any time and resume at a later date. At each stage in the migration, the integration environment continues to work and the overall process improves.

Summary

In this chapter, we learned the following:

- The latency due to nightly batch processing can be very costly to a business, both in capital expense and customer service terms.

- Batch processing does not really fit the needs of a company that needs to run 24/7 in a global economy.

- Refactoring to an ESB can provide a migration toward real-time data exchange, which removes the latency and reliability problems associated with ETL.

- An ESB can be adopted incrementally, in a nonintrusive fashion by using special file-drop services that mimic the interfaces of the previous batch processing solutions.

Java Components in an ESB

10

The ESB is a platform-neutral concept—theoretically, an ESB could be implemented without any Java involved. However, a good ESB should take advantage of Java components due to the widespread use of Java-based technology across many IT departments.

Although an ESB is not implemented on top of an application server, it does integrate with one very nicely. Chapter 11 illustrates a practical-use case of an ESB enabling asynchronous, loosely coupled integration with an application server in a portal environment. An ESB can draw from many of the individual technologies within the J2EE and J2SE family of specifications, such as JMS, JCA, EJB, JSP, JAAS, SAAJ, JSSE, JSP, JAXB, JAX-RPC, and JMX. However, they don't have to be used all together, all at the same time, at every installation of every component on the bus. There are a few individual Java specifications that warrant particular attention because they have a special impact on the operation of an ESB. This chapter will discuss the following specifications and their impact on making an ESB a more effective integration environment:

Java Business Integration (JBI)
> A specification being developed under the Java Community Process (JCP) that describes the way integration components, such as ESB services, can be plugged together in a vendor-neutral and portable fashion.

J2EE Connector Architecture (JCA)
> A specification that defines the use of a standard set of interface contracts for creating adapters to connect into, and interact with, enterprise applications.

Java Management eXtensions (JMX)
> A specification for remote management that defines the means by which an application can interface with a management infrastructure and management consoles. *Management* includes configuration data, commands for controlling lifecycle, and runtime alerts and event notifications for statistics gathering and health monitoring of remote applications and services.

Java Business Integration (JBI)

The Java Business Integration (JBI) initiative (a.k.a. JSR-208) is an effort within the JCP to define a specification describing the way integration components, such as ESB services, can be plugged together in a vendor-neutral and portable fashion. Members of the JBI Expert Group (EG) include BEA, Borland, CGE&Y, Collaxa, IBM, IOPSIS, Intalio, Nokia, Novell, Oak Grove Systems, Oracle, RIM, SAP, SeeBeyond, Sonic Software, Sun Microsystems, Sybase, TIBCO, Tmax, Vignette, and WebMethods.

JBI is considered an "enterprise" capability. However, the goal of the JBI EG is to not require the entire J2EE application server stack. JBI is primarily geared toward allowing vendors, whether application server based or not, to be able to plug together integration-enabling components in a portable and interoperable fashion. While JBI does not preclude the use of a J2EE server, a primary goal of JBI is to allow for a much broader adoption beyond the handful of J2EE application server vendors. The objective is to foster an ecosystem where any vendor with something to offer in the way of integration components and infrastructure may provide a JBI-compliant infrastructure, or plug their wares into one.

Figure 10-1 shows the high-level view of what JBI defines. The JBI model consists of a JBI container, which houses JBI Service Engines (SEs), which in turn hold services.

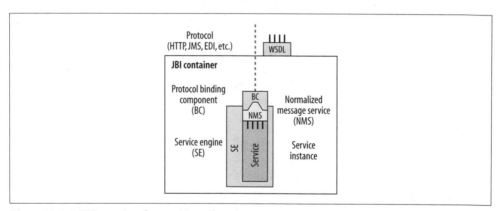

Figure 10-1. A JBI container houses SEs and services

A JBI container provides protocol independence through the use of a Binding Component (BC) and a Normalized Message Service (NMS). The binding component is responsible for interfacing with an external protocol. Binding components are custom-built for each protocol and are pluggable into the JBI container. This allows any JBI component to communicate over any protocol or transport (SOAP, JMS, EDI, etc.) simply by plugging in the appropriate binding component. The responsibility of the binding component is to consume and produce the protocol-specific message data and hand it off to the NMS to be "normalized" for consumption by the SE.

The NMS provides a common Service Provider Interface (SPI) for all services and SEs to write to. The NMS does not attempt to define the format of the message payload. Instead it focuses on sending and receiving messages, and providing a means of transferring and propagating transactional context and security context between the protocol and the SE.

A JBI container may house multiple SEs, as illustrated in Figure 10-2. In an intracontainer environment, SEs communicate using the NMS and go through a BC, which simply acts as a pass-through or *reflector*. No message normalization is required and no protocol conversion or serialization is to be performed because each side of the BC conversation deals with an already-normalized message. As illustrated in Figure 10-2, all SEs are described using WSDL.

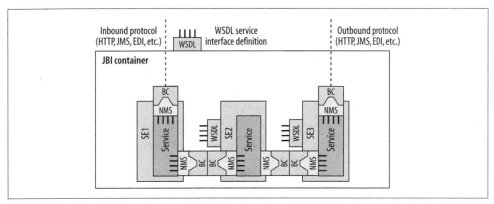

Figure 10-2. A JBI container houses multiple SEs

JBI as an ESB Container

JBI provides a means for integration services to be hosted in a managed environment that allows pluggable SEs from third-party vendors to interoperate with each other in a portable fashion. These SEs and their respective services can be anything that facilitates integration and process management. For example, an SE could be an XSLT-based transformation engine, a CBR service, or an orchestration engine based on WS-BPEL. These services could be provided by three different vendors, and still be able to work together in the same managed environment. The BCs may be provided by different vendors as well. For example, a JMS vendor could provide its own JMS BC for hooking into its messaging layer, and an ESB vendor could provide a JBI container, as illustrated in Figure 10-3. The same ESB vendor could also provide a BC for JMS, SOAP, FTP, and a variety of other transports. Figure 10-4 shows the JBI ESB container plugged into the ESB.

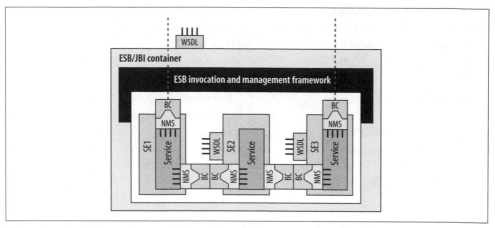

Figure 10-3. An ESB container as a JBI container

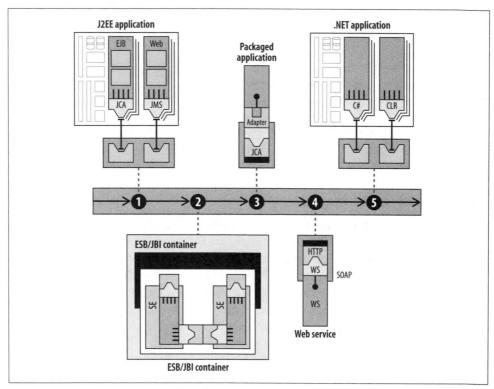

Figure 10-4. An ESB/JBI container plugged into an ESB

The adoption of JBI will help to foster and accelerate an ecosystem around pluggable, interoperable integration components. This will allow further industry momentum to build around a model of third-party services that can easily plug into an ESB environment.

JBI and Other Java Specifications

While JBI does not require a full J2EE stack, it does take advantage of as many of the components as possible. Individual specifications from the J2EE stack, such as Java Transaction API (JTA), JMS, JAAS for security, and JAXB for data binding between Java and XML, will be referenced within the JBI work.

Another JSR that is relevant to JBI is JAX-RPC 2.0. Historically, JAX-RPC has focused on the client server view interaction model within an SOA, where JBI focuses on how an integration component can be plugged into an integration framework as an event-driven service. The JAX-RPC 2.0 Expert Group is in the process of defining an asynchronous callback API in order to migrate the interaction model away from a purely client-server view toward more of an event-driven service model. The API is similar to work that began in the Apache Axis project in 2002. Because of the overlap between the team of people who did the proposal in Axis and the JAX-RPC Expert Group, those of us involved in the Axis project decided to defer the Axis work and wait for it to become standardized first through the JCP.

The JBI and JAX-RPC groups have decided to codevelop a common specification for the areas that overlap between the two technologies, such as asynchronous invocations and invocation handlers for passing transaction context and security context through their respective frameworks.

The J2EE Connector Architecture (JCA)

The J2EE Connector Architecture, otherwise known as JCA or J2CA, has become a popular means of connecting legacy applications to a Java environment using a standard set of contracts. JCA simplifies integration by providing the container contract between an application server or middleware integration broker to an application adapter, and between the application adapter and an application. A vendor-supplied or third-party application adapter that is JCA-compliant can simply plug into this container. JCA was designed to be implemented in an application server container, but can also be implemented in an ESB container.

JCA is to applications what JDBC is to database connectivity. It provides connection management and connection pooling, transaction control, propagation of security context, and a worker thread management and delegation model. A birds-eye view of the JCA architecture, shown in Figure 10-5, reveals the following components:

- A JCA container, which is intended to house a JCA Resource Adapter (RA). The container manages the contracts for thread pooling, connection pooling, and the propagation of transaction and security context.

- A Resource Adapter (RA), which is the component that interfaces with the application and implements the application-specific behavior for connection management, security, and transactional resources. This portion of the JCA is allowed to be proprietary on a per-adapter-type basis.

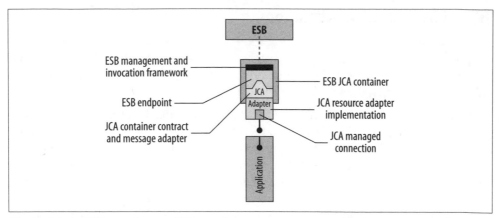

Figure 10-5. An ESB container as a JCA container

An ESB that supports a JCA container allows applications to be plugged into an ESB using a standard set of off-the-shelf adapters. These adapters can be made available from the application vendors themselves, such as SAP, or from vendors who specialize in providing adapters, such as iWay and DataDirect.

Domain Expertise

JCA automates the connectivity task of plugging adapters into middleware infrastructure by providing a standard set of contracts for plugging an application adapter into a managed container environment. This allows deployment and configuration tools to have a uniform approach toward integrating applications. However, it does not preclude the need for expertise on the inner workings of the applications themselves. Consider the JDBC and database analogy. When connecting to a database, JDBC simplifies and standardizes things such as connection pooling, transaction management, and security management. This does not eliminate the need for a database administrator who knows the intimate details of the tables and inner workings of the database. The same is true for JCA adapters. While JCA can automate some of the details of connectivity, application expertise is still required to achieve a successful integration; for example, you still need to know the impact of invoking the interfaces that an application exposes.

ESB to Application Server Connectivity

Beyond specialized application adapters, JCA can also be used to generically connect a JMS interface into an application server. JCA allows multiple application servers from different vendors to plug into a common JMS layer. Figure 10-6 shows two ways that an application server can connect into an ESB endpoint using JMS. The application server uses the JMS client API coded directly into an instance of a servlet, portlet, or Stateless Session Bean (SSB). The application server's EJB container may configure a Message-Driven Bean (MDB) to interface with the JMS topic or queue channel directly, without any special coding.

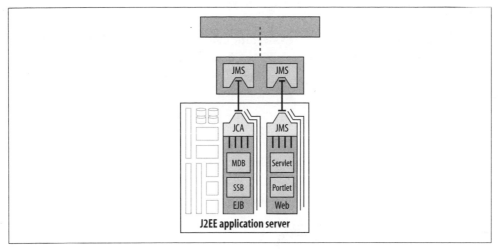

Figure 10-6. An application server can interface with messaging using either direct JMS APIs, or through a JCA 1.5 connection

 NOTE JCA is considered a "slang" acronym for the J2EE Connector Architecture. Chronologically, "Java Cryptography API" came first, and officially
owns the acronym of "JCA." However, early adopters of the J2EE Connector Architecture also used the acronym "JCA," and the usage has
stuck. This book uses JCA and J2CA interchangeably to refer to the J2EE
Connector Architecture.

Java Management eXtensions (JMX)

Java Management eXtensions (JMX) is a technology aimed at management and monitoring using the Java platform. JMX provides standard interfaces for connecting an
application with a management infrastructure and management consoles. The JMX
specification defines an architecture, programming design patterns, APIs, and a standard set of monitoring services.

JMX facilitates the integration of a management infrastructure with popular management consoles, such as IBM Tivoli, HP OpenView, and Computer Associates Unicenter.
JMX has been officially included as part of the J2SE 1.5 platform, and most Java middleware providers now expose JMX-based management facilities.

JMX can be used to easily instrument any resource in a scalable fashion. Resources may
expose configuration and runtime attributes, operations, and notifications. JMX
provides APIs to dynamically query a resource's management APIs, access attribute values, invoke operations (such as start, execute, monitor, configure, operate, and stop),
and subscribe to management notifications. This section will explore how a JMX-based
management infrastructure can manage a highly distributed SOA in an ESB
architecture.

A JMX Primer

From a high-level view, the JMX architecture consists of the following components, (illustrated in Figure 10-7):

- JMX Server, which is a Managed Bean (MBean) server that contains MBean services
- JMX clients
- Protocol adapters and connectors
- JMX connector interface
- Managed Beans (MBeans), which serve as the interface for managed resources (applications)

These components are described in the following sections.

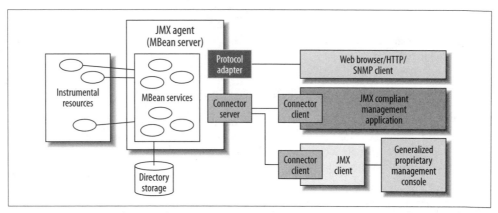

Figure 10-7. Overview of JMX architecture

JMX server environment

A management server, also known as an MBean server, provides a registry for MBean resources and MBean services. An MBean resource is a Java class that represents a resource to be managed or monitored. MBeans support interfaces that allow for instrumentation of a managed resource such that it can be enabled for receiving commands from and sending notifications to an MBean server.

JMX client protocol adapters

A JMX client is an application that controls JMX management servers by submitting requests, activating new services, and receiving notifications. JMX relies on protocol adapters and connectors to make the MBean server remotely accessible from outside the server's JVM. A protocol adapter exposes a protocol directly to a client. For example, an HTML adapter exposes an interface to a web browser using the HTTP protocol. An SNMP adapter exposes SNMP directly to management consoles that support it.

JMX connector interface

A JMX server may also be remoted using a *connector** interface. The MBean server exposes an MBean's management interface across the connector. It does not expose the MBean's object reference directly; rather, a JMX client can dynamically interrogate the management interface that an MBean exposes. The management interface, management requests, and notifications are sent across the connector between the client interface and the MBean implementation on the server.

The client side of the connector may be a specialized management console that was written from the ground up with JMX in mind, or it may be a client that acts as a proxy for JMX interfaces and uses some other proprietary means for communicating with a general-purpose management console. A connector implementation may use protocols such as RMI, IIOP, or HTTP. In the next section, "JMX Management in an ESB Architecture," we will explore how an ESB may use messaging as a transport for JMX management communications.

An MBean server containing MBean services, a set of MBeans that represent managed resources, and one or more protocol adapters or JMX connectors are collectively referred as a *JMX agent* or *JMX container*.

JMX MBean interfaces

An MBean interface contains metadata that describes the following:

Attributes
   Attributes include state information about the resource being managed. In an ESB environment this can include the following:

   - Attributes that indicate whether a remote service is in a ready state, or has been shut down or temporarily halted

   - Counts, such as the number of messages pending in a queue, or the number of active service instances in a service container

   - Settings, such that a remote JMX client can have a set of names and values that it can manipulate through operations

Operations
   Operations can include actions, or commands that can be executed on managed resources. In an ESB environment, these types of actions can be performed as commands issued to a remote service through its service container. This can include lifecycle commands such as shutdown, restart, suspend, and resume, and may also include commands to components of the ESB, such as telling a message queue manager to clear a specified set of undelivered messages from its queue.

---

* The use of the term "connector" in JMX parlance is not to be confused with a JCA "connector."

Notifications

JMX defines a notification model, with senders that broadcast notifications and listeners that receive notifications. Through the connector interface, notifications emitted by the MBean are propagated to JMX clients that have registered interest on such notifications by providing a notification listener callback object. Notifications can be generated either by managed resources or by the JMX-specified *monitor MBeans* that can be used to monitor an attribute value. Examples of notifications in an ESB environment include:

- Alerts based on certain thresholds being reached, such as the size of a message queue approaching its maximum specified size limit
- Connections into the ESB being established or dropped
- Message delivery timeout and subsequent routing to a dead message queue

JMX Management in an ESB Architecture

Most JMX implementations assume a client-server model where JMX connectors use RPC protocols such as RMI, IIOP, and HTTP to connect JMX agents with JMX clients. In an ESB architecture, the JMX connectors can be implemented using the ESB messaging layer, as illustrated in Figure 10-8.

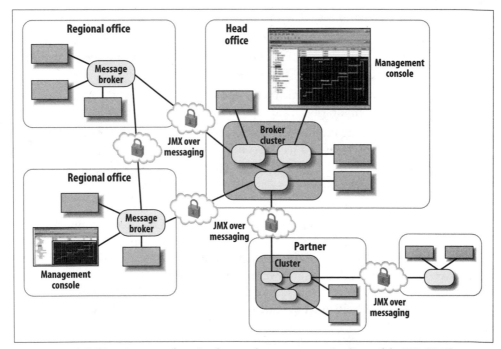

Figure 10-8. A JMX management layer implemented across a messaging layer of the ESB (JMS)

Figure 10-8 shows the underlying messaging topology of an ESB MOM core being used to link a corporate headquarters (the Head Office) with multiple regional offices and a business partner. Note that JMX management communications can be carried across the same secure messaging topology that is being used for the business-level communications. There are several advantages of using this approach over other protocols such as RMI or HTTP:

Messaging. Using JMS messaging, a management console may asynchronously push commands or configuration settings to multiple remote JMX agents.

Reliability. Management communications can enjoy all the benefits of asynchronous reliable messaging. For example, using reliable messaging and durable subscriptions, remote JMX agents may receive instructions even if the agent is temporarily unavailable.

Fault tolerance. If the message broker infrastructure supports fault-tolerant clusters with failover capabilities, the JMX communication can take advantage of that. If a message broker goes down for any reason, a backup broker can take over with no negative impact on the transfer of management data.

Centralized configuration. The MOM can be used to remote the configuration store (directory service) so that each JMX container does not need its own fully replicated directory service.

Firewall security. The deployment topology in Figure 10-8 shows that the only communication link that needs to be opened in the firewalls between the headquarters and other locations is the single link between the message brokers. The alternative (using a point-to-point protocol such as RMI) would likely require an unmanageable number of holes in the firewalls.

Authorization and secure access. The management console can gain access to all of the remotely managed agents, given that the proper security credentials are in place. In Figure 10-8, the management console at headquarters has authorized access to all of the remotely accessible nodes in the regional offices and the partner site. The management console at the remote partner site could intentionally be restricted to only have access to the local agents at that site.

Minimize network configuration. If you are going to set up a messaging infrastructure like this anyway, why maintain a parallel RMI infrastructure just for the management layer?

Of course, this approach of using JMX across a messaging infrastructure works effectively only if the ESB MOM core supports a fully connected distributed topology that is capable of linking remote messaging domains in such a fashion.

JMX-Managed Components in an ESB

In an ESB architecture, individual components of an ESB can be managed by a JMX agent. Figure 10-9 shows message brokers and ESB containers being managed by JMX agents that are using a JMS connector to communicate with each other. One of the message brokers is acting as a domain manager, which manages all of the other JMX agents that are within a designated realm of control. It serves as a domain manager because it has direct control and access to a directory service that holds all of the configuration information for the entire ESB segment.

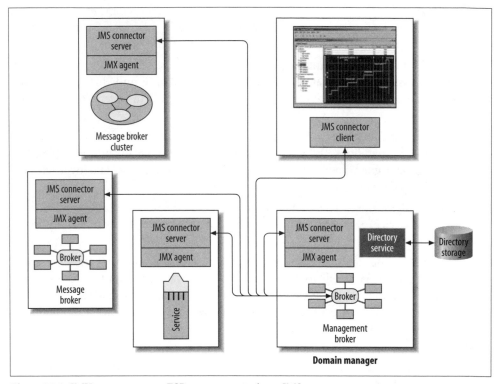

Figure 10-9. JMX agents manage ESB components using a JMS connector

Examples of configuration information that can be remotely managed include:

- Endpoint definitions for service interfaces, described using WSDL.

- Message channels, which have many characteristics to be configured. For example, the channel name; whether the channel is designated for publish-and-subscribe or point-to-point queuing; and message queue tuning capabilities such as a setting that specifies how much a message queue can hold in memory before it starts flushing its message to disk.

- Configurable settings for an ESB service, such as those discussed in Chapter 6. XSLT stylesheets, JavaScript helper functions, JAR files, process itineraries, WS-BPEL scripts, XQuery scripts, and CBR rules can all be specified using the management layer, and propagated out to remote service containers.

- Security information, such as allowable security credentials for access to endpoints. ACLs and QoP settings on individual message channels can be also remotely managed by the management layer.

Directory Cache

In a centralized hub-and-spoke EAI broker, there is an intrinsic advantage to centralized configuration in that all of the configuration information can be managed in a single place. However, such an architecture creates a single point of failure. In an ESB architecture, a directory service can push its content out to remote containers that maintain their own local caches of configuration information, as illustrated in Figure 10-10.

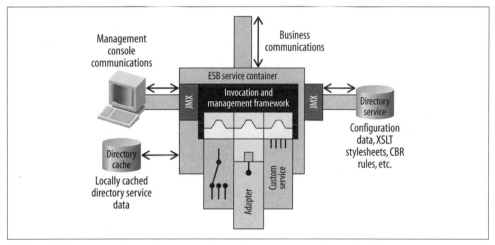

Figure 10-10. The ESB-managed component maintains a local directory service cache, thus eliminating the single point of failure

Any ESB-managed entity, such as a service container or message broker, can have its own local directory service cache. In Figure 10-10, the directory service and the management console are located elsewhere on the bus, and the directory cache is colocated with the ESB service container. As new information is updated in the directory service, it can be proactively pushed out to the remote directory service caches. This prevents the directory service from being a single point of failure. If the directory service becomes unavailable for any reason, the ESB service container can continue to function using its locally cached information.

Template-Based Remote Configuration Replication

Remotely managed ESB entities often have much in common with each other. For example, in the video-store scenario mentioned in Chapter 1, each of the remote stores has its own local messaging traffic and its own local service containers for integrating with the local point-of-sale kiosks. A common configuration template can be created for each store that describes the integration characteristics that all remote stores have, such as the local messaging channel definitions and the routing information that controls how messages flow between applications within a store and back to headquarters. Using a single management console interface, a configuration template can be created once and then subclassed for each location prior to being pushed out to all of the remote stores. This local configuration can be done by IT staff at headquarters through a remote management console.

If any change needs to be made to the shared configuration, it needs to be done only once by changing the configuration template, and the changes can then be made immediately available to all of the remote stores without disrupting the local configurations. This can potentially affect hundreds or even thousands of remotely managed ESB containers and message brokers. If the underpinnings of the management infrastructure are based on a message channel infrastructure, large-scale changes can be propagated efficiently. These changes would have been impractical or impossible if each site was connected to explicitly in a 1-to-1 fashion.

Summary

In this chapter, we learned the following:

- Although an ESB does not require a J2EE application server for its implementation, it can make extensive use of individual technologies from J2EE and J2SE.
- The JBI effort will provide a specification for plugging integration components into an interoperable integration environment. This will allow JBI-compliant integration components to be plugged into an ESB infrastructure as services.
- The JCA defines a standard set of interface contracts for creating adapters to connect into and interact with enterprise applications. An ESB can use JCA as a common way of plugging into application adapters through an adapter service type.
- JMX provides a means by which an application can interface with a management infrastructure and management consoles. In an ESB, a JMX-based management infrastructure can manage remote services and remote configurations from anyplace that is accessible by the bus.

ESB Integration Patterns and Recurring Design Solutions

11

This chapter will examine some common uses of an ESB in integration scenarios. The ESB concept already has a number of uses that solve some very common and challenging integration problems. While this is not an exhaustive list of all the integration patterns that are in use today, it should be enough to give you an idea of how an ESB can be used in real integration scenarios. For more information on integration patterns using an ESB, please visit this book's web page on the O'Reilly site, *http://www.oreilly.com/catalog/esb*.

In this chapter we will examine the following integration patterns:

- VETO and VETRO, which are commonly used ESB patterns that use message itineraries to perform Validate, Enrich, Transform, (Route,) and Operate functions.

- Two-step XRef transformation, which is a commonly used pattern for data transformation using a data cross-reference pattern. This pattern includes a two-step process for transformation: one step that uses XSLT transformation for structure and form, and another that uses a database lookup to translate the content.

- Flexible and scalable integration between an enterprise portal and a number of backend systems.

- An enterprise portal caching system using a "cache-forward" integration pattern.

- Federated query, which is a distributed data retrieval pattern using an ESB to query multiple backend applications and data sources across an enterprise.

The Preface describes this book's use of the pattern form to describe ESB integration patterns, along with an explanation of the diagramming techniques used to illustrate the pattern sketches.

The owner of an application can rely on the ESB to provide a uniform, consistent approach to sending and receiving data. An application plugs into the bus; it posts data to the bus; it is the responsibility of the bus to get the data where it needs to be, in the target data format that it needs to be in. An ESB separates the business process routing logic from the implementation of the applications that are being integrated. This shields the application owner from having to worry about things such as the routing of messages and the validation of data.

Messages can arrive into a business process from a variety of sources and in a variety of data formats. How does the ESB ensure that messages are validated and normalized so that they are in a usable format for each target system?

As we have seen throughout this book, a message itinerary can be a very powerful and flexible tool for intercepting the path of a message and performing operations on it, thus adding value to the integration environment. Through configuration and management tools, additional processing steps can be inserted as event-driven services into an XML processing pipeline.

The VETO Pattern

VETO is a common integration pattern that stands for Validate, Enrich, Transform, Operate (Figure 11-1). The VETO pattern and its variations can ensure that consistent, validated data will be routed throughout the ESB.

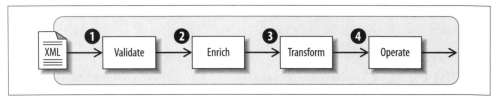

Figure 11-1. The VETO pattern

Validate

> The Validate step is usually the first part of any ESB process and can be accomplished in a number of ways. It's important that this step happen independently if possible; this removes the burden of validation from all of the downstream service implementations and promotes reuse. Building validation directly into the first service of a process makes it difficult to insert an additional service in front of it without requiring that the new service also provide its own validation.

> The simplest form of validation is to verify that an incoming message contains a well-formed XML document and conforms to a particular schema or WSDL document that describes the message. This requires that the service use a validating parser and always have available the up-to-date XML schema for a particular message type. The schema and WSDL can be kept in the directory service and managed remotely by the management infrastructure of the ESB. A service may also have scripting associated with it. For example, in Chapter 7, scripting was used to call the isPO( ) helper function that was made available to the service through its configuration (Figure 11-2).

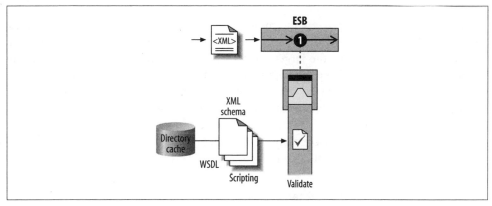

Figure 11-2. XML schema, WSDL, and validation scripts can be made available to a service through configuration

If the target data is not in XML format or if there is no schema or WSDL available, then a custom service can be used to validate the incoming message.

Enrich

The Enrich step involves adding additional data to a message to make it more meaningful and useful to a target service or application. As you recall from the PostalCode example in Chapter 4, the Enrich step was used to put the serviceLevel="overnight" attribute on the PostalCode element, and to put the new data structure with the additional digits beneath the PostalCode data element. The Enrich service could be implemented to invoke another service to look up additional data, or it could access a database to get what it needs (Figure 11-3).

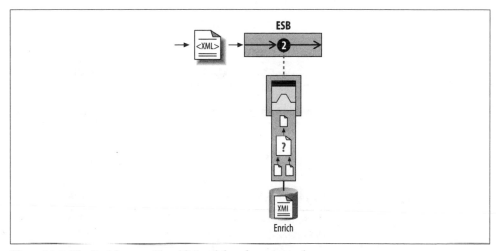

Figure 11-3. The Enrich step adds additional data from external sources

Transform

> The Transform step converts the message to a target format. This often involves converting the data structure to an internal canonical format, or converting from the canonical format to the target format of the Operate step. The target system may have its own built-in validation rules requiring that the transformation step modify the incoming data in order to prevent the target system from rejecting the message. In this sense, the transformation step is also providing prevalidation protection in a separate service that can be separately managed. While this may mean redundant logic in the short term, it provides more flexibility in the long term because it allows the Operate step to focus on business logic.

Operate

> The Operate step invokes the target service or interacts in some way with the target application. If the operation is a service that is written to conform to the agreed-upon canonical data format, the transformation converts from the incoming format to the canonical format, if it isn't already in that format. If the target operation is an enterprise application that requires its own data format, then the transformation step converts the message to the target format required by the application.

The VETO concept is profoundly simple, and is at the heart of what an integration architect does regularly with an ESB. An ESB provides an event-driven SOA to applications in an integration fabric. Regardless of the process routing and orchestration method being used—itineraries, sophisticated process modeling using an orchestration service, or the XML pipelining model discussed in Chapter 7—it is the VETO pattern and its variations that provide the overall value and flexibility to the integration fabric. The stages of the VETO pattern can be implemented as separate services that can be configured, reused, and independently swapped out for alternate implementations (Figure 11-4).

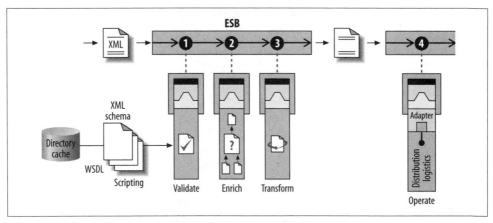

Figure 11-4. The VETO pattern as independent services

Variations: The VETRO Pattern

The VETO pattern has many variations. One such variation is the VETRO pattern, which includes a Route step such as a CBR service (Figure 11-5).

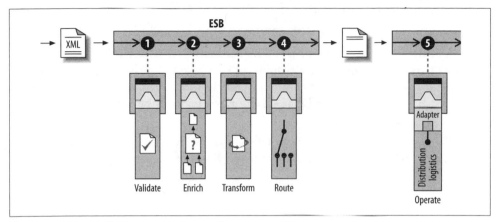

Figure 11-5. The VETRO pattern includes a Route step, such as a content-based router

In some cases the validate, enrich, and transform steps can be accomplished in one service implementation. The CBR service discussed in Chapter 7 used the script-based validation directly in the service itself instead of using a separate service. In many cases, this is not advised because it does not promote loose coupling and service reuse, and does not allow the validation to be separately defined and managed. However, it may sometimes be convenient, particularly if the context of validation can't easily be applied to other uses.

The Two-Step XRef Pattern

There may be times when integrating data across disparate systems requires structure-level as well as content-level transformations. For situations that require content-level transformations, where external data caches or relational database systems contain the necessary replacement data, a cross-reference lookup function is required to extract the appropriate data from the external source and use it to replace or enrich the document with its results. These high-level requirements can be satisfied by a single monolithic transformation service or by constructing two loosely coupled, autonomous services. The latter approach, which is better suited for service-oriented architectures, will be explored in this section.

In a typical transformation, XSLT and XPath are essential ingredients in XML-to-XML transformations, where the underlying engine parses and transforms the structure of a source XML document to that of the target. XSLT also provides prefabricated functions to manipulate strings and numeric values (e.g., Substring, Concat, and Sum) as well as offering the ability to write XSLT extensions that can then be used as part of an XSLT transformation. One particular extension can contain JDBC and SQL logic to access external stores such as an Oracle database (Figure 11-6). These are executed at runtime to perform lookup and replacement functions to satisfy content-level transformations. Although this design will work in most situations, it simply will not scale in midsized to large projects for several reasons:

- The XSLT is tightly coupled with JDBC, hindering reusability.

- XSLT extensions are processed as external callouts from a data-driven, callback-oriented parser. This can create a scoping and initialization problem, which makes it difficult to take advantage of common JDBC features, such as connection pooling, and to be able to create reusable service types that can be supplied with configurable runtime parameters.

- XSLT extensions can be difficult to debug and test, requiring redeployment of new classes and JAR files when changes are made. XSL alone is more dynamic.

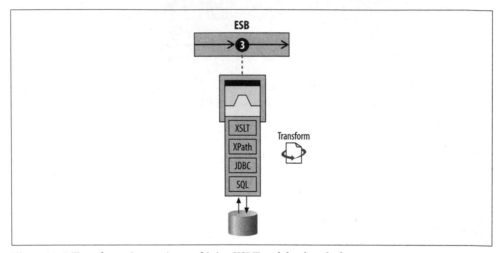

Figure 11-6. Transformation service combining XSLT and database lookup

Contrast this all-in-one approach to writing a composite process that consists of two autonomous services (Figure 11-7). This can be designed and developed to satisfy the requirements in a much more elegant fashion—one that fits nicely into an SOA model for mid- to large-scale projects.

The "Service Reusability" section of Chapter 7 explains the concept of reusable service types that can be instantiated with different configuration options. In this case, we have separated out the tightly coupled transformation service into two steps to separately address the problems of structure-level transformation and content-level transformation. Therefore, we can create two abstract service types that can expose configuration and runtime parameters that give each instance of the newly refactored services a unique identity. By breaking the solution out into two autonomous services, we can rapidly derive new instances of each service type. This promotes service reusability to

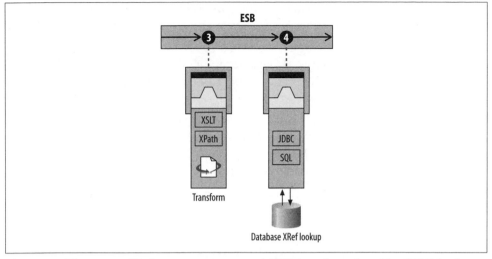

Figure 11-7. The two-step XRef pattern separates generic XSLT transformation with a JDBC database XRef lookup service

cost-effectively solve other business problems that follow the same use case and require structure- and content-level transformation using similar techniques.

Using this approach, even the database XRef service can be written once as a custom service type, and then customized with unique SQL statements as configuration parameters, as illustrated in Figure 11-8. Configuration parameters related to the database connection such the database name, JDBC driver information, username, and password can be configured. Configuration parameters that are supplied to the service instance are used to build, execute, and handle the returning result set.

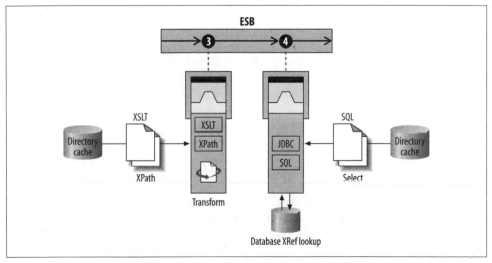

Figure 11-8. XSLT, XPath, and SQL statements are supplied to the service instance as configuration parameters

By decoupling both XSLT and JDBC/SQL operations into their own service and using an ESB process to tie them together, we now have a more strategic and scalable solution compared to the previous approach. This provides us with the following benefits:

A higher degree of code reusability. A generic XSLT transformation service can be applied to other use cases. A generic database lookup service can be applied in non-transformation contexts as well.

Accelerated development time. This approach allows concurrent development of service types, simplifies debugging and testing, and provides better isolation overall.

Faster database access. The database access service can exploit JDBC 2.0 in order to leverage connection pooling for faster database access.

Loose coupling. Problems that occur at the data access level do not affect XSLT operations.

Portal Server Integration Patterns

A *portal application* is normally used to pull data from multiple backend sources and represent it in a unified view via a web browser. The means for gathering the data from backend applications and databases into a portal environment is typically based on application servers and synchronous RPC-style communications. Like the ESB itself, this pattern arose out of necessity, based on the work of IT architects looking to solve problems they encountered with existing portal server infrastructures. Some organizations that started out using the typical portal server approach soon realized that it wouldn't scale to suit their long-term needs, and looked for an alternate architecture. They discovered that having an ESB as an integration strategy behind the portal server provides the ideal mediation between the portal server and the disparate backend data sources. This case study will explain the reasons why a default portal server architecture can break down or become unwieldy as the number of backend systems increases, and the span of time to fulfill the requests increases.

The ESB can act as a reliable buffering mechanism between the portal application and the backend systems. Through asynchronous communication, reliable delivery, and correlation, an ESB can improve the overall success rate of inquiries, improve throughput and responsiveness, and reduce errors. In addition, an ESB can provide a much more flexible backend integration layer than what can be provided by the portal server alone. Backend applications can use a variety of connectivity choices to plug into the bus and immediately begin to participate in an event-driven SOA with other applications and shared integration services.

The ESB architecture accommodates change. As new sources of information are brought into the realm of what the portal can access, an ESB allows these new sources to plug into the SOA and immediately start participating in the data sharing network simply by administratively configuring the new service to join into business processes.

Standards such as the JSR-168 "Portlet" specification and the OASIS Web Services for Remote Portlets (WS-RP) specification can help provide an API and a model for portal developers to build *portlets*, which are components that populate and render portions of a web page in a portal. The portlet can plug into the ESB and have a single interface to the entire backend system. This allows the portlet to rely on the ESB to normalize the data from all backend sources and feed it into the portlet. As data sources change over time, the portlet code can remain the same.

Because an ESB is very XML-aware, it can provide a much simpler interface from the perspective of the portal application. The ESB can perform much of the aggregation and semantic mediation instead of delegating it to the presentation layer or portal server. If the ESB is used to deliver all of the data to the portal server, the developer of the portlet consumer can simply focus on reformatting XML using XSL stylesheets rather than handling each data source as a unique format.

This section will explore the general advantages of using an ESB in a portal server environment. Later, two specific design patterns will be explored:

Forward Cache
    The ability to move data from distributed systems close to the presentation tier for low-latency, read-only access to the data.

Federated Query
    The ability to efficiently query multiple systems and aggregate the responses asynchronously at the presentation tier.

These patterns are explained in the context of a portal server integration scenario. However, they are generic enough to be used in other scenarios as well.

The Portal Server Deployment Architecture

Figure 11-9 shows a typical deployment model for a portal without an ESB. The portal provides a unified view of data that may originate from a variety of sources: for example, databases, applications, and other portals. These data sources can be deployed across multiple physically separate locations and can be based on a variety of platforms and technologies, including C, C++, J2EE, and .NET (or .NET predecessors).

The portal server provides the presentation logic for the users of the portal who use web browsers to look up information. This type of environment is used within many forms of Customer Relationship Management (CRM), including helpdesk applications, call-center applications, and even customer-facing applications where customers interface directly with portal-based applications to perform self-service queries. The portal server in this example is based on a J2EE application server platform. One of the operations the portal server performs is accepting web requests from a web browser, and using web page generation technology to dynamically format an HTML page as a response back to the user. A J2EE application server is well suited for this type of request/response handling and HTML page generation.

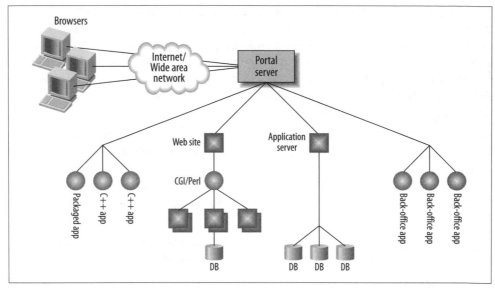

Figure 11-9. Portal infrastructure using a portal server that acts as an aggregation point for multiple data sources

The portal server also acts as the interface to a variety of backend systems from which data is extracted to populate the page generation engine. The interface to the backend systems can be accomplished in a variety of ways:

- Using JCA-compliant adapters that are supplied with the application server
- Putting web service interfaces on the backend data sources and using SOAP-over-HTTP to make web service requests
- Using JMS to reliably and asynchronously integrate with the backend systems
- Using a reliable SOAP protocol to reliably and asynchronously integrate with the backend systems

Sounds great, right? But what's wrong with this picture? There are challenges associated with this architecture that motivated several IT departments to adopt an ESB:

- The back-office system may be incapable of sustaining the peak loads required to support the frontend presentation tier. There is a risk associated with exposing the back-office system directly to the presentation tier. Placing a web frontend on an existing application and allowing all customers to suddenly start using the application directly can result in an increased volume of data and unknown amounts of traffic. An application that was once built for a single user, or a given number of users sitting in front of a terminal at predictable times throughout the day, may not be capable of handling these larger volumes of throughput. The portal server approach by itself does nothing to alleviate that situation.

- The latency for request/response could exceed the tolerances of the presentation tier. Some of the queries being executed could take longer than a typical browser request/response time to complete.

- In a distributed, SOA-based environment, careful attention must be paid to how systems interoperate, and what would happen in the event of failures or downtime. In many situations, preexisting systems are not capable of resending messages as necessary and providing the "in-doubt resolution" required to compensate for these failures. An ESB can offload this complexity from those systems.

- The back-office system could be in a different geography than the portal server. If links go down between the two data centers, the data should still be available to end users. Likewise, if the backend data source should become temporarily unavailable, the query should still be able to complete.

The first step toward achieving a solution for these issues is to deploy an ESB in between the portal server and the backend systems, as illustrated in Figure 11-10.

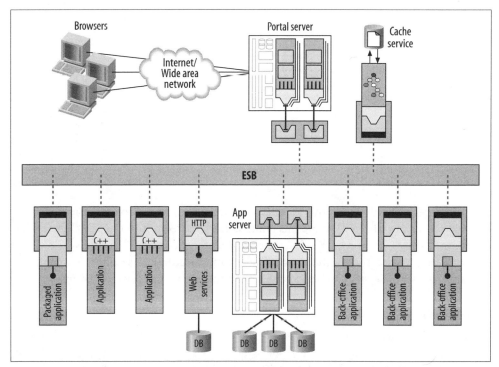

Figure 11-10. The ESB as the integration layer between the portal server and the backend systems

The general advantage of deploying an ESB in this fashion is that it provides a more flexible, enterprise-grade backbone to reliably link applications and services together into a cohesive event-driven SOA, capable of servicing the full range of integration scenarios required by most portals. Before continuing on to explore more about the ESB, let's revisit the non-ESB portal solution and examine some of its characteristics.

Portal Server Challenges

The typical portal server deployment architecture presents several challenges.

Synchronous sequential aggregation

Figure 11-11 shows a browser request being sent to a portal server, which in turn initiates a series of synchronous requests to a number of backend systems using web services interfaces.

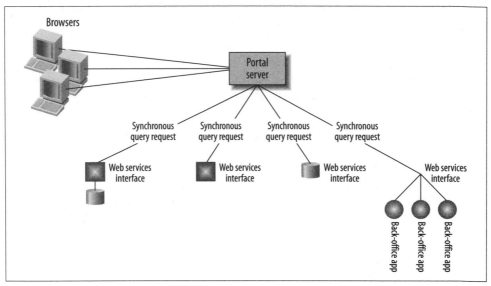

Figure 11-11. A portal invoking synchronous web services requests sequentially

Latency issues associated with this approach can make it an untenable experience for the end user of the portal. To illustrate this point, consider a request to the portal server that results in a query to four backend services. If each service takes 3 seconds to process, invoking these services sequentially would take a minimum of 12 seconds. Some queries that are executed using this model can take 20 minutes to several hours to complete.

Web services

Another quality of the approach illustrated in Figure 11-11 is the expectation that web services interfaces will be used as a one-size-fits-all solution. An integration solution needs to be capable of accommodating the needs of the application without doing a synchronized retrofit onto every application across an organization. It is not reasonable to mandate that all applications will switch over to web services interfaces on a certain date; coordinating such an effort on a mass scale with limited resources is nearly impossible, especially when factored in with the everyday priorities of an IT organization. Instead, it's much more reasonable to have a plan to eventually achieve a common interface description using WSDL and web services, and it is much less of a barrier for embarking on a portal integration project.

Concurrency via multithreaded request

To compensate for the latency issue, it is possible for a portal server to introduce concurrency by creating a separate thread for each request, and to have the thread block and wait on the synchronous call (Figure 11-12).

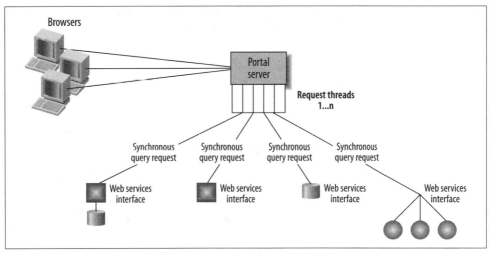

Figure 11-12. Introducing concurrency by creating separate threads that block on synchronous invocations

The multithreading allows multiple requests to be executed in parallel, thus reducing the overall latency to the longest individual query time rather than the sum of the query response times. However, this solution is not without its problems, and there are better ways to handle this situation using an ESB. There is still the possibility that a network link could go down, that one of the backend systems could be shut down due to failure or scheduled downtime, or that the portal server itself could go down (Figure 11-13).

If a failure occurs, the portal server may not be built to automatically retry the request. This could be done by manually creating a thread and going into a retry loop, which can result in a buildup of unused threads under high-volume usage. Also, if a failure occurs and the query has already been running for 10 minutes, it can be extremely frustrating for the end user to have to start over again.

Long-duration conversation management

The portal server may have implemented some form of stateful long-duration conversation management for web services interactions. However, this requires all backend systems to be enabled as web services, and to be enabled to support long-duration conversations. This still does not protect against failure modes, however. The portal

---

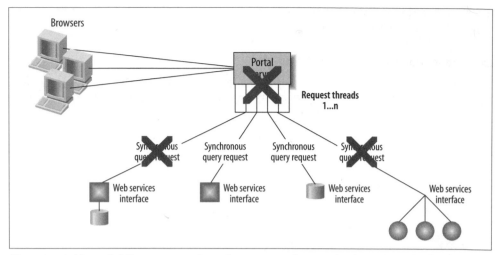

Figure 11-13. Network failure or system downtime can cause interruption in service and a frustrating user experience

server may manage persistent state for its side of the conversation, but that doesn't help with the conversational state of the remote service.

Asynchrony and reliability using JMS

One approach to providing asynchrony and solving the reliability problem without explicitly using an ESB would be to use JMS between the portal server and the backend data sources. This is a step in the right direction. A portal server that is based on J2EE may also come with a JMS provider in the box. However, this approach also suffers from the one-size-fits-all problem. The JMS provider that comes with the application server may support only Java clients, and you can't reasonably expect every backend application and data source that the portal needs to integrate with to switch over to Java and JMS interfaces.

Connectivity using application adapters

To allow more flexible options for backend applications or data sources to plug into the portal server, special adapters may be used. Many application servers offer integration capabilities by licensing third-party application adapters (the same adapters that can also be licensed by ESB providers) that are made for plugging into specific brands of applications, such as SAP or PeopleSoft. The downside of this approach is the requirement that the adapter be housed inside the application server container, leading to the "appservers everywhere" problem that was discussed in Chapter 6 (Figure 11-14). This is not always a terrible thing, if you really must have application servers installed at every location to host middle-tier business logic. However, if they need to be installed at every location across your organization simply to act as conduits to an enterprise application, an ESB can be a much more viable alternative.

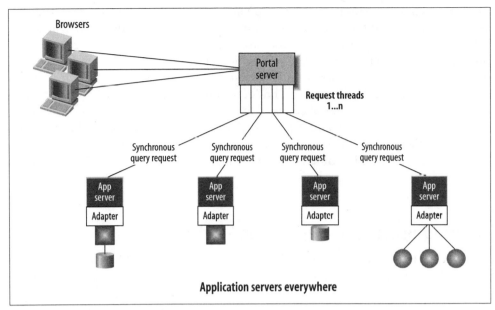

Figure 11-14. Appservers everywhere

You could piece together an alternative approach that combines the use of JMS and adapters, as illustrated in Figure 11-15.

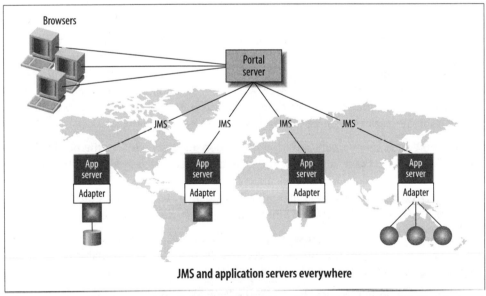

Figure 11-15. JMS implementations that are supplied with application servers do not provide adequate routing across geographically dispersed deployments

This approach is a step in the right direction in terms of providing asynchrony and reliability, but it still has the "appservers everywhere" problem. Another potential downside is that the JMS that comes in the box with the application server can typically provide asynchronous, guaranteed messaging capability only in a single network domain, and doesn't allow for a uniform and seamless namespace of destinations to scale across multiple departments or business units. Application server vendors have attempted to link multiple installations of their JMS messaging systems by providing a custom SOAP bridge to forward messages reliably between data centers, but this does not provide the end-to-end global accessibility that an ESB provides. Lastly, if the application servers being used in different departments are from different J2EE vendors, this presents the further challenge of getting them to work together using the JMS layer from one of the vendors.

Inserting an ESB as the Integration Backbone

The solution to the problems outlined previously is to install an ESB as an intermediate infrastructure between the portal server and the backend applications and data sources, as illustrated in Figure 11-16. An ESB provides seamless end-to-end asynchronous and reliable communications across a distributed environment. It also provides additional connectivity options, such as web services and application adapters, allowing flexible deployment of the services anywhere on the ESB. Furthermore, an ESB provides the event-driven SOA to plug in the added integration services when and where you need them, facilitating the extraction, routing, and transformation of the data as it moves across the bus between the portal server and the backend applications.

With the ESB layered in the middle, all links between the portal server and the backend data sources can now be asynchronous and reliable, without the downsides stated earlier. Because of the flexibility of choices in connectivity, the backend data sources can use any combination of JMS, C++, web services, FTP, and HTTP to integrate into the ESB backbone. This not only saves time in the integration project, but also potentially results in higher performance and reliability for legacy connections.

Remote ESB service containers can host application adapters without the need to install application servers at each remote location. In many cases, such as the SAP RFC adapter for the Availability To Promise application from Chapter 8, the remote ESB container can use a custom service to act as an application adapter, which makes the development and deployment of that integration point extremely lightweight and simple.

This architecture can scale across geographically dispersed deployments, allowing all data sources plugged into the bus to be accessible from anything else that is plugged into the bus, regardless of its physical location.

Lastly, inserting an ESB allows the use of the general-purpose integration patterns that will be explored in this chapter and in Chapter 12.

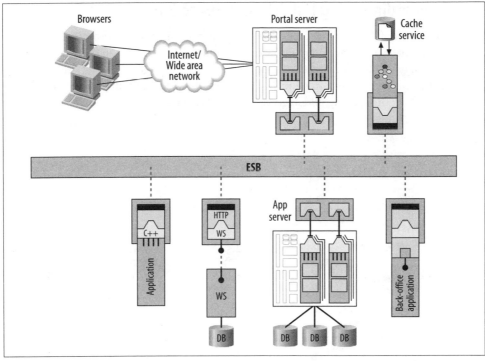

Figure 11-16. The ESB as the integration infrastructure between the portal server and the backend data sources

The Forward Cache Integration Pattern

The Forward Cache integration pattern allows data to be proactively pushed from the backend data sources to a data cache service that is located closer to the presentation tier. Caching data closer to the presentation services improves performance and can allow continuous access when backend sources are offline. An ESB can be used to intelligently and reliably route data from the backend sources to the cache service. Although this pattern is discussed in the context of an enterprise portal, it can be applied generally to any situation that requires the collection and aggregation of data across a diverse set of distributed applications and other data sources.

Two forms of populating the cache from the backend applications will be discussed in this section:

- Using reliable publish-and-subscribe messaging
- Using ESB process definitions to "skim" the data from the process and forward it to the cache by inserting fan-out services into key points within the process itineraries

Both variants of the Forward Cache pattern rely on the concept of *data forwarding*, which is the act of making a copy of a message and propagating it to a data caching service.

Data Forwarding Using Publish-and-Subscribe

The basic model of the forward cache is quite simple. Using persistent messages on publish-and-subscribe message channels with durable subscriptions, an ESB can reliably forward change notifications to the cache, as illustrated in Figure 11-17. The cache service can be implemented using the XML storage service (introduced in Chapter 7), which is used for the caching and aggregating of XML data.

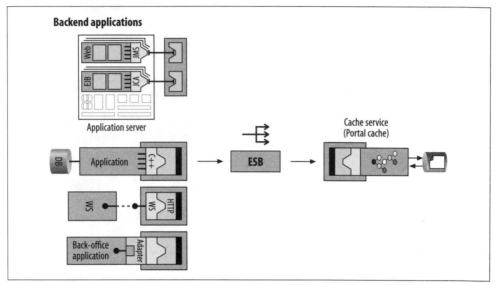

Figure 11-17. Applications plugged into an ESB send data on pub/sub topics to be consumed by a portal cache

Because the ESB is coordinating the data flow between the applications and the cache service instead of just being used as a message bus, a variety of backend technologies can participate in publishing their data using the connection interface that best suits their needs.

The key to this pattern is creating and managing the change notifications in remote applications and regularly routing them to the cache. Trying to predict the most commonly queried data can be difficult. If the cache service has the ability to expire unused information, the cache can use subscriptions to subscribe to a broad range of topics, and allow the unused data to expire.

Because an ESB is used to integrate the backend applications, each application interface can be designed to simply post data to the endpoint that the ESB exposes. The fact that a publish-and-subscribe channel is being used to deliver the data is a configuration detail that is managed through ESB administrative tools instead of being coded into each application. The type of channel and the details of how the data gets routed can be manipulated over time based on analysis of usage and data access patterns. The result is that many requests for information can be satisfied directly from the cache without needing to make a request to the backend data sources (Figure 11-18).

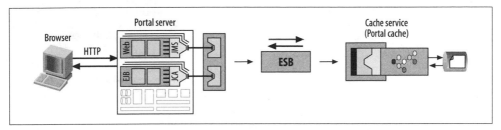

Figure 11-18. The portal server communicates with the portal cache through the ESB using a synchronous request/reply messaging pattern

The data being forwarded from backend data sources can be organized into topic trees using publish-and-subscribe channels to carry data. This allows the additional backend data sources to be easily joined into the data sharing network by selectively publishing to a particular topic branch within the topic hierarchy. As a result of designing the data channels this way, the portal cache can also subscribe to specific categories of data using wildcard subscriptions (Figure 11-19). If the portal cache will be used to aggregate data, it would likely use a broader subscription mask, such as Asset_Class.*, to receive everything that is published under that topic namespace (using the Asset_Class topic hierarchy example from Chapter 5, Figure 5-9), or it may narrow the selection by specifying the Asset_Class.#.Domestic.# and Asset_Class.#.International.# topic nodes individually. The individual systems on the backend may be much more selective, perhaps subscribing to the Asset_Class.#.Domestic.# topic node only. This selectivity allows you to reduce the overhead of the cache by limiting its scope.

The use of publish-and-subscribe channels in this type of pattern is another reason why a MOM is core to an ESB. However, this couldn't be accomplished with a MOM alone. Note that because an ESB is being used, one of the publishers in Figure 11-19 is actually an external web service.

Data Forwarding Using Itinerary-Based Routing

An alternative to the publish-and-subscribe method of populating the cache is to use ESB process definitions to route messages to the cache service. The process definitions can use topics, queues, or any other type of transport that can have an endpoint defined for it. As illustrated in Figure 11-20, a process itinerary can use a fan-out service to route data to another application and a portal cache in parallel. The fan-out service makes a copy of the message and sends it to an alternate endpoint.

A combination of process itineraries and publish-and-subscribe could also be used. The fan-out service itself could be implemented using pub/sub as the means for fanning out the data, and the exit endpoint of the fan-out service could be configured to use a pub/sub channel.

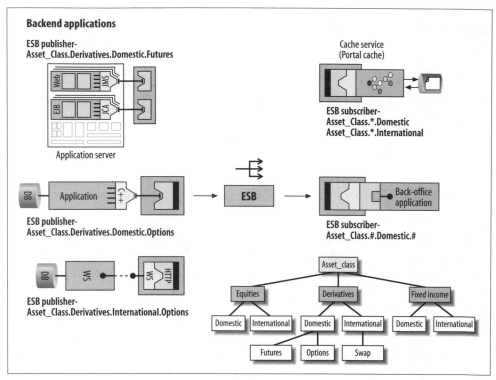

Figure 11-19. Wildcard subscriptions on hierarchical topic trees allow a cache to selectively listen for data that is being passed between backend applications on pub/sub channels

Other Considerations of the Forward Cache Pattern

The forward cache, as previously presented, is a relatively simple and straightforward approach if the only purpose of integrating the backend systems is to feed the portal with data. But it is highly likely that the backend systems could benefit in other ways by integrating and sharing data with each other. How does one take advantage of the effort put into the portal project and leverage that work into a more generic integration solution?

Integration first, portal second

Perhaps a better way to ask that question is "How can an integration project also be capable of populating caching services for access by enterprise portals?" One of the key benefits of the Forward Cache pattern is that it can be a side capability that is added onto an existing ESB integration strategy for backend data sources. The enterprise portal initiative may be the project that drives the backend integration, but it is likely part of a larger integration project. In that respect, you should be thinking about designing the integration strategy based on how the backend data sources and applications might best interact and share data with each other.

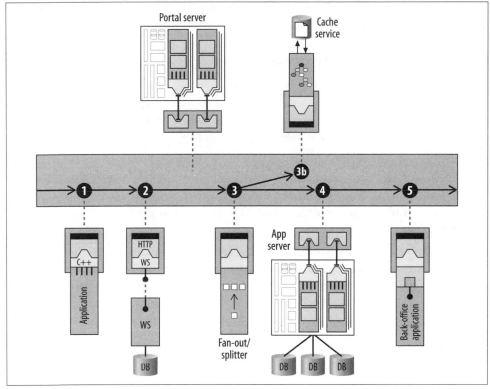

Figure 11-20. A process itinerary uses a fan-out service to route data to another application and a portal cache in parallel

If the backend applications are first integrated with each other using an ESB, then populating the portal cache with data can be accomplished by inserting listeners into the existing integration pathways that forward copies of message data directly to the cache update endpoint.

If the data sharing is being done by posting messages to publish and subscribe channels, the portal cache can easily join in the data sharing network by subscribing to those channels. If the integration and data flow are being done using more formal business process definitions, the portal cache can be populated by inserting fan-out services into key business processes that intercept a message and route a copy of it to the cache.

Federated Query Patterns

An action performed by an end user, whether through an enterprise portal application or a user-facing client application, often results in complex requests that need to query multiple backend systems. This process is referred to as a *federated query*. As we have seen, the Forward Cache pattern and its variations can make this process much more efficient.

Cache Push Versus Pull Patterns

The patterns examined so far have been based on a push model, where data is proactively identified to be pushed to a cache. Sometimes, however, the data in the backend system can't reasonably be pushed to a cache. The volume of data may be too great, or it may just not be technically or economically viable to trap all the updates necessary to maintain the forward cache.

Sometimes the data can't reasonably be cached at all, due to the rate of data change in the backend systems. Querying cached data that is frequently outdated can lead to data inconsistency and provide incorrect results. The federated query pattern has a *cache pull* variant that can address this issue.

Implementing the federated query real-time request pattern and its variations requires going out to the multiple backend systems and querying them in real time. The federated query patterns are based on the request/reply and reply-forward patterns, which were discussed in Chapter 5. The federated query pattern comes in at least two variants: *real-time request* and *long-duration request*. Which one you use depends upon the duration of the query.

The Real-Time Request Pattern

The federated query could be addressed without an ESB by utilizing multiple concurrent request/reply messaging patterns. A portal server (or an application) can use multi-threading techniques to fire off simultaneous requests to reduce the overall latency associated with querying multiple backend applications and data sources. However, this approach is not tolerant of failure conditions. An ESB can address concurrency and reliability issues by invoking the backend data sources as service requests using reliable publish-and-subscribe messaging channels (Figure 11-21).

The responses are sent back to the portal server directly from each remote data source, which runs as an event-driven service invocation, as illustrated in Figure 11-22. Because the portal server itself is plugged into the bus, it is accessible from every other process that is plugged into the bus. If the underlying implementation of the service invocation is mapped onto a point-to-point message queue channel, the portal server can have an MDB interface that listens on the point-to-point message queue.

In the *cache pull* variant of the federated query, the request will first go to the cache to see if there is any nonexpired data that can satisfy the request. If not, the federated query will be initiated. The replies from the federated query can be routed to an ESB process that updates the cache and then forwards it on to the portal server (Figure 11-23).

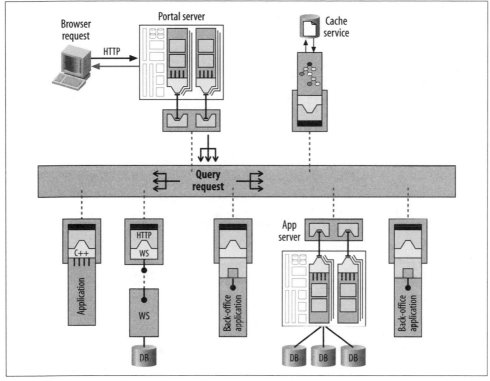

Figure 11-21. A portal request initiates multiple simultaneous requests to backend applications using publish-and-subscribe messaging across an ESB

The Long-Duration Request Pattern

The real-time request pattern works well, assuming that all of the data sources are immediately accessible and that the response to the query will complete within a reasonable amount of time. In practice, requests may take a very long time to complete. Here are some reasons why:

- Human input (a step in a process may involve manual intervention, such as approval)
- Requests deferred to off-peak hours
- Offline system or application
- Network outage

The long-duration request pattern builds on the real-time request pattern, but assumes that responses from services on the bus will return over a much less predictable period of time. This allows the portal user to browse to other areas of the web site while responses asynchronously aggregate in the user's session.

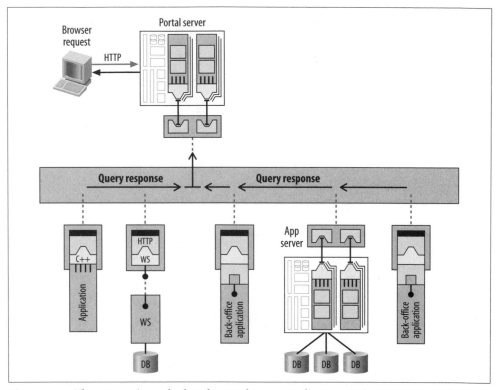

Figure 11-22. The response is sent back to the portal server as a direct service invocation across the bus, using a message queue to an MDB to receive the response

In this scenario, a user logs into the application and initiates an action that launches a query to the ESB. The ESB routes the request to the appropriate systems on the bus, and delivers the responses back to the same application or portal session. The user is then free to use other features of the application while the requests are accumulated. If the application is an enterprise portal, it requires the portal to have a user session feature that allows the user to log in at a later time and check for responses.

The XML persistence service that is used for the cache service may also be responsible for collecting the multiple responses and then forwarding them on to the portal. In that sense it acts as an aggregation point as well as a cache. All of these techniques require you to configure a "rule" that defines when the result set is complete, which in turn triggers the response to the original query request. Normally the rule is simply an XPath or XQuery returning a Boolean. The trigger may be a CBR step or may be built into the XML service.

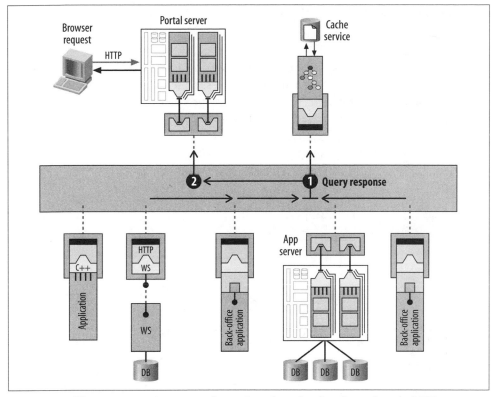

Figure 11-23. The responses go to a process that updates the cache, then forwards to the MDB

Federated Query Pattern Variations

There are several variations of the federated query patterns.

- The real-time and long-duration patterns can be combined. When the federated query is issued in this scenario, the portal waits for a fixed amount of time and then returns the aggregated results to the user. Any late responses are asynchronously aggregated by the portal and are available on subsequent requests by the user.

- The "response" event that gets generated from the aggregation service to the portal could be implemented as a single message that carries all of the data, or it could be an empty message that signals the portal server to issue another request to extract the data from the XML aggregation service.

- Before forwarding to the portal server, the multiple responses could be run through a VETO pattern that could consolidate the data and reformat it using XSLT into a form that is more suitable for consumption by the portal.

Federated query using itinerary processes

Variations of the federated query can be accomplished using ESB process itineraries rather than publish-and-subscribe messaging channels, as illustrated in Figure 11-24 and Figure 11-25. This gives you more control over how each subquery is handled, but increases the latency for the federated query if the subqueries are executed sequentially. To execute subqueries in parallel with an itinerary process, you need a specialized *join service* that can intelligently collect the multiple responses.

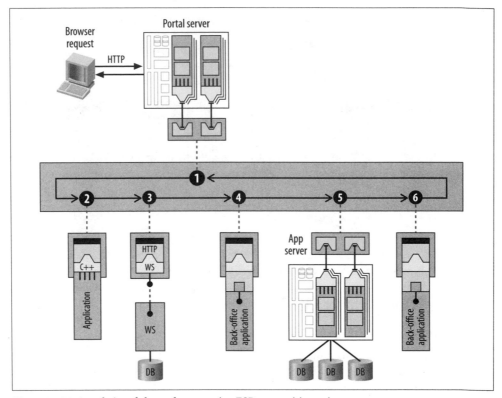

Figure 11-24. A real-time federated query using ESB process itineraries

Federated query using BPEL4WS and an orchestration service

An orchestration service is well suited for the branching out of multiple requests and for waiting for the responses to come back, as illustrated in Figure 11-26. Rather than using process itineraries and fan-out services, a process orchestration service can orchestrate more complex interactions such as splits and joins based on transition conditions. More information on the merits of an orchestration service versus process itineraries can be found in Chapter 7.

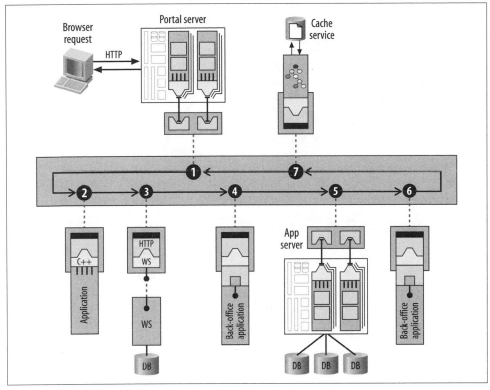

Figure 11-25. A cache pull federated query using ESB process itineraries

Summary

In this chapter, we learned about a few interesting integration patterns using an ESB:

- The VETO pattern and its variants are a simple, fundamental approach to building SOAs within an ESB environment.

- The two-step XRef transformation pattern can separate commonly used but distinct operations into loosely coupled service types that are reusable across a variety of situations.

- Portal servers by themselves have challenges associated with long-duration requests that span multiple backend applications and data sources, particularly if the backend applications are geographically dispersed.

- Inserting an ESB as an integration layer between the portal and the backend data sources provides a much more flexible backend integration layer than a portal server alone.

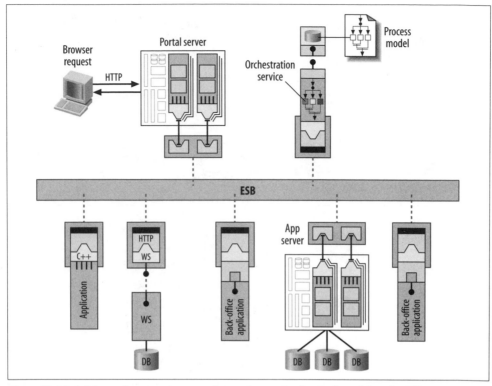

Figure 11-26. A federated query using an orchestration service that is plugged into the ESB

- Inserting an ESB as an integration layer between the portal and the backend data sources can improve the success rate of inquiries, improve throughput and responsiveness, and reduce errors through the following means:

  - Through asynchronous communication, reliable delivery, and correlation.

  - Using the federated query and its variations.

  - Using the Cache Forward pattern and its variations. ESB caching services can be strategically located across your enterprise, and can be populated with data in a variety of ways using intelligent routing techniques.

There are many more integration patterns to explore. Visit *http://www.oreilly.com/ catalog/esb* for the latest information on ESB integration patterns.

ESB and the Evolution of Web Services

12

This chapter provides an overview of the evolving web services specifications, and an explanation of how web services and ESBs will move forward together.

There is an evolving set of specifications being branded as the "Web Services Specifications," commonly referred to in this book as the WS-* family of specifications. Some of the WS-* specifications originated from standards organizations such as the W3C and OASIS, but a large majority are a result of an ad hoc collaborvation of vendors that usually includes Microsoft, IBM, and BEA. Other vendors and organizations, such as Global Grid Forum, RSA, SAP, Sonic, and TIBCO, also collaborate based on their particular area of expertise. For example, the WS-Notification Specification authors include Akamai Technologies, Computer Associates International, Fujitsu Laboratories of Europe, The Globus Alliance, Hewlett-Packard, IBM, SAP AG, Sonic Software, and TIBCO Software; the October 2003 WS-ReliableMessaging Interoperability workshops included BEA, IBM, Blue Titan, Microsoft, NEC, Sonic, TIBCO, and Systinet.

The goal of these ad hoc vendor collaborations is to eventually bring the specifications before a standards body, after a considerable amount of public feedback sessions and interoperability workshops have occurred. For some specifications, such as WS-Security, WS-BPEL, and WS-Notification, this has already happened. The reason behind this approach is that these companies feel that defining standards by committee is too slow and arduous, and that it is best to define the standards offline until they are "almost baked" before finally bringing them to a standards body for "ratification" with a broader community.

That being said, these standards are not being developed in a vacuum. In the case of WS-ReliableMessaging, WS-Security, WS-Policy, WS-Notification, and others, the sponsoring companies have been hosting specification feedback meetings and providing open invitations to interoperability workshops.

Some specifications that do originate from standards bodies have overlapping objectives with the specifications from the ad hoc vendor collaborations. Some examples of this include:

- The WS-Reliability specification, an output of the OASIS Web Services Reliable Messaging (WSRM) Technical Committee (TC), overlaps with WS-ReliableMessaging of the WS-* family of specifications.

- The WS-Policy specification, from the WS-* family of specifications, overlaps with a W3C SOAP 1.2 capability known as "Features and Properties" (F&P).

- WS-Eventing and WS-BaseNotification, both from the WS-* family of specifications, are almost identical in scope.

- WS-Addressing from the WS-* family of specifications, and WS-MessageDelivery, which is a W3C "member submission."

This overlap can sometimes even exist in multiple standards bodies. For example, the Web Services Choreography Working Group (WS-Choreography) was established in the W3C. Shortly thereafter, the Business Process Execution Language for Web Services (BPEL4WS) specification was brought to OASIS to form the WSBPEL TC. The two groups eventually decided to create official liaisons between them, and now have a fair amount of cross-membership.

An ESB should be capable of accommodating these specifications going forward, even if it means supporting multiple overlapping versions. To an ESB, these become more standardized ways to integrate with applications. When Microsoft supports WS-Reliable-Messaging in its Indigo platform, for example, an ESB should be able to support that protocol if it wishes to provide integration hooks into applications based on Indigo. However, an ESB implementation may also need to support WS-Reliability in order to integrate with applications from vendors who back that specification, such as Oracle, Sun, and SAP.

Composability Among Specifications

The word "composable" is used quite frequently in the WS-* family of specifications to refer to the way that the specifications depend on each other. Previous attempts at trying to build large, complex specifications that define the whole stack of interoperability in an all-or-nothing fashion, such as ebXML, have been unable to garner the widespread adoption their early proponents had hoped for. The WS-* family of specifications is broken down into small, interconnected specifications, which are more easily understood and implemented by a broader range of vendors, large and small alike.

Summary of WS-* Specifications

The set of WS-* specifications is still evolving. The following are brief descriptions of some of the important ones that have relevance to an ESB:

WS-Eventing
  Supports a publish-and-subscribe event model using web services. WS-Eventing provides a simple subscription model using WSDL interfaces, but has no notion of

message brokering and does not attempt to describe how topic namespaces are managed.

WS-Notification

Provides a family of specifications that includes WS-BaseNotification, WS-BrokeredNotification, and WS-Topics. WS-BaseNotification defines a subscription-based event model using web services, very much like WS-Eventing. WS-BrokeredNotification defines a model for how publish-and-subscribe messaging can be managed by message brokers, and how message brokers themselves can act as conduits for dispatching messages to their intended destinations. WS-Topics defines how a hierarchical namespace of publish-and-subscribe messaging topics can be managed and accessed. Subscriptions are treated as manageable resources with a lifecycle that is defined according to the rules specified by the WS-ResourceFramework family of specifications.

Both WS-Eventing and WS-Notification are intended to work with WS-Policy and WS-ReliableMessaging. WS-Notification has been brought to OASIS to form a Technical Committee (TC). TC members may introduce other possibilities such as "composability" between WS-Eventing and WS-BrokeredNotification.

WS-ReliableMessaging

Published by MS/IBM et al., WS-ReliableMessaging provides a SOAP-based reliable protocol that describes SOAP header elements and behavioral semantics for message acknowledgments, message retries, and fault handling for coping with undeliverable messages. The specification definition and input process have been broadened to include several feedback and interoperability workshops that have been open to the public. WS-ReliableMessaging has a high degree of overlap with OASIS WS-Reliability in terms of capabilities and functionality.

WS-Reliability

A product of the OASIS Reliable Messaging TC, WS-Reliability provides a SOAP-based reliable protocol that describes SOAP header elements and behavioral semantics for message acknowledgments, message retries, and fault handling for coping with undeliverable messages. Several test implementations have been provided by the TC members for the purposes of interoperability testing. WS-Reliability has a high degree of overlap with WS-ReliableMessaging in terms of capabilities and functionality.

WS Security (WSS)

An OASIS TC that specifies QoP, privacy, and message integrity through encryption and signing of XML documents, in part or in their entirety, WSS also includes mechanisms for associating security tokens, such as X.509 certificates and Kerberos tickets, with XML documents.

WS-Trust

WS-Trust is a companion specification to WS-Security that describes how to establish security tokens and derive and share security keys.

WS-SecureConversation

WS-SecureConversation establishes a shared security context and shared session keys based on security context. Shared security context exists for the lifetime of the conversation.

WS-Security will not be fully baked until WS-Trust and WS-SecureConversation are fully worked out and adopted by the security vendors and the major platform vendors.

WS-Federation

The goal of WS-Federation is to provide security, including authentication and authorization across federated security realms, using a single authentication mechanism.

WS-Addressing

WS-Addressing defines a set of constructs for endpoint references that represent From, To, RelatesTo (RefTo), FaultTo, and ReplyTo (and Reply Forward) addresses. WS-Addressing maps very well for use as a base for the metadata describing a message itinerary in an ESB.

WS-Policy

WS-Policy is a composable set of specifications (WS-Policy, WS-PolicyAssertions, WS-PolicyAttachments) that, collectively, are similar to SOAP 1.2 F&P. WS-Policy defines a means for expressing assertions about the capabilities of an endpoint, or the underlying capabilities of the service behind the endpoint. A web service client that wishes to communicate with the service endpoint should first query its properties to determine whether it is capable of supporting that endpoint's asserted "features." WS-Policy allows a service endpoint to specify preferences using a weighting system, indicating to a potential client multiple options of capabilities that can be used to carry out a conversation. For example, a service endpoint might expose a policy indicating that it supports both WS-ReliableMessaging and WS-Reliability as communication protocols, but that it prefers the client to use WS-ReliableMessaging if there is a choice. In addition, these policy preferences are packaged up in the SOAP envelope header to indicate to the receiving service endpoint which policy preferences the sender has chosen to use. This is not a negotiation protocol per se; it is a one-way exchange of information where the service endpoint asserts to a potential client sender that it supports certain capabilities, designated as required or optional. The sender must support the required capabilities or it will not be allowed to send a message to the endpoint (i.e., the endpoint will generate a SOAP fault).

SOAP 1.2 Features and Properties (F&P)

A product of the SOAP 1.2 Transport Binding Task Force (*http://www.w3.org/2000/ xp/Group/tbtf*) and an alternative approach to WS-Policy, SOAP 1.2 F&P makes use of the SOAP 1.2 extensibility model (*http://www.w3.org/TR/2003/REC-soap12- part1-20030624/#extensibility*), which allows two parties having a conversation over SOAP to mutually agree on capabilities of the endpoints. For example, they both may agree that they support WS-Encryption and that they can exchange encryption keys using an out-of-band means that is known to both sides of the conversation. Choosing a WS-Rel* protocol, as described in the WS-Policy explanation, can work here equally as well.

WS-BPEL

WS-BPEL is an OASIS TC that is defining the ongoing work of the Business Process Execution Language for Web Services (BPEL4WS) specification. BPEL4WS extends and subsumes its roots, which come from a combination of Microsoft's XLANG specification and IBM's Web Services Flow Language (WSFL) specification. BPEL4WS defines an XML grammar for describing an abstract business process and the constraints of a message exchange of business-level messages in an executable process flow. The first rendition of the specification focuses on peer-to-peer interactions between web services endpoints that are described using WSDL.

BPEL4WS can also be described as providing a schema for an instance of a business process from the point of view of a particular participant (service). The language defines business process sequences (flows) by describing *links* between participants and the interactions between those links.

The language supports constructs such as variable definitions, looping, and throw and catch blocks that can be transactionally scoped using compensating transactions. *Activities* define the interactions between links. Examples include the invoke, reply, compensate, and receive statements. Correlation sets are defined for linking "request" messages with "response" messages, and fault handlers are provided for handling the cases when good messages go bad. Parallel execution paths of business processes and conditional joins are supported in the language.

It should be noted that BPEL4WS is sufficient enough to describe an abstract definition of a business process, or the interaction steps between two partners. An actual implementation requires that vendor extensions be provided, or that an import/export facility be implemented. Biztalk 4.0 provides an import/export facility. An ESB could support either approach as well.

Adopting the WS-* Specifications in an ESB

An ESB implementation does not have to support all of the WS-* specifications in order to be an effective integration platform. If you recall from most of the discussion in this book, the majority of applications today are built upon neither J2EE nor .NET, and they won't all just switch over to web services interfaces in a day.

ESBs will generally support these specifications as they become more mature and are adopted in the industry. When they do implement these specifications, interoperability and integration through an ESB will become an even easier task. Using the full WS-* stack of technology as an alternate protocol between services, ESBs will provide better interoperability across services and provide endpoint connectivity without necessarily requiring the use of special adapters.

Table 12-1 lists the functionality in the ESB and existing standards that are reasonably mature and that have implementations that an ESB can utilize to provide interoperability among applications and services. It also gives an indication of which of the evolving WS-* specifications should be used in an ESB implementation as the specifications mature and are adopted by multiple vendors and platforms.

Table 12-1. ESB and the evolving WS- specifications*

ESB capability	Existing ESB technology	Evolving WS-* specifications	Notes
Secure communication channels	SSL, HTTPS	WS-Security, WS-SecureConversation	WS-Security not really useful without WS-SecureConversation and WS-Trust.
Authentication	PKI digital certificates	WS-Trust, SAML, WS-Federation	
Message payload encryption	Standard cypher suites	WS-Encryption	
Access control lists	LDAP, JMX, proprietary	XACML	
Publish and subscribe	JMS, proprietary	WS-Notification, WS-Eventing	
Service endpoint description	WSDL, proprietary, LDAP, JNDI	WSDL, WS-Policy, SOAP 1.2 F&P	
Reliable messaging	JMS, proprietary MOM	WS-ReliableMessaging, WS-Reliability	
Itinerary-based routing	WSDL, proprietary	WSDL, WS-Addressing	
Business process orchestration	Proprietary	WS-BPEL, WS-Choreography, proprietary	BizTalk 4.0 imports and exports. Other implementations use extensions to do anything concrete.
Transactions	JTA, JCA, XA, proprietary, compensating	WS-Coordination, WS-Transaction, WS-AtomicTransactions, WS-BusinessActivity, WS-CAF	

WS-* Does Not Imply Enterprise Capabilities

There are and will continue to be a number of implementations of web services stacks that are not sophisticated enough or scalable enough to support an enterprise-wide integration backbone. Simply supporting WS-Rel*, for example, requires only that two endpoints know how to perform a message exchange pattern that satisfies the send/acknowledge semantics that the specification defines.

An open source effort, such as the Apache Web Services project, may eventually support the whole family of specifications, but that does not mean that you should use it alone to deploy an enterprise-wide integration backbone. Implementing this family of specifications does not require or imply that the implementation supports, for example, a scalable implementation of clustered fault-tolerant message brokers that can act as a single virtual unit, and that are capable of intelligently routing messages across sophisticated deployment topologies.

WS-* Does Not Imply ESB

If a web services toolkit provides support for the WS-* specifications, it does not automatically imply that the toolkit is an ESB. A question I am often asked is, "When web services become more mature, will I still need an ESB?" or "What's the difference between an ESB and a bunch of web services linked together with a BPEL engine?" Of course, at this point in the book, the answer should be apparent. But I'll summarize the key points.

An implementation of a set of WS-* specs does not imply an ESB. The ESB concept is well suited for adopting the WS-* family of specifications as they mature and are adopted by more vendors. As the ad hoc collaboration of vendors implements more of these specifications in their respective platforms, their products will be able to interoperate with each other. This will not obsolete the use of an ESB, however; in fact, it will make the ESB concept more relevant, in that applications built upon those platforms will be easier to integrate into the common integration environment that is the ESB.

Support for the WS-* family of specifications does not imply anything about the underlying implementation. Recall the accidental architecture discussion from Chapter 2. Web services alone, without a proper architecture for a distributed integration network, does not buy you much except for a new set of protocols and interfaces to deal with. Simply applying web services interfaces and protocols to existing applications can quickly lead to a "standards-based accidental architecture."

A common misconception of an ESB is that it is just a MOM with SOAP and WSDL bindings. Providing an environment where the gap can be bridged between a proprietary MOM and a Web Services Reliable SOAP protocol is a step in the right direction, but it is only one part of what makes an ESB. It is analogous to having an Ethernet plug on the back of your computer—that alone does not make your computer automatically able to talk to every other computer. An entire network of switches and routers makes that part possible.

Part of what makes an ESB is an underlying *message bus*, which provides a network of collaborating message servers that can transparently route application data as messages across a variety of protocols. However, even a message bus by itself does not fully qualify as an ESB. An ESB provides an SOA across that message bus, and the highly distributed integration functions in a hosted lightweight container environment, which can operate independently of one another, without the need to install the entire stack of functionality in every place an individual integration component is required. This includes the capabilities of XML data transformation, content-based routing, orchestration and process flow, and application adapter interfaces.

Looking forward, the best possible outcome of the "coming of age" of the WS-* family of specifications is that, when combined with an ESB architecture, IT functions will have even more ways of integrating and interoperating with application endpoints.

Adoption of the WS-* family of specifications by the major application platform vendors will continue to make the model of message-driven application interfaces a reality. As more application endpoints provide support for these protocols, it will become easier to integrate them through an ESB integration fabric.

Conclusion

I hope you have enjoyed this journey through the ESB architecture and its applied use. Here are the key points you should take away from this book regarding what an ESB is and how it should be applied within an organization:

- The enterprise is far from integrated.
- An ESB provides the implementation backbone for an event-driven SOA.
- An ESB provides a loosely coupled, event-driven SOA with a highly distributed universe of named routing destinations across a multiprotocol message bus.
- An ESB is a standards-based integration platform that combines messaging, web services, data transformation, and intelligent routing to reliably connect and coordinate the interaction of significant numbers of diverse applications across extended enterprises with transactional integrity.
- An ESB is not an academic exercise; it was born out of necessity. It is based on mature technology that exists today, and is well suited for adopting the evolving interoperability technologies of tomorrow.
- An ESB is based on the philosophy that integration should be pervasive across an enterprise.
- Pervasiveness includes being suitable for any general-purpose integration project, no matter how large or how small.
- An ESB supports incremental adoption, which allows you to implement locally and integrate globally.
- An ESB provides the underpinnings for solving problems that scale beyond the barriers of EAI and into the realm of B2B and supply chains.
- The ESB concept is based on a highly distributed, lightweight, remotely managed service container, which allows the selective deployment of independently scalable integration components exactly where you need them.
- An ESB does not require installing a full application server stack or a full integration broker implementation at every site that requires integration components.
- An ESB is built upon a highly distributed, multiprotocol, standards-based message bus.

Appendix: List of ESB Vendors

The following is the known list of ESB vendors at the time of publishing. To be included in this list, vendors simply had to make a public statement that they have an ESB, intend to provide an ESB in the near future, or are using ESB terminology in their marketing materials.

I will do my best to keep this list up to date with subsequent reprints of this book.

BEA
Cape Clear
Fiorano
IBM
Iona
Kenamea
KnowNow
PolarLake
SeeBeyond
Snapbridge Software
Sonic Software
SpiritSoft
Wakesoft
webMethods

Bibliography

Analyst Reports

Gartner Predicts: 2003 (DF-18-7304). *http://www.gartner.com*. (Quote from Roy Schulte in Chapter 1)

Gartner Predicts: 2004 (118991). "Enterprise Service Buses are Taking Off." *http://www.gartner.com*.

IDC. *The Enterprise Service Bus: Disruptive Technology for Software Infrastructure Solutions* (Document #29132). *http://www.idc.com/getdoc.jsp?containerId=29132*.

IDC. *Integration Standards Trends in Program Development: It All Depends on What the Meaning of "Open" Is* (Document #30365). November 2003. *http://www.idc.com/*.

Books

Alexander, Christopher et al. *A Pattern Language: Towns, Buildings, Construction.* Oxford University Press, 1977.

Fowler, Martin. *Patterns of Enterprise Application Architecture*. Addison Wesley, 2002.

Hohpe, Gregor and Bobby Woolf. *Enterprise Integration Patterns*. 2004. Pearson Education, Inc. Figures: Aggregator, p.268; Content-Based Router, p.230; Control Bus, p.540; Message Broker, p.322; Message Channel, p.60; Publish-Subscribe Channel, p.106; Routing Slip, p.301; Splitter, p.259. © Reprinted by permission of Pearson Education, Inc. Publishing as Pearson Addison Wesley.

Kaye, Doug. *Loosely Coupled: The Missing Pieces of Web Services.* RDS Press, 2003.

Kreger, Heather, Ward K. Harold, and Leigh Williamson. *Java and JMX: Building Manageable Systems.* Addison Wesley, 2002.

Monson-Haefel, Richard and David A. Chappell. *Java Message Service*. O'Reilly, 2000.

Miscellaneous

The CIO Council's XML Web Services Working Group "Kickoff Presentation" at the XML/Web Services Technical Exchange Meeting/Conference at MITRE; Langley, Virginia. Brand Niemann, XML and Web Services Specialist, US EPA and Chair, XML Web Services Working Group, January 28, 2003: *http://web-services.gov/MITRE-XML%20Web%20Services%20Working%20Group12803.ppt.*

Sarbanes-Oxley Act of 2002
http://news.findlaw.com/hdocs/docs/gwbush/sarbanesoxley072302.pdf

Example EDI to XML from Chapter 4
http://www.gea.nu/ppt/xml-edi/XML%20vs%20EDI%20SMDG.ppt

http://www.google.com/search?q=cache:VgSZ68gdENkJ:www.gea.nu/ppt/xml-edi/XML%2520vs%2520EDI%2520SMDG.ppt+edi+to+xml+example&hl=en&ie=UTF-8

RosettaNet RNIF and PIP description
http://www.rosettanet.org/RosettaNet/Doc/0/GSDNEQEHTOK4T6AML84EL31VAD/RNIF2[1].1.pdf

jCO SAP Java connector
http://www.sap.com

jCO SAP Java connector FAQ
http://www.sapgenie.com/faq/jco.htm

Quote from John Udell in Chapter 1
http://www.infoworld.com/article/03/10/31/43OPStrategic_1.html

Web Services Specifications

Organization for Advancement of Structured Information Standards (OASIS)
http://www.oasis-open.org

World Wide Web Consortium (W3C)
http://www.w3.org/

SOAP 1.1 specification
http://www.w3.org/TR/2000/NOTE-SOAP-20000508/

SOAP 1.2 specification (XML Protocol) Work Group home page
http://www.w3.org/2000/xp/Group/

Web Services Description Language (WSDL) Work Group home page
http://www.w3.org/2002/ws/desc/

Reliable Messaging Interoperability Workshop (IBM, October 2003)
http://msdn.microsoft.com/webservices/community/workshops/rminteropwsOct2003.aspx

Reliable Messaging Feedback Workshop (Microsoft, July 2003)
http://msdn.microsoft.com/webservices/community/workshops/rmspecwsjul2003.aspx

Reliable Messaging Workshop Discussion list
http://groups.yahoo.com/group/WS-RM-Workshops/

WS-Reliability test implementations (RM4GS – Reliable Messaging 4 Grid Services)

- Fujitsu: *http://www.fujitsu.com/services/solutions/xml/activity/XML_wsr.html*

- Hitachi: *http://www.hitachi.co.jp/Prod/comp/soft1/wsrm/*

- NEC: *http://www.sw.nec.co.jp/soft/ws-reliability/download.html*

- WS-Security: *http://www.oasis-open.org/committees/download.php/3281/WSS-SOAPMessageSecurity-17-082703-merged.pdf*

- OASIS WS-Reliability (WS-RM) home page: *http://www.oasis-open.org/committees/workgroup.php?wg_abbrev=wsrm*

- WS-ReliableMessaging: *http://msdn.microsoft.com/webservices/default.aspx?pull=/library/en-us/dnglobspec/html/ws-reliablemessaging.asp*

- WS-Federation: *http://msdn.microsoft.com/webservices/understanding/advancedwebservices/default.aspx?pull=/library/en-us/dnglobspec/html/ws-federation.asp*

- WS-Trust: *http://msdn.microsoft.com/webservices/default.aspx?pull=/library/en-us/dnglobspec/html/ws-trust.asp*

- WS-SecureConversation: *http://msdn.microsoft.com/webservices/default.aspx?pull=/library/en-us/dnglobspec/html/ws-secureconversation.asp*

- WS-Addressing: *http://msdn.microsoft.com/webservices/default.aspx?pull=/library/en-us/dnglobspec/html/ws-addressing.asp*

WSBPEL

- Business Process Execution Language for Web Services v1.0: *http://www-106.ibm.com/developerworks/library/ws-bpel1/*

- OASIS WSBPEL Technical Committee home page: *http://www.oasis-open.org/committees/tc_home.php?wg_abbrev=wsbpel*

- OASIS Web Services for Remote Portlets Specification: *http://www.oasis-open.org/committees/download.php/3343/oasis-200304-wsrp-specification-1.0.pdf*

- WS-Policy vs. SOAP 1.2 Features and Properties discussion: *http://lists.w3.org/Archives/Public/www-ws-desc/2003Oct/0144.html*

Java Specifications

Java Community Process (JCP)
  http://www.jcp.org

Java Management eXtenstions (JMX) home page (Specification, Reference Implementation, and related JSRs), Sun Microsystems
  http://java.sun.com/products/JavaManagement

JSR 168, Portlet API home page
  http://www.jcp.org/en/jsr/detail?id=168

JSR 208, Java Business Integration home page
  http://www.jcp.org/en/jsr/detail?id=208

JMS home page
  http://java.sun.com/products/jms

JCA home page
  http://java.sun.com/j2ee/connector/index.jsp

Enterprise Java Beans home page
  http://java.sun.com/products/ejb/index.jsp

Java Server Pages home page
  http://java.sun.com/products/jsp/index.jsp

Java Authentication and Authorization Service (JAAS) home page
  http://java.sun.com/products/jaas/index.jsp

Soap with Attachments API for Java (SAAJ) home page
  http://java.sun.com/xml/saaj/index.jsp

Java Secure Socket Extension (JSSE) home page
  http://java.sun.com/products/jsse/index.jsp

Java Server Pages (JSP) home page
  http://java.sun.com/products/jsp/index.jsp

Java API for XML-based Remote Procedure Call (JAX-RPC) home page
  http://java.sun.com/xml/jaxrpc/index.jsp

Java 2, Enterprise Edition (J2EE)
  http://java.sun.com/j2ee/index.jsp

Index

A

abstract decoupling, MOM, 84
abstract endpoint, service container and, 110
accidental architecture
    departmental issues, 30
    integration and, 23, 28
    organizational issues, 30
    problems with, 30
acknowledging messages, 90
ACLs (Access Control Lists), 87
adoption by industry, 19
aggregator services, 138
Apache Axis, 8
application servers, 44
    ESB connectivity, 188
    integration brokers and, 118
    management, 121
    service containers and, 118
applications
    extensibility, 62–67
    portal applications, 204
architecture
    data exchange, 70
        canonical, 70, 72
    service-oriented, abstract endpoints
        and, 102
asynchronous conversations, orchestration
        services and, 142
asynchronous errors, 158
asynchronous processing, atomicity and, 180
asynchrony
    portal server deployment and, 210
    reliability, 88

at-least-once delivery, messaging, 89
at-most-once delivery, messaging, 89
atomicity
    asynch and, 180
    message-based, 180
ATP (Availability To Promise)
    manufacturer case study and, 57
    partner integration case study, 162
auditing, 115
authorization, JMX and, 193
autonomy of messages, 88

B

B2B (Business-to-Business), 1
BAM (Business Activity Monitoring), 16
    enabling functionality, 143
batch processes
    data synchronization, 170
    downtime, 170
    overnight jobs, 169
batch transfer, integration and, 23, 32
batch updates, 168
    latency, 168
BC (Binding Component), JBI, 184
best practices
    EAI, 34
    SOA, 34
best-effort delivery, 146
BPEL4WS (Business Process Execution
        Language for Web Services), 9
    conditional routing and, 134
    orchestration service and, 140

We'd like to hear your suggestions for improving our indexes. Send email to *index@oreilly.com*.

H

handling errors, 115
hands free processing (see STP)
hardware, disruptive hardware technology, 22
history of ESB, 45
hub-and-spoke integration brokers, 118

I

IBM, 7
impedance mismatch, solutions, 10
implementation
    services, code example, 114
    SOA, 35
    XML persistence services, 143
incremental adoption, 18
independently deployable integration
        services, 109
Indigo (Microsoft), 7
INOVIS TLE (Trusted Link Enterprise), 165
input data, managment interface, 112
insurers adopting ESB, 19
integration
    accidental architecture, 23, 28
    batch transfers and, 23, 32
    brokers, service container and, 110
    business partners, 41
    conventional approaches, 4
    distribution, 9
    EAI hubs and, 33
    economic drivers, 22
    economy and, 55
    enterprise connectivity, 28
    ETL and, 23, 32
    FTP and, 23, 32
    government and, 26
    IT and, 23
    partner flexibility and, 57
    pervasiveness, 2
    priorities and, 22, 24
    problems with, 23
    real-time
        case study, 173–181
        file interface removal, 181
        message-based atomicity, 180
        migration to XML, 179
        streamlined dataflow and, 179
    regulatory compliance, 22, 25
    RFID tags and, 22, 27
    Sarbanes-Oxley Act of 2002, 26
    services, independent, 109
    SOA and, implementation, 35
    standards-based, 53–55
    STP and, 22, 26
    Y2K preparation and, 23
integration brokers, 33
    application servers and, 118
    hub-and-spoke, 118
    service containers and, 118
integration fabric, 3
integration network, ESB as, 3
integration patterns
    cache-forward, 197
    Federated Query, 197, 217
        long-duration request, 219
        push model versus pull, 218
        real-time request pattern, 218
        variations, 221
    Forward Cache, 213–217
        itinerary-based routing, 215
        publish-and-subscribe, 214
    portal server, 204
    portal server deployment architecture
        and, 205
    reply-forward, 97
    request/reply, 96
    two-step XRef transformation, 197
    types, 197
    VETO, 197, 198–201
        Enrich step, 199
        Operate step, 200
        Transform step, 200
        Validate step, 198
    VETRO, 197, 201
    XRef, two-step, 201
interfaces
    JMX Connector Interface, 190, 191
    management, service container, 111
    MBean, JMX, 191
    messages
        loosely coupled, 81
        RPC-style programming, 78
        tightly coupled, 80
    messaging
        loosely coupled, 78
        tightly coupled, 78
    service, 113
introducing ESB, project level, 38
inventory, excess, 173
inventory management, manufacturer case
        study, 56

processes, state recovery orchestration
services, 142
producers, messaging, 84
project level introduction of ESB, 38
protocols
    adapters, JMX, 190
    bridging, 152
    direct handlers, 154
        asynchronous request/reply, 156
        service invocation, 155
        synchronous request/reply, 155
    SOAP protocol handler, 157
publish-and-subscribe messaging model, 85,
    90
    Forward Cache pattern and, 214
pull model/push model, Federated Query
    patterns, 218

Q

QoP (Quality of Protection), 116
QoS (Quality of Service), 116
    messaging, 89
queries, federated queries, 197
queues, messaging, 84

R

RA (Resource Adapter), JCA, 187
real-time integration
    data flow and, 179
    file interface removal, 181
    message-based atomicity, 180
    migration to XML, 179
real-time integration case study, 173–181
    data channels, 177
    data transformations, 177
    ESB insertion, 176
    process flows, 177
real-time request pattern, Federate Query, 218
real-time throughput, 16
refactoring to ESB, 37–41
reflectors, JBI, 185
regulatory compliance, integration and, 22, 25
remote configuration, 14
    template-based replication, 195
remote management, 14
replication, remote configuration, 195
reply-forward pattern, messaging, 97
request/reply messaging patterns, 96
retailers adopting ESB, 20

reusing services, 135
    composition and, 137
    configuration and, 135
    parameterization, 135
RFCs (Remote Function Calls), 163
RFID (Radio Frequency Identification)
    tags, 22
    integration and, 22, 27
    Tesco and, 27
    U.S. Department of Defense, 27
    Wal-Mart and, 27
RME (Rejected Message Endpoint), 131, 159
routing
    CBR (content-based routing), 69, 129–135
    conditional, BPEL4WS and, 134
    itinerary-based, 126, 127
        Forward Cache pattern and, 215
    patterns
        itineraries and, 138
        multi-itinerary CBR pattern, 139
        services and, 138
    XML, content-based, 67
RPCs (Remote Procedure Calls),
    programming, 78
RPC-style programming, message
    interfaces, 78
rule( ) method, 130

S

SAP adapter, 162
SAP JCo (Java Connector), 163
SAP RFCs, 163
Sarbanes-Oxley act of 2002, integration
    and, 26
Schulte, Roy, 7
scripting, orchestration services, 142
secure DMZ deployment, 160
security, 12
    MOM and, 12, 160
SeeBeyond, 7
servers
    application servers
        ESB connectivity, 188
        managing, 121
    JMX Server, 190
        environment, 190
    MBean, 190
    message servers, 77

W

Wal-Mart, RFID tags and, 27
web services, 1, 105
  partner integration and, 160–167
  portal server deployment and, 208
  protocols and, 150, 154
  SOA and, 3, 35, 45, 102
    bind/invoke, 126
WS-* specifications, 225
  adopting, 229
  composability among, 226
  enterprise capabilities, 230
WS-Addressing, 228
WS-BPEL, 229
WS-Choreography, 9
WSDL (Web Services Description
      Language), 8
  SOA and, 35
WS-Eventing, 99, 226
WS-Federation, 228
WS-Notification, 99, 227
WS-Policy, 228
WS-Rel*, 151
  interoperability, 149
WS-Reliability, 227
WS-Reliable Messaging, 227
WS-RP (Web Services for Remote
      Portlets), 205
WS-SecureConversation, 228
WS-Security (WSS), 227
WS-Trust, 227

X

XML (eXtensible Markup Language), 60
  benefits, 60
  caching
    federated query pattern, 142
    forward cache pattern, 142
  EAI and, 35
  EDI and, 61
  extensibility, 62–67
  human readability, 61
  messages, service interface, 114
  migration to, 179
  as native datatype, 16
  parsing and, 61
  persistence services
    aggregation and, 143
    federated query pattern, 142
    forward cache pattern, 142
    implementation and, 143
    reporting and, 143
  routing, content-based, 67
  transformation, content-based, 67
  XSLT and, 68
XML processing pipeline, 144
XML storage services, 142
XPath, 8
XQuery, 8
XRef integration pattern, two-step, 201
XRef transformation, two-step, 197
XSLT (eXtensible Stylesheet Language
      Transformation), 8, 68
  extending, 68
  two-step XRef pattern and, 202

Y

Y2K preparedness, integration and, 23, 44

About the Author

David A. Chappell (*chappell@sonicsoftware.com*) is vice president and Chief Technology Evangelist at Sonic Software (pioneers of the ESB). Dave has more than 20 years of experience in the software industry in a broad range of roles including architect, code-slinger, sales, support, and marketing. Dave has a strong background in a number of distributed computing models, and is well known for his writings and public lectures on the subjects of the ESB, Message Oriented Middleware (MOM), enterprise integration, and evolving standards and web services. Dave led the development effort for SonicMQ®, which has grown to become synonymous with enterprise messaging and the Java Message Service (JMS). He has published numerous articles on interoperability and integration technology in leading industry publications, such as *Java Developers Journal*, *JavaPro*, *Web Services Journal*, *XML Journal*, and *Network World*. He is noted for authoring popular books on JMS, web services, and ebXML.

Colophon

Our look is the result of reader comments, our own experimentation, and feedback from distribution channels. Distinctive covers complement our distinctive approach to technical topics, breathing personality and life into potentially dry subjects.

Emily Quill was the production editor and copyeditor for *Enterprise Service Bus*. Audrey Doyle proofread the book. Philip Dangler Marlowe Shaeffer, and Darren Kelly provided quality control. Mary Agner provided production assistance. Johnna VanHoose Dinse wrote the index.

Edie Freedman designed the cover of this book. The cover image is of assorted eggs from *Hewitson's British Oology*, 1833, from the collections of the Ernst Mayr Library of the Museum of Comparative Zoology, Harvard University. Emma Colby produced the cover layout with QuarkXPress 4.1 using Adobe's Minion font.

David Futato designed the interior layout This book was converted by Joe Wizda to FrameMaker 5.5.6 with a format conversion tool created by Erik Ray, Jason McIntosh, Neil Walls, and Mike Sierra that uses Perl and XML technologies. The text font is Adobe Minion; the heading font is Adobe Myriad Condensed; and the code font is LucasFont's TheSans Mono Condensed. The illustrations that appear in the book were produced by Robert Romano and Jessamyn Read using Macromedia FreeHand 9 and Adobe Photoshop 6. These illustrations are based on original art created by David Chappell, Jonathan Bachman, Gary Hemdal, and Hub Vandervoort.

Related Titles Available from O'Reilly

Java

Ant: The Definitive Guide
Eclipse: A Java Developer's Guide
Enterprise JavaBeans, *3rd Edition*
Hardcore Java
Head First Java
Head First Servlets & JSP
Head First EJB
J2EE Design Patterns
Java and SOAP
Java & XML Data Binding
Java & XML
Java Cookbook
Java Data Objects
Java Database Best Practices
Java Enterprise Best Practices
Java Enterprise in a Nutshell, *2nd Edition*
Java Examples in a Nutshell, *3rd Edition*
Java Extreme Programming Cookbook
Java in a Nutshell, *4th Edition*
Java Management Extensions
Java Message Service
Java Network Programming, *2nd Edition*
Java NIO
Java Performance Tuning, *2nd Edition*
Java RMI
Java Security, *2nd Edition*
Java ServerPages, *2nd Edition*
Java Serlet & JSP Cookbook
Java Servlet Programming, *2nd Edition*
Java Swing, *2nd Edition*
Java Web Services in a Nutshell
Learning Java, *2nd Edition*
Mac OS X for Java Geeks
NetBeans: The Definitive Guide
Programming Jakarta Struts
Tomcat: The Definitive Guide
WebLogic: The Definitive Guide

O'REILLY®

Our books are available at most retail and online bookstores.
To order direct: 1-800-998-9938 • *order@oreilly.com* • *www.oreilly.com*
Online editions of most O'Reilly titles are available by subscription at *safari.oreilly.com*

Keep in touch with O'Reilly

1. Download examples from our books

To find example files for a book, go to:

www.oreilly.com/catalog

select the book, and follow the "Examples" link.

2. Register your O'Reilly books

Register your book at *register.oreilly.com*

Why register your books?
Once you've registered your O'Reilly books you can:

* Win O'Reilly books, T-shirts or discount coupons in our monthly drawing.
* Get special offers available only to registered O'Reilly customers.
* Get catalogs announcing new books (US and UK only).
* Get email notification of new editions of the O'Reilly books you own.

3. Join our email lists

Sign up to get topic-specific email announcements of new books and conferences, special offers, and O'Reilly Network technology newsletters at:

elists.oreilly.com

It's easy to customize your free elists subscription so you'll get exactly the O'Reilly news you want.

4. Get the latest news, tips, and tools

www.oreilly.com

* "Top 100 Sites on the Web"—PC Magazine
* CIO Magazine's Web Business 50 Awards

Our web site contains a library of comprehensive product information (including book excerpts and tables of contents), downloadable software, background articles, interviews with technology leaders, links to relevant sites, book cover art, and more.

5. Work for O'Reilly

Check out our web site for current employment opportunities:

jobs.oreilly.com

6. Contact us

O'Reilly & Associates
1005 Gravenstein Hwy North
Sebastopol, CA 95472 USA

TEL: 707-827-7000 or 800-998-9938
      (6am to 5pm PST)

FAX: 707-829-0104

order@oreilly.com
For answers to problems regarding your order or our products. To place a book order online, visit:

www.oreilly.com/order_new

catalog@oreilly.com
To request a copy of our latest catalog.

booktech@oreilly.com
For book content technical questions or corrections.

corporate@oreilly.com
For educational, library, government, and corporate sales.

proposals@oreilly.com
To submit new book proposals to our editors and product managers.

international@oreilly.com
For information about our international distributors or translation queries. For a list of our distributors outside of North America check out:

international.oreilly.com/distributors.html

adoption@oreilly.com
For information about academic use of O'Reilly books, visit:

academic.oreilly.com